The Therapeutic Use of Self

The Therapeutic Use of Self: Counselling Practice, Research and Supervision is a ground-breaking examination of the individual therapist's contribution to process and outcome in counselling.

Counselling training courses tend to pay very little attention to what it is about the individual counsellor that governs their level of effectiveness. Using many powerful case examples and extensive research findings from the author's own work, this book presents the counsellor's evaluation of their own practice as the main vehicle for the development of insight and awareness into individual 'therapeutic' characteristics. It addresses many of the taboos and infrequently discussed aspects of therapy, such as:

The value of therapist failure

Breaking the rules of counselling

Working beyond the accepted boundaries of counselling.

The Therapeutic Use of Self: Counselling Practice, Research and Supervision will act as a spur to individual counsellors to acknowledge, develop and value their own unique contribution to the counselling profession.

Val Wosket is a senior lecturer and Head of Scheme for Counselling Studies at the University College of Ripon and York St John. She is co-author of *Supervising the Counsellor: a Cyclical Model*, with Steve Page (Routledge 1994).

The Therapeutic Use of Self

Counselling practice, research and supervision

Val Wosket

London and New York

First published 1999 by Routledge
11 New Fetter Lane, London EC4P 4EE

Simultaneously published in the USA and Canada by Routledge
29 West 35th Street, New York, NY 10001

© 1999 Val Wosket

Typeset in Times by Graphicraft Limited, Hong Kong
Printed and bound in Great Britain by Clays Ltd, St Ives Plc

British Library Cataloguing in Publication Data
A catalogue record for this book is available from
the British Library

Library of Congress Cataloging in Publication Data
Wosket, Val, 1954–
    The therapeutic use of self : counselling practice, research, and
supervision / Val Wosket.
        p.   cm.
    Includes bibliographical references and index.
    1. Psychotherapy—Methodology.   2. Psychotherapist and patient.
3. Psychotherapists—Psychology.   I. Title.
RC480.5.W67   1999
616.89'14—dc21   99–13989
                                                                                          CIP

ISBN 0–415–17090–7 (hbk)
ISBN 0–415–17091–5 (pbk)

This book is dedicated to those who have
honoured me by telling me their stories

Contents

Acknowledgements

I would like to express my gratitude to the following people who have directly or indirectly helped with the creation of this book.

My colleagues Alan Dunnett, Gordon Jinks, Sue Copeland, Mary Connor and Alison Perry who cheerfully bore the brunt of my absence from college during a writing sabbatical. Marie Whittaker and Eileen Ashmore for their permissions and contributions. My mother, who found herself acting as unpaid research assistant when she had thought she was coming to stay with me for a holiday. Steve Page who acted as my writing review partner and, as ever, provided feedback that was unstintingly supportive whilst being rigorously challenging. Professor Chris Butler who provided encouragement and helped me with the research funding which paid for a term's writing sabbatical. My client, called here Rachel, who inspired the research study presented in Chapters 3 and 4. Other clients and supervisees who gave their explicit permission for examples from our work together to go into the book. The counsellors and psychotherapists who responded to my research questionnaires and, in many instances, volunteered far more than was asked of them.

Finally, I would like to acknowledge the support and forbearance of my partner, Paul Baker, who possesses two rare gifts: that of making me laugh when I get too serious about myself and this writing business, and that of the therapeutic use of fishing. His experience of being abandoned by me for long periods during the writing of this book was made infinitely more tolerable by the catching of a record carp.

The author and publisher wish to thank the copyright holder for permission to include the extract from Emily Dickinson's poem 'The props assist the house'. This is reprinted by permission of the publishers and the Trustees of Amherst College from *The Poems of Emily Dickinson*, Thomas H. Johnson, ed., Cambridge, MA: The Belknap Press of Harvard University Press, Copyright © 1951, 1955, 1979, 1983 by the President and Fellows of Harvard College.

Preface

The seeds of this book were contained in the sense I had a few years ago of having lost my way as a counsellor. In the years that followed my initial training, which relied heavily on the Skilled Helper model of Gerard Egan (1997), I went through what seemed like several metamorphoses in order to try to arrive at an accurate definition of myself as a therapist. For a while I thought I might be eclectic, and then that I had become an integrationist. Eventually I tried the then newly coined term 'relational' (Holmes *et al.* 1996) in my search to find a label that accurately reflected how I conceived of the counselling process and my part in it.

All of these were milestones to be passed in search of new signposts. Though they pointed the way they didn't take me to a place where I felt comfortably located. I felt confused about my professional identity. If I couldn't find an approach or model that I felt adequately summed up what I did, did this mean that I was hopelessly lost as a therapist? At the same time I seemed to be using fewer and fewer interventions that I could attribute to a particular school of counselling. I knew I had strayed from the confines of a pure approach or style and I suspected that I had also managed to cast myself adrift from the twin harbours of eclecticism and integrationism. I could no longer state with confidence when I was integrating something, or what I was integrating into what. Either I was losing my grip or something else, which I couldn't quite make sense of, was happening.

I puzzled over this in supervision and shared with my supervisor my disquiet over the suspicion that I was becoming a theoretical and procedural outcast from every respected and recognised school of counselling. Even the literature I read which did not appear to favour one approach over another still stressed the importance of having a theory from which to practise – even if it didn't make much difference what that theory was (Lambert and Bergin 1994; Duncan *et al.* 1992). At times I became really worried that I must be losing my way if the familiar markers were disappearing at such a rate.

Although experiencing what felt like a disintegration of my therapeutic identity, as far as I could see my clients didn't appear to be suffering any fallout from this. On the contrary I had the sense that I was engaging at a deeper level with my clients and achieving more successful outcomes, even with individuals with seemingly intransigent difficulties. Although I felt that I had lost the ability to name what I was doing, what I *was* doing seemed, more often than not, to be working. And, in general, I felt more consistent and sure-footed in my counselling practice than I had previously been.

Often, during this period, I felt liberated and exhilarated in my counselling practice. Just occasionally I felt dogged by a sense of doubt and unease – not necessarily arising from the work itself but from the shadow of my orthodox training. Without too much effort I could summon up spectres whispering: 'You are getting too involved with your clients' . . . 'You are encouraging client dependency' . . . 'Your boundaries have slipped' . . . 'You are meeting your own needs in the way that you are working with clients'. Fortunately I had a very experienced and sound supervisor who had come to know me very well, over a number of years, and had witnessed the unfolding of my practice from careful orthodoxy to experimental, client responsive, unorthodoxy. She was cautiously (sometimes very cautiously) encouraging and this helped.

Reflecting on all this, it seemed that two aspects of my clinical practice stood out and appeared to be interrelated. First, I had largely stopped using specific techniques and interventions that I could identify as hailing from particular schools or models; second, in place of these I was using responses that seemed to 'well-up' from inside me rather than being selected from external sources. In essence I was increasingly listening to myself and utilising responses that arose from two particular aspects of this listening: the first was the sense I had of myself as I lived the relationship with the other person, and the second was a growing reliance on what had worked from past, and sometimes idiosyncratic, experience.

Then, whilst researching material for this book I came across the work of Donald Schön (1983, 1987) on 'The Reflective Practitioner'. Immediately I knew that here was someone who could throw light on what I was groping towards. Here was a serious researcher and academic who appeared to recognise and value the kind of process I found myself in and even give it a name: 'Reflection-in-Action'. These are some of Schön's words that spoke directly to my own experience:

When we go about the spontaneous, intuitive performance of the actions of everyday life, we show ourselves to be knowledgeable in a special way. Often we cannot say what it is that we know. When we try to describe it we find ourselves at a loss, or we produce descriptions that are obviously inappropriate. Our knowing is ordinarily tacit, implicit in our patterns of action and in our feel for the stuff with which we are dealing. It seems right to say that our knowing is *in* our action.

(Schön 1983: 49)

This book is an attempt to make explicit some implicit knowing of the sort to which Schön refers, particularly as it pertains to the use of self in the conduct of counselling and psychotherapy. I do not now claim allegiance to any named school or approach to counselling, although I acknowledge a debt to many. I now feel so convinced that the best of my knowing about how to be a counsellor is determined by what I know and use of myself that I wish to invite other therapists to consider themselves and their work in the same light. This book is that invitation.

Introduction

I decided to write this book because, after a number of years spent training and supervising counsellors and psychotherapists, I suspect that there are many therapists out in the field who are not working to their full potential. I also suspect that while there are a few outstanding and innovative therapists at work, there are also many more who are struggling to find ways to liberate and express their full therapeutic capacity.

Supervision and accreditation are the ways we appear to have chosen to regulate counselling and raise it to the status of a profession. In the processes of both accreditation and supervision the locus of evaluation is external. Since this is the case, the danger exists that the therapist will be selective in what they reveal to the eyes of a supervisor or accreditation panel in order not to jeopardise their chances of approval. I would like to see the profession growing to maturity in a climate of openness and risk taking where practitioners are expected to develop their own internal frames of evaluation before giving themselves and their work over to the scrutiny of 'experts'. To this end, in the pages that follow, I will be championing the cause of the practitioner-researcher who is committed to the value of learning from ongoing research of their own clinical practice.

The decision to write this book was influenced by my increasing sense that a whole vital area of counselling and psychotherapy practice is not openly discussed and infrequently finds its way into books, journals and research studies. This is the area that I have termed unorthodox practice. Unorthodox practice, in the sense that I am using the term in this volume, occurs where experienced therapists depart from the norms and conventions of their previous training and put themselves out on a limb to work in original, innovative and intuitive ways. It is important for the reader to understand that I am discussing what I consider to be the legitimate practice of unorthodox procedures by experienced therapists who have 'served their time' following a disciplined, rigorous and extensive training in psychotherapeutic theory and practice. In no way am I intending to imply that inexperienced therapists short-cut this route and initiate idiosyncratic ways of working which derive from foreshortened or superficial training, naïvety born of ignorance, or a perverse and inflated sense of omnipotence.

Perhaps those of us who work in progressive and unorthodox ways are reluctant to admit to this from fear of disapproval or opprobrium – both from the public and from others within the profession. Dissonance within the professions of counselling and psychotherapy has historically been fuelled by competition and rivalry between contending schools. It is only in recent years, as I summarise in Chapter 1, that there are signs that therapeutic pluralism is giving way to a new atmosphere of rapprochement between the different schools and approaches. Maybe we are reluctant to rock this new found boat in which there might be a place for all of us by opening up the possibility that the way forward for the profession may now be to direct our attention to the contributions of individual therapists and away from the common factors to be found across all schools of therapy.

If we begin to take serious note of the research (Blatt *et al.* 1996; McLennan 1996) which indicates that therapists who share similar training backgrounds, levels of experience and operating procedures are differentially effective and some have clients who consistently get better while others have clients who consistently do not – and some of whom even seem to get worse – we are raising all sorts of spectres for the profession. For instance, if it seems that we cannot train people to be equally effective as therapists, might not prospective employers of counsellors start to require practitioners to provide evidence of their effectiveness and then weed out those who don't quite seem to match the success rates of others?

I *do* think that counsellors in general need to be more accountable for what they do and to evaluate their own practice more thoroughly and I give examples of how this can be done in Chapters 3 and 4. A number of authors (Herron and Rouslin 1984; Howard 1996; Samuels 1992; Spinelli 1994) remind us that psychotherapy and counselling are activities that are yet to be clearly defined. Herron and Rouslin (1984: 1) suggest that:

> the fact that people keep coming to us despite the murkiness surrounding us, and them, lessens our incentive to concern ourselves with definition. We sort of know what we do, since we do it, and

our patients sort of know because it happens to them. That is not good enough, even when such obscurity has certain satisfactions for all parties concerned. Therapists must increase the honesty factor about what is known and what is not known.

I agree that counsellors, generally, need to be clearer about what they do. However, I approach the topic of counsellor accountability from a position that I hope will encourage therapists to research and evaluate their own practice because of the benefits for themselves and their clients in so doing, not because the spectre of professional disgrace hovers uncomfortably over one shoulder. My belief is that many counsellors could become more effective if they sometimes directed their attention away from the models and processes originally taught to them and more towards acknowledging their own unique helping attributes. Just as I believe that each client we meet has a unique potential for growth and healing, so I believe that every competent counsellor has their own uniquely healing characteristics. To discover our true potential as therapists I think that we need to look to ourselves and our clients and be prepared, on occasion, to take what Peck (1989), paraphrasing Robert Frost, has called 'the road less travelled'.

As a child I loved doing jigsaw puzzles. From a young age I tackled with total absorption and great patience the most difficult puzzles that would take days to piece together from apparently undifferentiated, but in actuality, uniquely different pieces. I still recall the small but tangible sense of achievement I would feel whenever suddenly, unexpectedly, one piece clicked or slotted into place with another in an unmistakable match.

The conceptualisation and writing of this book have been very much like doing a large and fragmented jigsaw puzzle – except that I didn't have the finished picture on the box lid to guide me in placing the pieces as I went along. Some of the pieces were found in conversations with colleagues and students, some took shape from reading or preparing workshops and lectures. Others started joining up and forming patterns in the self-reflection that occurred in, or as a result of, my own supervision and therapy. By far the greatest number of pieces, and the ones that connected different parts of the puzzle so that the semblance of a whole picture began to emerge, were supplied by my clients and supervisees. It is because of what they have taught me that this book has its final shape and form. It is not a shape that is imposed or has had the pieces cut to fit. The picture has emerged without my knowing how it would eventually look and the process has been one of adventure and discovery. I know that for many readers there will be pieces missing and I hope that they will be able to recognise the shape of these and be inclined to fill them in for themselves.

Chapter 1 sets the scene for subsequent chapters by giving a very brief account of the notion of the self as the term is intended to be understood throughout the book. It then goes on to consider issues of professionalisation and the therapist's use of self, proceeds with a survey of current and future trends and developments in the field of counselling, and ends with a consideration of the individual counsellor's contribution to process and outcome in therapy. Chapter 2 discusses aspects of the use of self within the counselling relationship under the rubric of 'the counsellor's edge of awareness' and considers how therapeutic strategies and interventions can be tailored to the client's way of being in the relationship. Chapter 3 looks at counselling research and the use of self, with particular focus on the practitioner-researcher paradigm, and introduces the research study that is the subject of the following chapter. Chapter 4 presents data and findings from an extended research study into the therapeutic use of self. Chapter 5 promotes the notion of healing impairments in relation to the use of self through a consideration of the imperfect counsellor and the growth and learning that can occur through mistakes, omissions and failures. This chapter and the two that follow contain research findings from a postal survey of therapists that invited them to record their experience of unorthodox practice and learning about the self. Chapter 6 looks at the use of self through 'rule breaking' in counselling and questions some of the myths and assumptions governing conventional therapeutic protocol. Chapter 7 considers the use of self in relation to working at the boundaries in counselling through looking at the significance of work that takes place around the 'edges' of the therapeutic frame. Chapter 8 presents aspects of the shadow side of the use of self and examines some of the functional and dysfunctional ways that therapists attend to their own needs in the conduct of their work. Chapter 9 concludes the book with some thoughts towards the use of self in counselling supervision.

Material in the book is intended to be exploratory rather than definitive. To precisionists and traditionalists the ideas presented in this book may appear inconsistent and meandering. To others I hope the way that I have written and what I have covered will be seen to mirror the creative ambiguities and unexpected twists and turns that the therapeutic encounter itself is wont to take.

Though by no means an exhaustive review, this book is intended to be a useful source book on what has been written and researched in relation to the use of self in counselling and psychotherapy. I have tried to write this book with a personal voice and style – and at times this has felt (and still feels) risky. I have attempted to tell my own truth about being a counsellor even when this may seem halting, hesitant, contradictory, inconsistent and stumbling. In this sense I have striven to communicate with the reader in what is sometimes called an 'experience-near', rather than an 'experience-distant' mode of writing.

The book contains elements of research, theoretical discussion, clinical practice and autobiography. An exposition of the therapeutic use of self requires both detached and personal perspectives. Alongside what I hope appears as a fairly rigorous treatment of issues, I have therefore included some personal material which I hope the reader will find illustrative rather than self-indulgent. I cannot write about the use of self in therapy without writing about myself as a therapist. I have included many examples from my own practice as a counsellor and supervisor as I do not think that theoretical conceptualisations alone can convey the living impact that the use of self may have on work with clients and supervisees. These days I work mainly, but not exclusively, with clients who need the benefit of a long term and committed relationship. My clinical examples are therefore largely drawn from my work with clients whom I saw over months or years, rather than weeks. Nevertheless I hope that what I have to say is of relevance to those who work in shorter time-frames.

Within this book I use the terms counselling and psychotherapy interchangeably. The question of whether there is a clear and viable distinction to be made between counselling and psychotherapy has received renewed attention recently as part of the wider debate about professionalisation and the status of therapists (Clarkson 1994a; Feltham 1997a; Horton 1997; Lidmila 1997). A number of writers have put forward a range of arguments in support of the view that the dichotomy is spurious and based largely on tradition, myth, assumed status and territorial self-interest (Dryden and Feltham 1992; Ellingham 1996; Feltham 1995; Howard 1996; Kwiatkowski 1998; Lomas 1981; Patterson 1974; Patterson and Watkins 1996; Peavy 1996; Spinelli 1994). I share this view because it seems to me that if I define what I do by the distinctions offered by those who support the dichotomy, then I practise both psychotherapy and counselling. Sometimes I undertake long term therapy with clients who appear to emerge from the work that we do together with an altered self-concept, temperament and world view – this seems to be what is often deemed to be psychotherapy. On other occasions I work short term with a problem-management perspective that gives the client some relief and redress from immediate difficulties but leaves the personality largely unchanged – this I understand some to define as counselling. To me, the difference in the way that I work is defined by what the client brings to me and the manner in which I respond. Though I call myself a counsellor, I do not wish to exclude those who call themselves psychotherapists and I often resort in the book to the inclusive term therapist.

Wherever possible, and in the majority of cases, I have gained the permission of clients and supervisees to include case material. Where this has not been possible because I am no longer in contact with the people concerned I have disguised details and been careful not to include personal features. In all cases names have been fictionalised and identifiable details expunged. Whilst it is possible that individuals may recognise themselves in what I have written, I think they will be the only people able to do so with any certainty. I hope they will see that I have written about my work with them with care, respect and anonymity and in doing so have honoured, rather than betrayed, our relationship. My client, called here Rachel, whose therapy is written about at length in Chapter 4 provided written permission for the material to be included. In addition she read and approved the drafts of Chapters 3 and 4. As she did this over two years after the therapy finished, I believe her permission was granted as free as it is ever likely to be of any vestiges of the power imbalance that invests any counselling relationship and may leave its traces for some time afterwards.

This book goes to press at a time when fundamental questions about the conduct and efficacy of counselling and psychotherapy are being raised by authors of the psychotherapeutic literature, by the public, by the medical profession, and by the media (e.g. McKinstry 1997; Persaud 1993; Weldon 1997). Some of these questions are highly critical in tone and dispute the very foundations and assumptions upon which counselling rests. In what are troubled times for the profession, I intend this to be a hopeful book that attempts to raise a phoenix from the ashes of these discontents by re-attaching therapy to its roots within the individual helper.

The book is aimed primarily at students in advanced training and therapists who have finished their training and are looking for ways to broaden, deepen and reinvigorate their clinical practice. It is likely to appeal to counsellors and psychotherapists who regard themselves as broadly humanistic, eclectic or integrative. I hope that it may also have something of value to say to therapists who may identify themselves with the more psychodynamic and cognitive-behavioural ends of the counselling spectrum and who have recognised the value of involving themselves more fully in their way of being with clients. I have endeavoured to avoid using too much approach-specific language so that therapists of all persuasions may find their own language in the words I have used. I hope, in addition, that trainers, supervisors and researchers who are open to a range of perspectives on the way that we understand, teach and evaluate counselling and psychotherapy will find here food for thought, if not for persuasion. Helping professionals from allied disciplines and professions may find material here that holds the potential for enriching their encounters with clients, patients and helpees by encouraging them to examine the unique contribution they themselves can make to the helping relationship. My principal hope is that this book will stimulate you to look with fresh eyes at your current work and the way that lies ahead for yourself and your clients.

Chapter 1

Towards an approach to counselling based on the use of self

> If psychotherapy is to forge its future, it must begin with the end of theory.
>
> (Karasu 1996)

In this first chapter I do not intend to outline a model of counselling. This may come as something of a relief to readers who, like myself, feel that the world of counselling and psychotherapy already has a surfeit of schools, approaches and models. In any case, as Collier (1987: 53) has dryly remarked, 'accounts of the "what I do in therapy" variety usually come to grief on the twin reefs of egoism and tedium'. Therefore, instead of recounting what I do as a counsellor, I intend to start this book with a review of recent literature on the use of self in therapy and then present a rationale for why I think greater attention should be given to the therapist's use of self. I will also offer some thoughts on where the use of self might fit into current trends and future developments in the field of counselling and psychotherapy.

Recent developments in the field have seen something of a burgeoning of interest in the therapist's use of self. Several publications have focused exclusively on this aspect of the therapist's contribution to process and outcome in psychotherapy (Andrews 1991; Baldwin and Satir 1987; Lambert 1989; Real 1990; UKCP 1997) and others have recently highlighted the self of the therapist as an important determinant in the therapeutic encounter. But what, precisely, is meant by the term 'the therapeutic use of self'?

TOWARDS A DEFINITION OF THE SELF

Before proceeding further I will hazard a working definition of self in the sense that I will be using the term in this volume. This is not an easy task as the question who, or what, is the self is one that has long vexed philosophers, novelists, poets, psychologists and sociologists and continues to intrigue authors of the psychotherapeutic literature today (see, for example, Baldwin, D. 1987; Bragan 1996; Brazier 1993; Erwin 1997; Gergen 1996; Hobson 1985; Holdstock 1993; Stevens 1996b). Erwin points out that the term 'self' has many different connotations and meanings within the psychotherapy literature amongst which are: a person, the ego, the mental apparatus, the whole or the core of the personality, a set of self representations or an inner agent or entity. The situation is further confounded if we consider that in much that is currently being written about the self, as Erwin (1997: 47) has commented, it is not always clear 'whether the author is really postulating an inner self, or is merely speaking metaphorically, or perhaps just writing carelessly'.

A number of writers have emphasised that the self is primarily constructed through interaction with others (e.g. Andrews 1991; Cashdan 1988; Friedman 1992; Howe 1993; Laing 1977, 1990; Mann 1994; Stevens 1996a). This is a view espoused particularly by feminist psychologists and arises from their assertion that identity for women is principally constructed from their sense of self in relationship with others (Zweig 1996). This view is not, however, limited to a feminist perspective. Cashdan (1988: 47) proposes that 'the child does not begin life with a self but incrementally constructs one through socially engaging others', while Laing asserts that 'every relationship implies a definition of self by other and other by self' (Laing 1977: 86). A sense of identity, according to these writers, is initially and profoundly formed by the relationships one experiences as an infant and further refined by the cultural and historical context in which one develops. 'The seed of one's self-concept is the internalization of how significant others, beginning with parents, have communicated *to* one, *about* one, in the past' (Andrews 1991: 8). As Laing puts it 'one's first social identity is conferred on one. We learn to be whom we are told we are' (Laing 1977: 95).

I share the view that while the sense of self is initially formed by early relational configurations it is not forever fixed and defined by these. A number of contemporary writers who have considered the notion of self in psychology and psychotherapy emphasise its fluid and reflexive nature (e.g. Andrews 1991; Cashdan 1988; van Deurzen-Smith

1988; Gergen 1996; King 1996; Mann 1994; Peavy 1996; Stevens 1996a; Wetherell and Maybin 1996). According to Andrews, initial self-concept does not necessarily remain fixed but is constantly being adapted and refined in response to environmental factors.

> [T]here is an active, in-motion quality about the sense of self. It is not only that a person 'has' a self-concept, an image of personal qualities and characteristics; in addition, he or she is continually testing, confirming, extending, and reconceiving that image in each new situation. The sense of self is as much *verb* as *noun*. And it is this fluidity of self-conceiving – the fact that the self concept is sustained by an ongoing definitional process – that makes psycho-therapy possible and fruitful. The central function of the therapist is to help the client channel that process.
>
> (Andrews 1991: 6)

In the chapters that follow I take this view of the self-in-process. This is the perspective espoused by Carl Rogers (1967, 1980, 1989) who con-sidered the self to be a fluid, growing, changing phenomenon, full of the possibilities of becoming, rather than a fixed and fully formed entity. For Rogers the pre-eminently important environmental factor for the client in the process of becoming is the person of the therapist.

Thus in a good enough therapeutic relationship clients may redefine themselves. Winnicott (1965, 1986), in promoting the idea of 'good enough' mothering, has observed that 'in the therapeutic child-care situation', where inadequate mothering is corrected by therapeutic intervention, 'one is often rewarded by the emergence of a child who is for the first time an individual' (Winnicott 1965: 17). Winnicott has further asserted that 'what we do in therapy is to attempt to imitate the natural process that characterizes the behaviour of any mother of her own infant' (ibid.: 19–20). The same process may apply to the adult client who will emerge from a therapeutic relationship in which they have been well cared for with a more integrated and differentiated sense of self. More about the 'good enough' therapeutic relationship is said in Chapter 2.

So it appears, if this view of the self is adopted, that being in a relationship has the potential to both limit and liberate the self. The majority of our clients will initially present as if the self and its atti-tudes and behaviours are fixed and I see it as a primary function of the therapist to intervene in such a way that the client experiences their self-concept unfreezing and becoming open to change and development. To begin to let go of what one has long considered to be certainties about oneself can be frightening and disorientating for the client and the daunting task for the therapist is to provide the right balance of care and safety with sufficient disconfirmation of the client's fixed or false sense of self to effect dissonance that can then lead to growth and healing. This takes patience, sensitivity and tenacity on the part of the therapist. If, as I believe, such a process of redefinition of self applies to the client in the therapeutic relationship it will also apply to some degree to the therapist as co-creator of the relationship. The way that therapeutic work impacts on the self of the counsellor provides one of the great motivators and rewards of our profession. This proposition is discussed further in subsequent chapters.

USE OF SELF AND THE PERSON OF THE THERAPIST

It is important to note that in what follows I am making a distinction between the *person* of the therapist and the therapist's *use of self*. Because the person of the therapist pervades the therapeutic relationship, some aspects of who the therapist is unavoidably become accessible to the client to a greater or lesser degree. Therapists inadvertently reveal themselves in innumerable small ways as they present themselves to clients through such aspects as dress, accent, age, voice intonation, skin colour, involuntary changes in movement or facial expression, mannerisms, the furnishings and state of orderliness of the counselling room, and so on. Yet inadvertent self-disclosure is not the same thing as intentional use of the self.

Vanaerschot (1993: 49) has commented that 'the important part of the therapist's attitude is not the fact that, in his contact to the client, the therapist eliminates himself as a person, but the very way in which he applies himself'. Rennie (1998: 103) makes a similar observation in pointing out that the therapist may be '*present* as an attentive listener . . . but *absent* as a personality' (original emphasis). Rennie suggests that Carl Rogers, despite his unsurpassed skills of empathy and attentive listening, for the most part kept himself aloof in the therapeutic encounter and showed a marked reluctance to explore his impact on clients (whilst displaying sustained interest in how clients impacted on him).

If the therapist's personhood is a given presence in the therapeutic encounter, their *use* of self is evident in the way that they *extend* aspects of their personality with the intention of influencing the client. Use of self involves the operationalisation of personal characteristics so that they impact on the client in such a way as to become potentially significant determinants of the therapeutic process. Most extended training courses in counselling and psychotherapy now include a substantial component of personal growth work whereby students are required to address aspects of self-development (Connor 1994). A growing number of courses have a requirement that students undertake a period of counselling or therapy whilst in training in order to deal with their own personal issues that arise in the process. Few, if any, explicitly address the topic of the therapist's use of self by guiding students through a systematic and rigorous educational process designed to help them identify, research, evaluate, enhance and integrate attributes of self in order to begin to meld these into their own unique and individual styles of counselling.

PROFESSIONALISATION AND THE USE OF SELF

Now that counselling and psychotherapy have reached the proportions of an industry (Bond and Shea 1997; Thorne 1995), moves to regulate that industry are in full swing. The professionalisation of counselling appears to be proceeding apace with the advent of registration, licensing and accreditation procedures and the emergence of training standards related to the assessment of competence, as pioneered by the Lead Body for Advice, Guidance, Counselling and Psychotherapy (AGC and PLB 1995).

One danger inherent in the increased clamour for accountability and professionalisation is that the therapist who takes an individualistic and unorthodox stance will have their voice ignored or, worse still, find themselves scapegoated and driven underground. Clarkson and Aviram (1998) have suggested that orthodox adherence to established theory is one way in which innovation is stifled and existing power structures within the profession are shored up. Hutterer (1993: 280–1) has written about the pressures to conform apparent within the 'trend towards instrumentalism and technology' that has become evident in the world of counselling in recent years. He sees this trend being fuelled by 'economic demands and competition between distinct therapeutic schools' and considers that it is the pressure to be successful which, in turn, has promoted 'closed and narrow views of effectiveness'. The trend has led to a growth in technical eclecticism and the popularisation of time-limited interventionist approaches, particularly cognitive-behavioural ones. The therapists who are most likely to lose out if this trend continues are those who eschew the power of technique in favour of viewing the therapist as the primary instrument of healing.

My informal conversations with experienced practitioners suggest that in this climate there may be a vibrant underground of therapists who are working in more personally determined ways and my own research (see Chapters 5, 6 and 7) confirms this. Duncan *et al.* (1992) have identified a pragmatic process of professional development that takes place for many therapists as they 'discover the need to reassess their assumptions about their clinical practices after experience shatters the illusions provided by their chosen orientations' (p. vii). They point out that no model of therapy is without its limitations, nor is wholly accommodating of the numerous exigencies of clinical practice. Once the model acquired in training has been thoroughly tested and found wanting, seasoned therapists who wish to grow in professional stature will naturally re-engage in a renewed search 'for a reliable but flexible intellectual framework to guide the therapeutic process' (p. x). Kottler (1986: 15) puts a time-scale to this process and suggests that 'the first decade of our professional life is spent imitating the master clinicians before we ever consider what we really believe in our hearts'.

Whenever I bring up the subject of unorthodox practice in the company of one or two therapists I find agreement that there is a place for this and often 'private confessions' that people work in progressive and personally determined ways in their own practice. Yet within large gatherings or the public domain I experience less of a readiness for therapists to admit to unorthodox or innovative work. The research reported in Chapters 5, 6 and 7 of this book records my invitation to experienced therapists to give a voice to what I consider to be the healthy sub-current of dissent that I have come to believe is vibrantly alive within our ranks.

I sense that healthy unorthodoxy has been driven underground in no small measure by the recent backlash of media criticism, much of it vituperative (McKinstry 1997 and Weldon 1997 provide typical examples of this), which has cast its shadow across the profession. Wary of this shadow, counsellors and psychotherapists are becoming squeamish about admitting publicly to aspects of their work that may be misconstrued, for example touching clients or engaging in regressive work, from fear that they may summon up such demons in the public mind as induced memories, abuse of power, exploitation and charlatanism. I fear we are in real danger of succumbing to our own version of what might be termed 'therapeutic correctness' which has crossed the Atlantic and arrived from America on the crest of the wave of litigation culture that has washed over that land (Hedges *et al.* 1997). Virginia Hilton (1997a) sees a contraction in the profession in the United States based on fear, which has come about through attempts by therapists to minimise exposure to litigation and false accusations of unethical practice. She suggests that an 'unfortunate consequence' of this professional contraction 'is that for many therapists it means a loss of spontaneity, of creativity, and a resulting loss of joy and satisfaction in their work' (p. 5).

If a tidal wave of litigation phobia washes up on our shores and serves to further whip up the strong winds of professionalisation that are already sweeping through our ranks, I suspect we will be in danger of a similar contraction. Thus in the clamour for standardisation, evaluation and audit that is following hard on the heels of the movement to professionalise counselling (House 1996, 1997; Mowbray 1995) many therapists may decide it is safest to eliminate improvisations and idiosyncrasies from their practice on the assumption that these will be construed by others as poor practice, or worse.

If professionalisation is concerned with making counsellors more accountable, then I think there are ways of doing this – some of them very simple – that extend beyond generalised standards of training and accreditation. As Pilgrim (1996: 15) has noted, in any case, 'the notion that registration can protect the public in a simple and direct way remains naïve' in the face of the potent combination of power and intimacy that invests all therapeutic relationships with the potential for abuse. One way we can begin to address this power asymmetry is to encourage our clients, the consumers of counselling, to require us to be more personally accountable. I think we should be educating prospective clients to ask more searching questions of counsellors as well as providing them with information sheets about what counselling is. Currently, few members of the public have little if any appreciation of what to expect from good practice.

Whenever someone asks my opinion about contacting a counsellor I recommend that they ask the therapist not only 'what approach do you use?' but also 'how do you know that this is effective?' I also suggest to prospective clients that they ask to see the therapist's code of practice and ask questions about their supervision arrangements. I encourage them to contact several counsellors and compare responses to their questions before deciding whom they would like to see. I recommend that they take account of the openness with which their questions are received as well as the answers given.

Others have gone further even than this. Miller (1997) suggests that at first interview a client should not fight shy of asking the therapist what made him or her choose their profession and of asking if the therapist is prepared to give concrete evidence that demonstrates that he or she has provided a number of people with '*lasting help*' (p. 143, original emphasis). LeShan (1996: 93) suggests that prospective clients should ask the therapist how much intensive personal therapy they have had and, 'unless the answer is (at least) a couple of years, go to the nearest exit at once'. He further advises that one way to gauge the attitude of a therapist 'is to ask whether he or she has either a sliding scale of prices per session with the spread between the highest and the lowest large enough to make a real difference or else contributes at least one half day a week to a free clinic' (p. 135) and adds that he would not refer to a therapist who did not meet one of these conditions.

These assertions might be viewed as fairly extreme and they certainly make the assumption that the client who is asking has the resources to make a choice about which therapist to see. However they also make the point that clients have the right to ask their therapists to account for the way in which they work and, wherever possible, make decisions based on the responses they get. Szymanska and Palmer (Palmer and Szymanska 1994; Szymanska and Palmer 1997) have developed checklists of issues for the client to consider that set out useful guidelines to help her or him work out whether or not they are getting a good deal from their therapist.

FUTURE TRENDS AND DEVELOPMENTS

I sense that counselling and psychotherapy are poised at a new frontier that may lead us into territory that lies beyond that which has been traditionally mapped out by orthodox theory and practice. If this is so we will need new maps to help us navigate this undiscovered land. I think the sketching of one possible map has been achieved by those who advocate rapprochement through the identification and application of common, or nonspecific, therapeutic factors that appear to occur in all the major approaches to counselling and psychotherapy.

The common factors paradigm

The idea that effective outcomes in counselling and psychotherapy are determined not by approach-specific strategies and procedures, but rather by common therapeutic factors occuring across all schools, is one that has been around for over thirty years and is now gaining ascendance.

After years of vigorously debating whether or not psychotherapy works at all (Eysenck 1952, 1966; Lambert *et al.* 1986; Rachman and Wilson 1980), and if it does, what works best for whom in what contexts and doses, the majority of commentators appear to have reached a guarded truce (Howarth 1989). Research findings seem now to suggest a consensus that counselling and psychotherapy are generally effective, but not differentially so (Bergin and Garfield 1994; Kazdin 1986; Luborsky *et al.* 1975; Shapiro and Shapiro 1982; Sloane *et al.* 1975; Smith and Glass 1977; Smith *et al.* 1980; Stiles *et al.* 1986). Indeed, in a recent edition of their landmark *Handbook of Psychotherapy and Behavior Change* Bergin and Garfield (1994) go so far as to propose that the evidence now accumulated in favour of what they call the 'equal outcomes phenomenon' is 'massive' (p. 822).

This research has uncovered the relative equivalence of contending schools of therapy whilst identifying that equivalence as lying within the province of shared process and relationship variables (Miller *et al.* 1997; Norcross and Grencavage 1989). These are variously identified by different writers but most frequently cited are those factors which combat demoralisation in clients and therapists, such as an emotionally charged, confiding relationship with the therapist; the provision of new learning experiences for the client; the enhancement of a sense of mastery and self-efficacy in the client, and the morale-raising properties of therapeutic myths and rituals (Frank 1961, 1971, 1989a). They are deemed to be common or nonspecific in that they are considered to influence all approaches across the board (Connor-Greene 1993; Duncan *et al.* 1992; Goldfried 1982a; Kottler 1986; Miller *et al.* 1997; Patterson and Watkins 1996; Shepherd and Sartorius 1989; Strupp and Hadley 1979; Wills 1982). A recent publication (Miller *et al.* 1997) that has extensively reviewed the research on common factors has narrowed them down to four broad categories – two of which belong to the client rather than to any expertise the therapist can claim. The four factors that Miller and colleagues identify as constituting the 'unifying language' (p. 16) of psychotherapy are: (i) extratherapeutic factors belonging to clients and their environments; (ii) the therapeutic relationship or alliance (iii) therapeutic techniques, and (iv) expectancy, hope and placebo – by which they mean 'that portion of improvement that clients experience simply by making their way to therapy' (p. 30).

The common factors paradigm, as it gains credence, should not be used as an excuse for woolly and ill-defined operating procedures. The danger then exists that this route, far from bringing us to closer understanding, will take us further away from, knowing and fine-tuning what are the most effective strategies for helping clients. The danger is likely to be minimised if recommendations are followed such as that made by Goldfried (1982b: 382) who has suggested that the common factors route could be extended through research studies designed to uncover and identify successful 'clinical strategies' that occur consistently in the work of effective therapists across a range of orientations. He suggests that such studies would be targeted 'at a level of abstraction between theory and technique' (ibid.) and therefore avoid the highest level of abstraction (theoretical and philosophical formulations) and the lowest (specific techniques) both of which have proved to offer limited paradigms for developing inclusive frameworks. Research into identifying effective clinical procedures at this intermediate level of abstraction would need to take account of contextual issues, including the view that psychotherapeutic variables cannot be meaningfully divorced from the situational context created by each unique therapeutic dyad (Butler and Strupp 1986). They would also need to address the notion that the matching of the therapist's interpersonal stance with the client's characteristics may be a crucial factor in determining successful outcomes (Beutler and Consoli 1993).

The common factors paradigm has achieved credibility following three decades of frantic research activity directed towards a comparison of counselling approaches. What seems to have been overlooked to a marked degree in all this activity is the possibility that it may have proved impossible to uncover consistent and conclusive evidence of the differential effectiveness of one modality as measured against another because outcomes might depend more on how effective the individual counsellor is in using the approach, than on some inherent advantage in the approach *per se*. To illustrate this point Strupp (1986: 125) uses the analogy of the surgeon's knife and suggests: 'it is largely meaningless to examine the surgeon's scalpel to discover why a particular operation was successful, but one may learn a great deal by focusing on the manner in which the surgeon (compared to, say, a layperson) employs it'.

In general, research evidence that purports to show the equivalence of various theories and approaches to psychotherapy suffers from what Kiesler (1966) has memorably termed 'the myth of therapist uniformity' in that it tends to flatten out individual therapist variables that may influence process and outcome and affect how different theories are applied by different therapists. So it seems to me an insupportable generalisation to say, for example, that behaviour therapy is more effective than psychodynamic therapy because such an assertion fails to take account of the multifarious variables that affect how one person might do behaviour therapy, compared with how another would do it. As research has indicated, there will be demographic variables, such as the therapist's age, race and gender as well as idiosyncratic ones such as perceived expertness, trustworthiness and attractiveness which all affect process and outcome (see, for example, Atkinson and Schein 1986; Atkinson *et al.* 1981; Cash and Kehr 1978; Driscoll *et al.* 1988; Heppner and Dixon 1981; Heppner and Heesacker 1982; Strong 1968). Even Hans Eysenck, the arch critic of psychotherapy (Eysenck 1952) and champion of behaviour therapy, in an interview late in his life (Feltham 1996a: 430) expressed the view that 'the method may be less important than the person in many cases [and] that some people are good therapists and others are not'. He called for research studies to investigate this proposition in order that 'we should know just how important the therapist is and how we can select those who are gifted'.

In parallel with the attention that is at last starting to be paid to the role of the individual therapist in influencing change, recent research has pointed to the significance of client variables. This research indicates that 'all psychotherapies may be successful, but with different types of clients' (Beutler and Consoli 1993: 417) and that therapist and client matching is an important predictor of outcome (McLennan 1996; Miller *et al.* 1997; Norcross 1991; Talley *et al.* 1990). Additional variables related to the client and the setting, for example the nature and severity of the client's problem, if they are seen in a 'laboratory' or clinical setting, duration and frequency of the therapy, are all likely to have a significant impact on outcome. Yet Aebi (1993) notes that client preferences have not normally been taken into account in experimental research studies where clients are usually randomly assigned to therapists.

Paradoxically, it may yet prove that what comes from the person of the therapist, rather than their use of models and techniques, provides whatever equivalence of effectiveness that actually exists across approaches. This notion is given credence by research findings and reports which support what has come to be known as the paradox of equivalence – the notion that experienced therapists, regardless of orientation, are more similar than different in the way that they practise (Barlow *et al.* 1984; Brady *et al.* 1982; Bugental 1987; Clarkson 1992, 1995; Crits-Cristoph *et al.* 1991; Fiedler 1950; Goldfried 1982a; Norcross and Grencavage 1989). Further evidence is provided by reports and studies which indicate that experience rather than theory drives the practice of more seasoned therapists (Clarkson 1994a; Skovholt and Rønnestad 1992) and that paraprofessional (i.e. minimally trained) helpers may be equally effective to professionally trained therapists

(Berman and Norton 1985; Christensen and Jacobson 1994; Dawes 1994; Durlak 1979; Hattie *et al.* 1984; Howarth 1989; Russell 1981; Stein and Lambert 1984; Strupp and Hadley 1979).

I strongly suspect that maybe it is not so much that all *psychotherapies* are equivalent. Instead (and this is a crucial difference) it may be that the *most consistently effective therapists* are in many respects equivalent and that equivalence derives more from factors such as clinical wisdom and the enlightened use of self, than from the utilisation of techniques and systematic treatment procedures. This viewpoint is given credence by recent research contributions that identify 'the therapist as an important variable mediating change, semi-independent of technique and orienta- tion' (Bergin and Garfield 1994: 825). Thus it may well be that whilst the external and clearly visible trappings of experienced therapists vary in their splendour and finery, they are actually all wearing something much more similar, and I suspect more homely, closer to the skin. And if the fable of the Emperor's New Clothes (Anderson and Grimm 1985) were to be re-written in this context we might find the observant child watching the procession declaring not: 'But he has got nothing on', and instead: 'But he's wearing the same underwear as everyone else!'

Perhaps as well as considering 'what approach is most effective and what can we learn from it?' it might have been profitable for more researchers in the last few decades to have asked 'which therapists are most effective and what can we learn from them?' There are signs that researchers are at least beginning to acknowledge the relevance and significance of this question (e.g. Goldfried 1982b) even if it has yet to be seriously taken up by the research community. An encouraging sign in this direction is given by Wilson and Barkham (1994) who have remarked that 'it is likely that future research into psychotherapist effectiveness (that is, skilfulness) may show considerably more dif- ferentiation of outcomes than have comparisons between theoretical orientations' (p. 55). The subject of the individual therapist's contribu- tion to process and outcome is discussed below.

Beyond eclecticism – towards a deconstructionist view of therapy

A number of contemporary practitioners and researchers seem to have largely abandoned the search for effective counselling models and approaches based on traditional, orthodox theory (e.g. Dawes 1994; Karasu 1996; LeShan 1996; Spinelli 1994). Others are calling for more flexible and client responsive approaches to therapy which are empirically guided and pragmatically determined, rather than theory bound (Duncan *et al.* 1992; Egan 1997; Howarth 1989; Mays and Franks 1985; Miller *et al.* 1997). In their most recent review of current trends and future developments in psychotherapy, Bergin and Garfield (1994) recognise the demise of 'traditionally dominant theories of personality and therapeutic change' (p. 821) in favour of 'minitheories' which, at a more pragmatic and micro level, concern themselves with what appears to work for which clients, with what problems, in which contexts.

A number of these writers have put forward the view that orthodox theory seems to have led to a dead end and that integrative and eclectic approaches, though currently popular, may prove to lead us up another blind alley from which much groping in the dark may ensue but further illumination and progress is unlikely (Feltham 1996b, 1997b; Howarth 1989; Patterson and Hidore 1997). Karasu (1996) takes a deconstructionist view (by deconstruction Karasu means 'the breaking down of form to find new meaning' [p. vii]). He argues that we need to dismantle and re-evaluate much that has come to be regarded as reliable theory underpinning the various schools of counselling and psychotherapy because a considerable amount of this is untested myth and assumption that is as likely to limit and constrain the clinical capabilities of therapists as it is to enhance them.

> Theories . . . steer one's observations by providing direction and focus, forming boundaries for what is included (and thereby necessarily excluded). Because a theory naturally confers restraints, it can force closure upon what one looks at and sees and, in a more extreme sense, consciously or unconsciously suppress information by eliminating whatever appears inconsistent or competitive with preferred existing beliefs. In this way theories may reify that which is favored or familiar, and, wittingly or unwittingly, obliterate the unfavored and unfamiliar.
>
> (Karasu 1996: 15)

Whilst I would contend that a solid and thorough theoretical grounding is an indispensable component of good counsellor training, I agree with Karasu that an over-reliance on theory may diminish what we have available within our natural helping repertoire and that too many therapists appear to wield their preferred theories and models of helping without sufficiently questioning the premises and assumptions upon which they are founded. Friedman (1992) suggests that therapists should be prepared to abandon theory when original and creative responses to clients are called for. 'Although no therapist can do without a typology, at a certain moment the therapist throws away as much of his typology as he can and accepts the unforseeable happening in which the unique person of the patient stands before the unique person of the therapist' (p. 176).

Karasu (1996) sees the power and potential of psychotherapeutic theories as resting in their 'mythic proportions' as 'legends that endure because they contain collective inspirational value' (p. 27) but warns that if taken as literal truths they are as likely to corrupt as to inspire. Spinelli (1994) takes a similar position and argues that psychotherapy theory largely consists of a number of untested assumptions that have the principal function of investing practitioners and the process of therapy 'with a sense of *special and unique authority and wisdom*' that reinforces 'the unnecessary *mystification* of therapy' (pp. 14–15, original emphases). Maslow (1982) cautions against the danger of theoretical conceptualisations becoming invalid where they are based on abstractions of knowledge rather than being derived from experiential learning gained in the clinical context. According to Mann (1994) the attraction of theory lies in its qualities to reassure, rather than in any inherent ability to carry forward universal truth. Thus he asserts that 'theory is a tidy workshop where we find relief from the complexities of practice. Entering it, we leave behind some of the unruliest truths. They do not fit or cannot behave or do not lend themselves to polite discussion' (p. 113). Crouch (1997) has pointed out that in order for it to become meaningful, counsellors need to make over theory to imprint their own personal stamp upon it. He regards the 'true test of a theory [as] – can I make it come alive, can I make it a part of my personal, and then my practitioner "bones"?' (p. ix).

Whilst Karasu acknowledges that (temporary) allegiance to a theory is important in promoting and fuelling the active placebo element in therapy, he suggests that the creative tension for therapists is to believe in their theories sufficiently to foster personal conviction and confidence whilst remaining receptive to alternative ways of understanding and implementing the therapeutic process that will come with experience, exposure to influences from contending schools, and from studying research findings. I would contend that perhaps *the* most potentially formative influence that may supersede allegiance to a theory is that provided for the therapist by taking opportunities to engage in ongoing research and evaluation of their own practice. This argument is carried forward in Chapters 3 and 4.

It may be that future generations of counsellors and psychotherapists come to view eclecticism and its sibling, integrationism, as sounding a death knell over a psychotherapeutic landscape that has become too densely populated with models and approaches to sustain further healthy growth. Counselling and psychotherapy face a crisis of identity as the explosion of pluralism exposes the inability of the profession to agree on a universally accepted body of theory and knowledge (O'Hara and Anderson 1996). As Goldfried and Pradawer (1982) have pertinently observed 'there comes a time when one needs to question where fruitful diversity ends and where chaos begins' (p. 3).

Though attempts at numbering them vary, it is frequently estimated that there are currently 300 to 400 different theoretical approaches to counselling and psychotherapy alive (if not kicking) and that 20 to 30 of these can be regarded as mainstream. It may well be that the current burgeoning of eclectic and integrationist paradigms comes to be seen as a last ditch attempt to achieve an impossible synthesis from what, in actuality, has become a desperately fragmented and confusing field where, in a glut of contending models, each is clamouring to be recognised (to paraphrase Lewis Carroll and Luborsky and colleagues [1975]) as the best in the race and to receive its prize. Norcross and Grencavage (1989) have seen the current proliferation of different psychotherapeutic orientations as heralding an imminent crisis given that 'the field has been staggered by over-choice and future shock'.

Karasu proffers an extreme view in predicting the complete demise of theory as the organising paradigm for the conduct of counselling and psychotherapy. His apocalyptic vision pictures the last therapist wandering a transtheoretical field of victory in which all adversaries professing particular theoretical allegiance are vanquished and 'the final surviving clinician is the one who shall endure all of the conceptual schisms and schemas that predated him. He does not need theory to buttress his being' (Karasu 1996: 132). In his deconstructionist vision of the future the progeny of this lone survivor will be those therapists who are able to distance themselves from the primacy of theory and create new transtheoretical paradigms based on pragmatic discovery and innovation. Although he doesn't elaborate his ideas about this in detail, Karasu foresees a fresh start to the profession if it can make a clean break from what he considers to be largely discredited, if entrenched, therapeutic myths and assumptions.

If eclecticism and integrationism are to survive as meaningful concepts I think they need to be seen as having the inherent capacity of evolving differently for individual therapists as they develop unique ways of organising, understanding and intervening in the therapeutic process. Then, in the words of Fear and Woolfe (1996: 410), 'it is possible that our journey as counsellors towards a personal integration simply parallels the work done by our clients'. This is a view mirrored in McLeod's (1993) assertion that 'a more fertile approach to understanding integrationism may be to view it as a personal process undertaken by individual counsellors and therapists' (p. 105). A counsellor's personal integration will be achieved through a process derived from the way they have developed and integrated, amongst other things: an image and concept of the person; an understanding of the origin and perpetuation of client problems; an understanding of psychological disturbance and health; an understanding of the principles of therapeutic change; a repertoire of counselling strategies and interventions, and an understanding of the underlying goals of therapy. The acquisition of these will be influenced by an understanding and awareness of their own cultural history and an appreciation of how it differs from that of others, together with awareness of the core values that inform their way of working. Most importantly, these ingredients of personal integration will be mediated by the practitioner's understanding of their own individual pathology and experience of their own healing process.

Mahrer (1989: 146) envisages a loss of integrity for the profession in a scenario where 'each therapist would very nearly be doing his or her own individual brand of therapy'. I think, however, that to a large extent this is already happening – and that in many cases integrity is thereby enhanced rather than lessened. Effective and personally authentic counsellors and psychotherapists do not operate as quiescent clones of their early trainers or the founders of their favoured approaches. I would hope that every therapist worth their salt refines and develops their early learning in the light of experience, perceived client need and their own personal characteristics and preferences.

Through their extended (ten year) research into the evolving professional self of the therapist, Skovholt and Rønnestad (1992) have identified a post-training process for practitioners that they describe as a 'loosening and internalising mode' (p. 103). In this process, which they suggest can last for twenty or thirty years, the therapist faces a challenge 'to individually decide which elements of the professionally imposed rigidity to shed and which elements of the internal self to express' (p. 104) and the task can be painful. Avoidance of this demanding and uncomfortable stage of authentic professional development can occur where practitioners adopt an alternative route which Skovholt and Rønnestad term 'the Pseudo-development path' (p. 103). Individuals who opt to take this easier path 'continue in an external and rigid mode' (p. 103) in which they come to emulate more and more closely and inflexibly an acknowledged master or distinguished proponent of their chosen approach. In consequence there is a continued and rigid external orientation to processes and procedures advocated by a particular theoretical school or model and this, in turn, leads to 'a growing alienation between the authentic personal self and the evolving professional self' (p. 103).

Skovholt and Rønnestad suggest that therapists who tread the hazardous path leading to greater authenticity will experience loss along the way as much of what seemed, at an earlier stage of development, to convey therapeutic truth and certainty needs to be shed to maintain personal and professional integrity. The shedding of the external frame includes 'elements of the professional role that are incompatible with one's own personality' (p. 109) and, as inauthentic aspects of self are sloughed off, a more natural and congruent self, more able to acknowledge the reciprocal nature of therapeutic work, emerges. 'The healthy evolution of the Professional Self permits the therapist/counselor to consistently meet one's own needs within an ethical, competent role. There is more flexibility and more creativity in, for example, applying clinical knowledge to unique client problems' (p. 105).

In suggesting that counsellors learn to work in personally determined ways I am not advocating that therapists merely fly by the seat of their pants in following wherever the wind of whim and mood takes them. Let me restate that what I am suggesting is that clinicians work out and declare their own personal and rigorous therapeutic rationales and procedures that are based on sound initial training in existing theory and practice and then further elaborated by ongoing research and evaluation of their own practice. I say more about what I consider to be the obligations of the practitioner-researcher in Chapters 3 and 4. The intention of this book is to present a client-responsive approach to therapy that draws significantly on the use of self. Such an approach is best conceptualised as a process rather than a fixed stance, and one that mirrors an understanding of the self as process, as outlined above.

In current counselling and psychotherapy training, research and practice there are two developments which at first glance appear to sit uneasily together and point to a possible future schism. The first is the emphasis on outcome and evaluation that is skills based and rests upon common and agreed competencies, as evidenced by movements such as the current development of National Vocational Qualifications by the Advice, Guidance, Counselling and Psychotherapy Lead Body (AGC and PLB 1995) and the British Institute of Integrative Psychotherapy (BIIP 1997). The second is the trend towards highlighting the significance of the therapeutic relationship in determining outcome (see Chapter 2) through emphasis given to the personal contribution of the therapist. Rather than focusing on skills, techniques, and specific interventions, this viewpoint on what determines effective therapy points to the importance of counsellor characteristics and the therapist's 'way of being' with the client.

The danger inherent in these conflicting perspectives is that in the training and deployment of counsellors a wedge may be driven between reflection on self and the skills-based delivery of treatment programmes, with either coming to be seen as essentially excluding and negating the other. In this book I attempt to create a bridge between these two essentially dichotomous positions by formulating a paradigm based on the use of self that straddles both camps through conceptualising the skilled and intentional operationalisation of the therapeutic relationship as the most powerful determinant of outcome. The paradigm encompasses both evidence-based competencies and intuitive interpersonal procedures in that it utilises research and evaluation to uncover how each practitioner may best tailor the therapeutic relationship to meet the needs of their clients. The foundation and wellspring of this paradigm is the individual therapist.

THE INDIVIDUAL COUNSELLOR'S CONTRIBUTION TO PROCESS AND OUTCOME IN THERAPY

The move away from the search for differential components of effective therapy has led some authors of the psychotherapeutic literature to begin to re-evaluate the individual counsellor's contribution. In some ways, as Mahoney and Norcross (1993) point out, this involves taking the hoary old research topic of interactions between therapist and client off the shelf and giving it a dusting down. However the subject is given a fresh tweak since the focus of study has now moved from issues of transference, countertransference and objective detachment to issues of mutual influence and reciprocity between therapist and client. One of this new breed of relationship researchers, Frank (1989a), has extensively studied the contribution of nonspecific factors in psychotherapy outcome and process and concluded that the therapist's personal characteristics are of fundamental importance in determining how the nonspecific components of therapy will be utilised to the client's benefit.

Moves to give greater credence to the individual therapist's contribution to effective psychotherapy are apparent in the growing number of books and articles that view the therapist's human qualities and common wisdom as more important in determining efficacy than learned theory or techniques. Lomas (1981: 2) sees the essence of this as considering the balance between the 'ordinary' and the 'special' in the practice of a profession which 'depends more on experience, courage, and imaginative open-mindedness than on anything else'. He suggests we consider a somewhat radical shift in perspective that acknowledges the validity of unrehearsed responses to troubled people by changing 'the paradigm for our work . . . to that of friendship rather than the application of scientific theory' (p. 6).

Feltham (1997b: 123) expresses a view that is gaining popularity, though one that is probably still more acceptable to clinicians than to theoreticians and funded researchers, that 'individual clinical giftedness, so overlooked as a factor in therapy, may well be more significant than any pedagogic theory'. Lambert's (1989) review of the individual therapist's contribution to psychotherapy process and outcome concludes with the cautiously worded (if to some, revolutionary) proposal that 'it would seem defensible to recommend treating the individual therapist as an independent variable in factorial research' (p. 482). He further clarifies this line of thinking in making the specific suggestion that future research should focus on 'the behavior and outcomes of exemplary therapists who produce either negative or positive results' (p. 483). McConnaughy's view, gleaned from an extended review of the literature on the person of the therapist, similarly indicates that researchers may need to change tack to take account of individual therapist variables now that the search to uncover differential effectiveness between schools of therapy has proved fruitless.

> It is possible that each school has a within-group variance (determined by the qualities of the individual therapists) that is greater than the between-group variance (determined by theoretical orientation), and that it is not the techniques or theoretical strategies per se that are curative. The finding of no differences lends itself to the thesis that the therapists themselves as persons are more influential than their theoretical orientation or technique.
>
> (McConnaughy 1987: 307)

McConnaughy's view has already begun to be reflected in findings where researchers and commentators have shown a keener interest in the individual therapist. Kline (1992), in his discussion of methodological problems in studies of psychotherapy, contends that variance among therapists is infrequently acknowledged in research studies, yet what evidence there is suggests that it may be a major contributing factor in determining outcome. His observations are borne out by a landmark study conducted by Luborsky and colleagues (1985) into therapist success and its determinants. The study uncovered 'wide variations in the effectiveness of the [9] individual therapists' involved and 'profound differences' in individual therapists' success rates with the patients treated (p. 602). Findings from data analysed in their study suggested to Luborsky and colleagues the following potentially significant conclusions:

> that the *effectiveness of a given therapy can vary considerably depending on the group of therapists providing the treatment.* This is turn suggests that the therapist is not simply the transmitter of a standard therapeutic agent. Rather, the therapist is an important, independent agent of change with the ability to magnify or reduce the effects of a therapy. This, of course, may be obvious to clinicians who are in the position of making referrals to colleagues; however there has been little quantitative evidence to support this clinical impression.
>
> (Luborsky *et al.* 1985: 609, original emphasis)

Overall, they conclude from their findings that 'the major agent of effective psychotherapy is the personality of the therapist, particularly the ability to form a warm, supportive relationship' (p. 609).

In an important addendum to a major research project (Shapiro and Firth 1987) which studied the comparative effectiveness of 'Prescriptive' and 'Exploratory' therapy, Shapiro and colleagues (1989) further analysed their outcome data and concluded that one outstanding therapist was in fact responsible for advantages that had initially been attributed to the type of treatment. In their discussion they admit that differences between individual therapists, which had initially been regarded as 'nuisance variables' (p. 383) to be eliminated as far as possible from the study, actually turned out to be the determining factors in differential effects found between the treatments compared: 'The first Sheffield Psychotherapy Project was not designed as a study of therapist effects, but rather a view to controlling these. With hindsight, the differential effectiveness revealed by the present analysis testifies to the failure of our attempt to design therapist effects out of the study' (Shapiro *et al.* 1989).

This was a well designed and controlled study and the implications of this re-attribution of effects are significant. Their findings indicate that it may be impossible to eliminate individual therapist variables from clinically relevant research studies. Furthermore their re-evaluation raises the possibility that attempts to disregard the individual therapist's contribution may constitute a major source of invalidity in process and outcome research. This is a notion that has far reaching implications for the research community as not only does it call for a change in the emphasis and direction of future psychotherapy research, it also calls into question the validity of numerous previous research studies that have reported findings where individual therapist variables have been disregarded. In the fourth edition of their major review of the effectiveness of psychotherapy Lambert and Bergin (1994) begin to address this issue in suggesting that the role of the individual therapist has been under-emphasised. They now consider that 'the individual therapist can play a surprisingly large role in treatment outcome even when treatment is being offered within the stipulation of manual-guided therapy' (p. 181). They note that 'this issue has been ignored to a surprising degree' and suggest that 'intriguing possibilities for new discoveries' lie in further researching the subject (p. 175).

It goes without saying that the individual therapist contributes to process and outcome in a relationship, not in a vacuum, and Patterson and Hidore (1997) have recently revealed the heart of the dilemma that now faces the research community in considering the ineffable nature of the therapeutic relationship as a focus for study. They suggest that within all forms of psychotherapy the:

> universal presence of a psychological relationship constitutes an obstacle to research attempting to study the influence or effect of other factors, such as specific techniques, apart from the relationship. The relationship cannot be eliminated and is difficult to control. Because of the inability to control the relationship scientifically in experiments, evidence is unclear concerning the impact of various techniques. Do the techniques work, or is the relationship alone the change agent despite the techniques?
>
> (Patterson and Hidore 1997: 176)

Approaches to counselling that give due prominence to the therapist's use of self have the potential for moving us beyond the current diversification (some might say disintegration) of approaches engendered by therapeutic pluralism and of taking us back to the healing power of the individual clinician (LeShan 1996; Peavy 1996). By moving forward in this way we may even be closing a circle and returning to an earlier time and culture of helping where the factors that generated restorative growth and therapeutic change were deemed to be the unique character- istics of the individual healer or practitioner. Interestingly, in a recent book considering the future of counselling and psychotherapy (Palmer and Varma 1997), Wessler and Wessler (1997) revisit the roots of therapy and remind us that those who counselled in earlier epochs, whether they were called priest, shaman, sage or elder, relied on accumulated wisdom and experience to guide and advise others. The development of the use of self is essentially about the development of clinical wisdom in the therapist. Whilst clinical wisdom may start with theories and models, it moves far beyond these to encompass a rich, potent and varied blend of life experience, self-awareness, technical and procedural expertise, ethical judgement and perspicacity, together with a sound understanding of one's own limits of knowledge and competence.

Despite the resurgence of interest in the individual therapist's contribu- tion, little has so far been written or researched on how the therapist might develop the use of personal attributes in their counselling prac- tice. The growing bank of literature on the personal development of counsellors and trainees (see Chapter 5) tends not to make explicit links between the therapist's personal characteristics and their style of counselling. Rather than looking, *per se*, at the personal growth and self awareness of the counsellor, this book will, instead, concern itself with exploring where the interface of the self of the therapist impacts on his or her work with clients. The following chapter borrows a term popularised by Gendlin (1981, 1984a, 1984b) to begin to look at where aspects of the person of the counsellor encounter the person of the client in such a manner as to be deemed therapeutic. It is suggested that at the interface of this encounter is often to be found a remarkable potential for growth, change and healing.

Chapter 2

The counsellor's edge of awareness

I am inclined to think that in my writing perhaps I have stressed too much the three basic conditions (congruence, unconditional positive regard and empathic understanding). Perhaps it is something around the edges of those conditions that is really the most important element of therapy – when my self is very clearly, obviously present.

(Rogers, in Baldwin 1987)

In talking about the counsellor's 'edge of awareness' I am borrowing a term from Gendlin who, in his work on focusing (1981, 1984a, 1984b, 1990, 1996), uses the expression to describe the outer edge of the client's awareness where the 'felt sense' of what is just becoming accessible to consciousness is experienced. This may be an underlying feeling, sensation, image, metaphor or thought. As Leijssen (1993: 129) has explained, when counsellors work at the client's edge of awareness they find themselves 'waiting in the presence of the not yet speakable and being receptive to the not yet formed'.

The edge of awareness is a concept that can be applied to the counsellor's experience as well as to the client's. For the therapist who works at their edge of awareness this can mean reaching beyond conscious competence to aspects of yet unfathomed capability, where new possibilities for working are forming only in that precise moment of being with the client. This is how Gendlin (1990: 210) describes focusing in relation to the client's edge of awareness and I think it can apply equally to the counsellor's process: 'The word "focusing" means to spend time, attending to that inwardly sensed edge. When that happens in the silence, the next thing and the next come gradually from deeper and deeper'. As Gendlin observes, this may sound mysterious until the therapist comes to know that awareness is in itself a process rather than a fixed state.

According to Bugental (1987), the seasoned therapist who is able to work at their edge of awareness is a true artist rather than a technician: 'True art is only to be found on the edge of what is known – a dangerous place to be, an exciting place to work, a continually unsettling place to live subjectively' (p. 95). In considering Bugental's words, it seems important to reiterate here that I am talking about counsellors who are able to confront the unknown in themselves and their clients from a secure base of training and personal awareness. Those who have not undergone the disciplined study and application of a core theory of counselling are likely to find themselves stumbling around in the dark when they leave familiar territory, rather than feeling their way to new levels of competence.

Yet there is a paradox at the heart of this assertion. For to be at our most effective as therapists I believe we must, to a large degree, liberate ourselves from the conceptual thralls of our training. At the same time it is crucial that we retain the discipline and safety which that training has given us. As trainees move from being novices to become seasoned practitioners the scaffolding provided by their training may be less and less relied upon. Gradually it is dismantled as the counsellor comes to graft sufficient aspects of their own particular therapeutic attributes on to their unique personal infrastructure. As the scaffolding is removed, the external shape of the new structure that is revealed may bear little, if any, resemblance to the initial form which was provided by the training experience. These lines from Emily Dickinson's poem *The Props assist the House*, though they describe the emergence of the soul rather than the therapeutic self, suggest how this process might unfold:

> The Props assist the House
> Until the House is built
> And then the Props withdraw
> And adequate, erect,
> The House support itself
> And cease to recollect
> The Auger and the Carpenter –

The theoretical formulations and clinical strategies we learned in training can only take us so far. Recent research supports this notion in revealing that techniques may account for only 15 per cent of change in counselling and psychotherapy, while relationship factors count for around 33 per cent (Miller *et al.* 1997).

The professional paradox here, as I see it, is that the completion of training constitutes a point of departure more than a point of arrival.

Casement (1985) has noted the limiting aspects of what is learned in training in observing that 'by listening too readily to accepted theories, and to what they lead the practitioner to expect, it is easy to become deaf to the unexpected. When a therapist thinks that he can see signs of what is familiar to him, he can become blind to what is different and strange' (p. 4). The essential nature of this paradox, then, is that it is only possible for us to break free safely from our learned responses when we have successfully integrated a good and useful training. As Hunter and Struve (1998: 76) assert, 'progressive therapeutic techniques will be effective only if they are used to enhance an already solid foundation of good clinical psychotherapy skills'.

Hobson, I think, has identified with some clarity the interface where the edge of awareness of counsellor and client dovetail with the therapist's technical training when he says that 'psychotherapy is mainly a matter of mutual exploration of emerging meanings. Most techniques are means of diminishing fear and of promoting courage to engage in a joint exploration in which two or more people venture into the unknown alone and yet together' (Hobson 1985: 11). Models and theories are only as adaptable and flexible as their existing epistemology allows. As a socially constructed phenomenon any theory or model of counselling or psychotherapy will have elements of circularity that determine its limits and its limitations. The self of the therapist, in contrast, is almost infinitely adaptable in having the ability to respond differentially to individual clients and a variety of therapeutic challenges. If we are open to moving beyond what our theory and training have taught us we are capable of responding to our clients in ways that we do not know we possess until they are drawn from us by each inimitable relationship with each unique client.

A PERSONAL PERSPECTIVE ON THE USE OF SELF IN THERAPY

In order to illustrate my thesis I will add, from time to time, some personal notes which I hope will give the reader some sense of how the use of self might actually take shape in the counsellor. I do this not so much from self-indulgence as from a wish to be congruent and to share something of the process that I think has been at work in forging my own development as a therapist. I consider it to be an essential exercise for any counsellor to reflect deeply, carefully and frequently on the links between their own psychological makeup and their activities as a therapist. To do so brings an important facet of the counsellor's edge of awareness into fuller view.

There is a natural correlation between the personal characteristics of the counsellor and the way their style and approach develops. This may manifest as an extension of, or as a reaction against, perceived personal attributes, depending on whether they are viewed (consciously or unconsciously) as desirable or otherwise. For instance, a counsellor who views themselves as having been deprived of a full range of emotional expression as a child by parents who disapproved of the free expression of feelings, may become a very 'feelings oriented' therapist in order to compensate (perhaps unconsciously) for this deficit. The danger then is that clients who prefer to work with ideas rather than feelings are insidiously induced by such a therapist to adopt a more feelings mode of engaging, without explicit negotiation or agreement having taken place. This is an abuse of power whether it is deliberate or uncalculated. In other instances the correlation between personal characteristics and the *modus operandi* of the counsellor may show itself as a complementary and therapeutically desirable extension of those qualities.

The division is not always clear cut. To illustrate: I am the child of a dominant and controlling father and a passive mother. I learnt from an early age to be wary, cautious and tentative in my relationships with others – a response formed from the necessity to accurately read and predict my father's moods, feelings and inclinations, and to respond accordingly. This ability could make all the difference between approval or a stinging rebuke. The positive legacy of this is that I think it has helped me to develop a sensitivity to the moods and needs of others that has resulted in reasonable amounts of empathy, intuition and a rather precise ability to attune my responses to the client's emotional 'wavelength'. On the other hand, I have on occasion been overly sensitive with clients and have held back when the client might have benefited from a more robust response from my own fear of a rebuke. At other times the controlling father within me can show itself in competitive rivalry, for instance, whenever I catch myself (or more likely my supervisor catches me) sparring intellectually with clients in a bid to win them over to my viewpoint and show them how clever I can be.

An important part of the work that a counsellor needs to undertake in their personal therapy and supervision is a sifting through of their own psychologically determined responses and a rigorous examination of how these may impact on their counselling work. With greater awareness choices can then be made about which aspects of self to coax and encourage into fuller expression as legitimate parts of the professional persona and which to keep a watchful eye on to ensure they do not undermine any therapeutic potency that the counsellor may possess. I am aware that aspects of my own personal history, such as that alluded to above, constitute a profound influence on the way that I work as a counsellor, and no more so than in how I view and conduct myself within the therapeutic relationship.

THE COUNSELLING RELATIONSHIP AND THE USE OF SELF

It has become commonplace to speak of the centrality of the counselling relationship in determining therapeutic outcome (see, for instance: Bergin and Garfield 1994; Butler and Strupp 1986; Callaghan *et al.* 1996; Cashdan 1988; Clarkson 1992, 1994a, 1994b, 1995, 1998; Friedman 1992; Hobson 1985; Holmes *et al.* 1996; Hycner 1991; Kahn 1997; LeShan 1996; Lewin 1996; Luborsky *et al.* 1985; Miller *et al.* 1997; Norcross 1986; Patterson 1974; Patterson and Hidore 1997; Patterson and Watkins 1996; Peck 1989; Rogers 1994; Smail 1978; Strupp 1989; Strupp and Hadley 1979; Woolfe 1996; Yalom 1980). It would seem that Patterson and Hidore (1997: 70) now speak for many when they comment that: 'Nearly everyone accepts the assumption that the relationship between the therapist and the client (or the therapeutic alliance) is the main factor in psychotherapy'. The interest that a number of researchers are currently displaying in the therapist's interpersonal stance and how it aligns with the client's attachment style is an indicator of the importance now being accorded to the quality of the therapeutic alliance as a predictor of outcome (Callaghan *et al.* 1996; Dolan *et al.* 1993; Lazarus 1993; Mahoney and Norcross 1993; Mahrer 1993; Norcross 1993; Rappaport 1991).

Clients make use of the relationship offered by counsellors in different ways. Sometimes the client appears not to need anything added which would make the counselling relationship overtly different to any other good, attentive, human relationship. Most of us have had clients who appear to need us to do little more than sit and listen to their stories and yet who clearly experience our listening as significantly therapeutic. It appears that what such clients need is *enough* of a good relationship – that is one which provides consistency, stability, a secure sense of attachment and unconditional care and attention – to have the experience of it radiating through them, like warmth from the sun, until they are sufficiently saturated to carry the warmth away with them. Perhaps they do this in the form of what Geller *et al.* (1981–2: 127), citing Schafer (1968), term ' "benignly influential" and enduring subjective representations of the therapeutic relationship'. Or perhaps it is, as Friedman (1992) suggests, that individuals need to be confirmed in their uniqueness by others who are different from them and that a good, ongoing, therapeutic relationship provides this confirmation. It goes without saying that with such clients we need to be cautious about ending too quickly on the mistaken assumption that the relationship is getting too cosy, or that the client is not benefiting, because we are not being sufficiently active.

Other of our clients may need the skilled operationalisation of the relationship, by the therapist, to make any difference. Here effective counsellors need to use sensitive interventions to call upon the client to *live in* the relationship, rather than merely basking in its warmth. A key strategy that can be used to bring the relationship powerfully alive is immediacy, which is discussed later in this chapter. Whilst retaining strong ego boundaries, therapists need to be able to loosen their egos sufficiently to allow their clients to make use of the relationship in the way that they need to. There is a crucial difference which therapists need to learn between being *used* and being *made use of*. The former means allowing myself to be exploited, the latter means to give myself freely and willingly in a disinterested way that allows the client to make best use of me to promote their own growth and healing. An example may serve to illustrate this important difference.

A number of years ago I undertook a research study (Wosket 1989) investigating four of my clients' experience of counselling. One participant, called here Nina, talked explicitly in her research interview about the way she had made use of me (as opposed to used me). Here is an excerpt from that interview in which we have been talking about what helped Nina to build trust in her counsellor.

NINA: [W]hat else helped – although at times I'd get really angry – would be I felt sometimes I was being so awkward, just to be awkward, but you'd still be sitting there and, you know, I'm thinking 'why isn't she getting angry – why is she just putting up with me?' But then it meant that I knew you'd still be there. So it meant I could go deeper or come up with stuff I really didn't want to look at, but knew I had to.

VAL: It sounds like something about stability.

NINA: Mmm . . . it was kind of gradually getting into things. You know, you'd start off with something not quite as heavy, or not quite as painful, or not quite as deep, and it's kind of a testing. You know,

I'd see what [pause] ... I suppose it is seeing, you know, how does she react if I brought this up. She reacted like that when I've done that, and she reacted like that when I've been like that – so it's safe and it's OK to be like this. It *is*, kind of, a testing. When I've felt as if I was being really awkward in sessions and thinking 'you haven't got anywhere – you're just being so stupid and so awkward'. But then I've been able to go deeper because I know that you're still there. And it was that kind of thing that allowed me to, kind of, go deeper.

[Later in the interview Nina brings this stage of the counselling up again]

NINA: I've just gone back over and thought 'I've been such a *bastard*, how on earth did you put up with me?' Because I do see this as work. I mean I came here to work – and I think I see it now as a kind of testing. How much can you put up with me and ... can you accept me whether I'm working or not working, or being nice or ...? [sentence not finished].

The words of this client serve to illustrate a point made by Beutler and Consoli (1993: 418) who have indicated that adaptability in the relationship 'requires a willingness on the part of the therapist to consider his/her interpersonal stance both as a malleable therapeutic force and as behaviors over which one can acquire planned control'. The ebb and flow of the relationship as proffered by the therapist will therefore involve both a loosening that allows the client room to experiment with ways of relating and, at other times, a tightening that evidences direction and purpose.

The power of the relationship in counselling hinges on the fact that it is normally the *only* relationship that the client and counsellor have. Many of us, as trainees and inexperienced counsellors, go through a stage of attempting to develop an ongoing relationship with a client whom we particularly admire or like. It usually only takes one experience of this to realise that counselling and social relationships don't mix. Part of the seasoning of the therapist is the giving up of the possibility of other relationships with people we often come to care deeply for. This is one of the 'necessary losses', to use Judith Viorst's term (Viorst 1987) that the therapist has to learn to endure over and over again.

A number of important inferences derive from the exclusivity of the therapeutic relationship. The therapeutic relationship because of its newness is not in itself contaminated by old patterns, grudges, betrayals, unfinished business, loss of hope or fixed stances. This makes it fertile and virgin territory for whatever the client needs to plant in it. At times this may be facsimiles of past relationships, or it may be fantasised hopes, fears and expectations that come from the client's previous experience. Yet this ground may also contain the seeds of latent and new possibilities that have remained outside the client's experience until they are brought to life through, and in, the special relationship with the therapist.

Clients frequently come into therapy with a history of fixed and unyielding relationships that contribute to a perception of the other in a relationship as adopting a series of absolute stances. The client has learned to define themselves and their relationships, often from a very early age, in an absolutist way in response to this experience. For example, 'my father is often angry with me, therefore I must be bad' may easily become, for the adult, 'if this person is angry with me they don't like me', or 'I can never feel angry with people I like'. For such a person experiencing and surviving angry moments with their therapist (both when they feel angry with the therapist and also when they experience the therapist being angry with them) can be nothing short of a revelation and is often a real turning point that enhances and deepens the therapeutic alliance. Here is an example of what I mean.

As we moved towards the end of the counselling session I knew that my client was very troubled and wanted to tell me what was distressing her whilst, simultaneously, finding it impossibly difficult to do so. I tried to reassure her that I would be able to hear whatever it was but she left without telling me and was clearly very upset. She came back still upset and I said to her that I thought she might be angry with me because I had encouraged her to disclose and had not managed the ending of the session very well. She, in turn, said that she had left feeling upset because she thought I had been angry with her for not disclosing. We talked about being angry with one another and I said: 'If I *had* been angry with you I would still care about you and I know that if you felt angry with me it wouldn't mean that you stopped caring about me'. To this she replied: 'I've never experienced that before. I've never thought that could happen in a relationship'. My client had experienced only fixed and absolute stances in her previous primary relationships – notably from one angry and punishing parent and one discounting and neglectful parent.

Her journey through counselling came to contain two distinct threads that were interweaved yet seemed like separate stories. One was the story of her abusive childhood; the other was the story of our relationship.

As the second narrative was played out she learned, for the first time, that relationships can be negotiated and that feelings can be of many colours and that within those colours exist an infinite range of shaded tones, and not only black and white. Among the colours she discovered and learned to differentiate between were those of joy and sadness; hope and despair; anger and love; shame and exaltation; rage and tenderness; humiliation and pride; collaboration and avoidance; wariness and trust; the compulsion to die and the wish to live.

There is a precision to the therapeutic relationship that separates it out in time, place and quality from other relationships and interpersonal experiences in the client's life. There is a certain clarity and distillation that belong to the time-limited and intimate nature of the therapeutic meeting. There is certainty and therefore some safety in the knowledge that it will run its course, will end and start again within clearly defined boundaries. It has its own rhythm and momentum. These things can give a sense of experience encapsulated and protected from the vicissitudes of life outside. Here the client (and the counsellor) can choose to let go of some of the complications of other relationships and activities in what is often experienced as a resting or creative space – even a place of sanctuary. Whilst it can have a timeless and floating quality, the fact that the session is clearly constrained by time boundaries can give the quality of the relationship within it a vibrant intensity in which time seems precious and must not be wasted on insubstantial issues. Thus the intimacy of the therapeutic dyad contains a paradox. Whilst the intimacy is constrained and restrained by time boundaries and codes of conduct, meaning that it is both a partial and a transitory intimacy, it also often affords a unique opportunity for a deeper and in some ways more lasting intimacy than do all or some of the client's (and maybe also the counsellor's) relationships outside counselling.

There can be excitement, tension, anticipation and exhilaration within the relationship that, at times, make it not unlike an intimate sexual encounter. The client is encouraged to divest themselves of their defences and social trappings in a way that may leave them feeling exposed and vulnerable. Similarly the counsellor will normally divest themselves of any social veneer and façade and may, at times, also feel revealed and laid bare. Kottler (1986: 9) describes the therapist's part in the pairing thus: 'The therapist uses only his naked self (figuratively of course) as the instrument of treatment, a condition that requires tremendous self-control and exacts considerable vulnerability'. For the therapeutic hour counsellor and client are locked in close physical proximity in an exclusive pairing, free from intrusion and behind closed doors. Some-times this can feel like a 'dangerous liaison' where the lines between psychological closeness, physical proximity and sexual intimacy are hard to discern and disentangle, for both counsellor and client. When this occurs, I think the counsellor normally does well to stay with the heat rather than take flight by getting out of the kitchen or lowering the temperature. I feel sure that I have done some of my best work as a counsellor when I have stayed with the heat in this way, as it is at such times when I feel most alive and receptive and in tune with myself and my client. Yet such occasions need to be handled by the counsellor with great sensitivity, awareness and propriety if both counsellor and client are to be protected.

In writing about the abuse of power in the helping professions, Guggenbühl-Craig (1979) has considered the difference between de-structive and constructive elements of sexuality within the therapeutic relationship. Sexual impulses, he suggests, are destructive when they are bent on harming either party. With therapists, Guggenbühl-Craig asserts, 'it is one of the oldest charlatan tricks to try to bind . . . patients by awakening sexual desire' (p. 62) whilst often 'a patient's sexual longing for her analyst is nothing more than her desire to destroy him professionally' (p. 61). If such impulses are not recognised and pursued with 'great psychological earnestness' (p. 62) by the therapist they are likely to be acted out compulsively and will then have a seriously destructive effect on the therapy. By way of contrast, Guggenbühl-Craig suggests that a different kind of sexual dynamic that is both legitimate and constructive may invest the relationship and enhance its potential to benefit the client.

> The situation is very different when the awakening of sexual desire in patient and analyst is an expression, a bodily aspect, of a basic-ally positive relationship. This is far less dangerous, since neither party is essentially interested in destroying the other and the sexual fantasies are nothing other than the expression of a fruitful rela-tionship, which is bound to have a positive effect on the therapy. Such fantasies may be safely permitted to continue and to develop, for the urge to live them out is not so strong.
>
> (Guggenbühl-Craig 1979: 62)

A client was referred to me for counselling, by his tutor, because of his 'attitude problem'. I searched for a way of liking him despite his aloofness, intellectualising and determination to keep me away from his feelings. The liking came first through the fleeting glimpses I saw, in his eyes, of a hurting child. I learnt to look at his eyes rather than listen to his words. My liking for him increased and began to include a sense of enjoying his physical presence and with this came an awareness of feeling sexually attracted to him. Whilst initially I felt that I 'ought' to try to suppress this response, I eventually came around to allowing it to be part of my experience and feelings when I was with him. I enjoyed being with him and the sexual energy was part of this. As far as I can tell, this doesn't mean that I conveyed to him in any overt sense that I felt attracted to him, although he may have picked it up in other ways. However, because I allowed this to be part of my experience when with him, I am sure that he felt my liking of him in a more tangible way. If I had kept the part of me that found him attractive out of the session I believe I would have been incongruent and he would not have experienced my liking of him so clearly and so fully.

There were risks around for both of us as this dynamic unfolded. As the therapy progressed I found it quite seductive to be told repeatedly by him that I had seen inside him and knew more about him than anyone else. I guess the risk for him would have been if he had interpreted my liking of him as an invitation for a different kind of relationship. At times it felt as if there was the sense of a special pairing and an intimacy that excluded others in our meetings. Two containing factors were especially important here for me (and therefore for my client). First, I knew, as certainly as I am able to know anything about myself, that I would not act out my attraction to this client in any way that elicited (or responded to) an invitation to engage in a different kind of relationship. I think the client at some level knew this and trusted me. If I hadn't felt secure in holding my own boundaries I think he would have sensed this and perhaps have needed to check or test out whether I could hold them. Second, I was receiving regular and careful supervision on this work and my supervisor was keeping a close eye on the welfare of the client and my handling of myself in the relationship.

The client, towards the end of counselling, referred to his experience of feeling liked by me. Six weeks after starting to counsel him I had reviewed the work with my supervisor who supported my feeling that I should offer him a further period of counselling. I then re-contracted to work with him for a further six months. When we came to our last session he spoke about this re-contracting and said that it had been very important for him that I had offered to see him beyond the initial six week contract. He said that because he knew I wasn't obliged to do this it had indicated that I was choosing to be with him and that I found him 'worth bothering about'. He told me that this had been significant for him and had marked a turning point in his counselling.

I realise that in presenting only my own perspective on this experience I may be laying myself open to being criticised for naïvety, subjectivity and incongruence. In my defence, I can only say that I chose not to raise the sexual dynamic with my client and invite a discussion about it because, as far as I could tell, it was not an issue for him and was not undermining the therapy. We did talk about liking one another in what seemed a clear and honest way. At the end of the therapy he asked me if he could return for counselling in the future if he had further difficulties on his course. His tutor told me several months later of positive changes he had observed in my ex-client's relationships with both himself and his peers and he also informed me that my client had secured a very good job at the end of his course that involved working with people in a helping capacity. This clinical vignette is included, not to encourage others to follow my example, but to stimulate debate on what is often considered to be a contentious area in counselling and psychotherapy. The topic of sexual dynamics in counselling is covered more fully in Chapter 8.

Love and dependency in the counselling relationship

I suspect, when it really comes down to it, that my primary motivation and ability as a counsellor rest on my capacity to love. I imagine I am not alone in thinking such thoughts, although I believe that many therapists may be reluctant to state publicly, as Lomas has, that 'the therapist's love for his patient often plays a significant part in healing and may even be the crucial factor' (Lomas 1981: 7). Peck (1989: 81) has defined love as: 'the will to extend oneself for the purpose of nurturing one's own or another's spiritual growth'. By love in the counselling relationship I mean the ability to care deeply enough about the other person to commit myself fully and unconditionally to their process of change and development without requiring anything for myself *that might diminish the other person in return*. Brazier (1995: 204) puts it like this: 'to do therapy, it is essential to be able to love without resentment'. I am not saying here that my clinical work does not meet my own needs – at times it most certainly does – and the many ways that this can happen are scattered throughout this book. What I am suggesting is that what I receive in return from my client as a by-product of my own investment in the relationship is not something that I *require* of the client in order to satisfy some unmet need in myself. As Hillman (1979: 18) has stated: 'needs in themselves are not harmful, but when they are denied they join the shadow side of counseling and work from behind as demands. . . . Demands ask for fulfilment, needs require only expression'.

Kreinheder (1980), in words attributed to his mentor, Kieffer Frantz, conveys the quality of the intimate and loving relationship that is possible in therapy and which can change both counsellor and client.

> 'If you are going to be a healer,' he said, 'then you have to get into a relationship. There is a person before you, and you and that other person are there to relate. That means touching each other, touching the places in each other that are close and tender where the sensitivity is, where the wounds are and where the turmoil is. That's intimacy. When you get this close there is love. And when love comes, the healing comes. . . . So I would say that the thing to do is to be intimate. Enter quietly into one another. Use all the empathy you can muster. Say what you think and what you feel. Talk about yourself and each other and your feelings and fantasies. Encourage the projections. Explore the full range of what happens when two people find intimacy. That is the greatest thing that is available to human beings. That is the experience a therapist can offer his patient, an experience that will transform the lives of both of you.'
>
> (Kreinheder 1980: 17)

These words from Kreinheder's paper on 'The healing power of illness' describe the unique quality of the love with which a therapist may honour their clients. Kahn, in commenting on the meaning of love in the work of Carl Rogers, makes a useful distinction between the Greek terms *agape*, the form of love meant here, and *eros*, a more worldly love.

> Eros is characterized by the desire for something that will fulfill the lover. It includes the wish to possess the beloved object or person. Agape, by contrast, is characterized by the desire to fulfill the beloved. It demands nothing in return and wants only the growth and fulfillment of the loved one. Agape is a strengthening love, a love that, by definition, does not burden or obligate the loved one.
>
> (Kahn 1997: 39)

Rogers himself defines the term *agape* as love which 'respects the other person as a separate individual, and does not possess him. It is a kind of liking which has strength, and which is not demanding' (Rogers 1994: 94). Rogers more frequently refers to this core condition of the therapeutic relationship as positive regard. Yalom has picked up on the risk of unorthodoxy involved in caring for our clients in this way.

> During the course of effective psychotherapy the therapist frequently reaches out to the patient in a human and deeply personal manner. Though this reaching out is often a critical event in therapy, it resides outside official ideological doctrine; it is generally not reported in psychiatric literature (usually because of shame or fear of censure) nor is it taught to students (both because it lies outside of normal theory and because it might encourage 'excesses').
>
> (Yalom 1980: 402)

Hobson (1985) equates love with tenderness towards clients and sees it as the animating force that determines the quality of our interventions: 'Without tenderness the noise of our talk does harm' (p. 280). Some clients, especially, seem to need our love in order to heal. The clients who need us to love them are usually those who cannot be *reasoned* into feeling healed. Many clients with fixed and pernicious ideas about themselves and their world will be able to benefit from cognitive-behavioural counselling approaches that can help them free up and reframe their understanding and thinking. Yet I suspect I am not alone in having clients who appear fundamentally unyielding to this approach and may repeatedly lament: 'I can see the reasoning, but I still *feel* I'm to blame'. With such clients all our valiant attempts at challenging the irrationality of their core beliefs may founder.

It may be that the client has too great an investment in holding on to a fixed belief that constitutes the core of their identity. Andrews (1991) provides a cogent rationale for this hypothesis.

> The self-image is embedded in a boundary-maintaining system, and information that disconfirms that image is often perceived as a threat. ... People will selectively counteract, avoid, or discount feedback that suggests that they are not who they think they are. This establishes a negative feedback loop that tends to return a system to its original equilibrium after a disturbance.
>
> (p. 12)

So, for instance, to give up the idea that it must have been my fault that I was abused as a child and that I was to blame because I was unlovable, can be more threatening to the psyche than the possibility that I deserved to be loved and that the parent who should have loved me seemed to hate and exploit me instead. Clients who are faced with the Herculean task of coming to terms with this kind of reality often cannot give up the hope of having a parent who loved them unless there is the possibility of finding a more authentic loving in the therapist. Clients who feel loved by their therapist may find that aspects of their negative self-concept start to shift and dismantle despite their best efforts to sustain them intact.

The client who has a deep and fundamental belief in their own badness will frequently do their utmost to ensure that the therapist confirms this view of the self. They will set out to 'prove' how unworthy and undeserving they are of the therapist's love and acceptance. It is therefore of the utmost importance that the therapist is persistent, consistent and reliable in their loving attending, in the face of the client's best efforts to provoke a different response that would confirm their self-image as someone who is profoundly unlovable. The leverage of change comes with the cognitive dissonance (Festinger 1957; Strong 1968) which is created through this loving attending. If it is sufficiently consistent and unshakeable the client, despite themselves, will come to trust the therapist and his or her judgement. The dissonance may first take the form of puzzlement: 'Either there is something about me you are not seeing (that is, my badness) or my reasoning is at fault. Because I *know* that I'm a horrible person, it must be that you are wrong – and yet normally I can trust your judgement'.

It would be naïve and overly optimistic to expect that the client will easily switch to believing that because the counsellor seems to like them, they must therefore be a likeable person after all. However, the lever will eventually come to find some purchase in the slender fissure that gradually opens up between the client's perception of themselves and the different experience of themselves that is mirrored increasingly in the relationship with their therapist. Whilst the head may continue to reason that the person is unlovable, the heart will experience feeling loved and cared for. Gradually, the client will comes to internalise the therapist's love and integrate it as love for the self.

It seems to me that the majority of counsellors have become frightened of the concept of love. Perhaps to them it smacks of unprofessionalism, over-involvement, erotic countertransference or the encouragement of dependency. And dependency is *certainly* not to be tolerated. As Lewin (1996: 77) has observed 'sometimes being dependent is so stigmatized as to be represented as a form of destruction' in which caring for the client is perceived as 'both a burden and an embarrassment'.

I want to write next that I have never had a problem with unresolved dependency with my clients as long as I have not required or demanded of them that they detach themselves from me before they are ready. And, as I write it, I am aware how arrogant such a statement may appear. None the less, my clinical experience has led me to believe that unless interfered with in some way it is a natural process for developing adults to separate from their care givers and that, similarly, the client who is growing towards autonomy in a healthy counselling relationship will naturally develop the will to disengage from the counsellor. Herron and Rouslin (1984: 150) have identified this process in observing that 'separation occurs throughout the therapeutic process' and not merely at its end. It is important to note that I am talking here about individuals who have shown themselves to be appropriate candidates for psychological therapy through requisite intake and assessment procedures and not about those individuals who have such a fragile sense of self that they are unable to sustain an adequate boundary between self and other during periods of therapeutic intervention.

This being said, it is my experience that some clients who are perfectly appropriate candidates for therapy initially need to experience a closeness with their therapist that verges on merging, rather than be expected to be self-responsible and separate from the outset. The therapist in such cases comes to represent and provide a part of themselves that the client may have lost or have never known. The counsellor becomes what is sometimes termed an 'auxiliary ego' and stands in for this aspect of the client – whether it is loving attention, acceptance, or perhaps a thinking part of the self – until the client re-owns it, or even comes to know of its existence for the first time.

The most needy and dependent clients are the ones who tend to come to therapy dragging behind them a series of fateful and doomed relationships. Their very neediness drives others away. These are people who have not had their dependency needs sufficiently attended to in childhood. It is not their fault that they become adults with 'holes in their souls' (Bradshaw 1991) and the therapist should not treat them as if they are wrong to have attachment deficits. Tait (1997) has observed that the attachment needs of adults whose dependency needs were not met in childhood tend to be overlooked by therapists or regarded simply as transference phenomena to be interpreted. The therapist's role with such clients is to calmly, strongly and acceptantly tolerate the extent of the client's neediness so that she or he learns that the therapist is able to do what the neglectful parent did not do – that is to bear what can seem like an insatiable need for love and attention and hold up under the pressure.

This process follows sound learning theory. An individual who, as a child, has been exploited, invalidated, ridiculed, discounted, ignored or neglected may not know how to love, comfort, accept and listen to themselves or pay attention to their own feelings. They come to discover these gifts to the self in what the therapist gives them in a close and loving relationship – and one that does not have to lead to irredeemable dependency. Having 'fed off' the therapist in this way the client will start to pull away and reintegrate as a separate and more complex person once they have taken what they need. The danger arises if I begin to doubt myself or my client or get scared or defensive and try to force a premature separation.

Bowlby (1969) makes an important distinction between dependency and attachment which is of relevance here. He argues that 'the value implications of the term "dependency" are the exact opposite of those that the term "attachment" not only conveys but is intended to convey' (pp. 228–9). Whilst dependency means that a child or grown-up relies on another to support aspects of their existence, and is a term frequently used pejoratively in relation to adults, attachment is a value neutral term describing close involvement or affinity with another person. Unfortunately, as Bowlby observes, the two terms are frequently confused and used interchangeably in therapeutic terminology. What can then happen is that therapists react to clients who are closely attached to them as if they are dependent upon them in some unhealthy and leech-like manner.

Counsellors who cannot tolerate fierce attachments are likely to attempt to prise the client away, as if they are some sort of limpet, perhaps in the mistaken belief that termination is the same thing as growthful separation. No matter how gently we try to detach a limpet from a rock it will only cling harder as it senses our attempt to dislodge it. It is then only the force of a blow that will make it relax its grip. Similarly, clients in terror of enforced separation, may cling on more desperately to counsellors who, in turn, are fearful of such attachment, until they are wrenched asunder by the equivalence of a blow from the therapist. This may come in the guise of a confrontation, decreased availability, or through increasing coldness or aloofness. I have even heard of it happening where a client arrived for their counselling session to find a note pinned to the door by the counsellor saying that they were unable to see the client any longer. There are, of course, also counsellors who are fearful of abandonment or of not being needed who will encourage unhealthy dependency in clients who would other-wise be ready to detach themselves and move away.

Aspects of love within the therapeutic relationship, when discussed at all, are usually alluded to under the rubric of reparenting, or what has come to be known as corrective emotional experience or the reparative relationship (Casement 1990; Clarkson 1995). In this paradigm, which has its roots in the psychoanalytic literature but now spans a number of approaches to counselling and psychotherapy, the therapist is seen as a substitute parent who can somehow stand in for and make reparation for neglectful, disruptive, abusive or smothering parenting that the client has experienced as a child. Whilst I believe that aspects of the relationship we can provide for our clients may be experienced as similar to that which a better parent might have been able to give them, I seriously doubt that we can provide an experience that is wholly reparative in any transforming sense. To do so would mean that we would have to fulfil all the client's unmet dependency needs from child-hood and adolescence and to feel that we can, or ought, to attempt this would have us posturing on either, or both, of the twin spurs of omnipotent grandiosity or undisciplined over-functioning.

If we cannot actually reparent, I think we *can* provide a model of good parenting from which the client can compare the upbringing they have had with what they might have expected to receive had they been better cared for as a child. As well as nourishing the client, the experi-ence of being in such a relationship can help him or her to think about what was, and what might have been. This can be a truly restorative process having the potential of giving access and release to powerful feelings such as grief and anger that provide a pathway to healing. The primary function of the counsellor is to bolster and reinforce the possibility that the client can then come to act towards themselves as the 'good enough' (Winnicott 1965, 1986) parent they have become acquainted with in the therapist. It is fundamentally important that the counsellor is able to help the client see that the ingredients of good parenting are generalisable and may be found within the client them-selves, rather than being the sole preserve of the therapist. The danger inherent in a perspective that invests the counsellor with the power of reparenting is that the client may locate their growth and healing in the therapist rather than in their own transforming powers of regeneration. It may stroke my ego to think that I have provided for the client in a way that their original carers lacked but the narcissistic glory I derive from this may well come at the expense of my client's autonomy and independence.

THE INTERNAL CLIENT OF THE COUNSELLOR

Casement (1985) has written wisely and fully about the 'internal supervisor' of the therapist and this concept has greatly influenced the development of approaches to counselling supervision. In similar vein I would like to suggest that the concept of the 'internal client' of the therapist has much to offer as a way of understanding the therapist's use of self and how this can be developed to the benefit of both client and counsellor. What I mean by the therapist's internal client is that part of the self that grows, is affirmed and, on occasion, is healed by the work that is done with clients and patients.

Whilst a good deal has now been written about the dangers of counsellors exploiting their clients and inappropriately meeting their own needs through the work that they do (Bugental 1964; Goldberg 1986; Guggenbühl-Craig 1979; Hillman 1979; Page 1999; Ram Dass and Gorman 1985), less has been written about the benign opportunities that counselling work affords the therapist for healing, growth and personal development. The oversight is curious given that a number of studies indicate that many therapists choose the profession in response to (and in some ways as a continuation of) their own experience of being a client, and that ongoing growth and healing become significant motivating factors for the work that they do (Kottler 1986; Miller 1997; Wosket 1990). Brazier (1993: 75) has gone so far as to suggest that 'the activity of being a therapist is intrinsically growth promoting' and that 'therapy is more consistently good for therapists than it is for clients'.

Many authors of the psychotherapeutic literature have written about how clients can impact on therapists through awakening their dormant issues. Aponte and Winter (1987) are two writers who explicitly develop this theme in terms of the therapist's use of self. They suggest that undertaking therapeutic work with clients 'jostles [the therapist's] own personal issues in ways that few other encounters do' and that the frequency of this process 'moves a therapist to seek to resolve his own life issues, especially as his dilemmas are inevitably brought to the foreground by the people he is seeing' (p. 94). Aponte and Winter see this process unfolding within the therapeutic environment which, by its very nature, provides unique opportunities for transforming aspects of self for the therapist as well as for the client.

> There are aspects of the persona of the therapist that are specific-ally, and often only, revealed to the clinician through his conduct

of therapy. Furthermore, he is not locked into the same person-specific struggles in his work that he has with his own family. He is often more able to pursue change in his work context than at home or in his own personal therapy or analysis. As a consequence, *providing treatment* acts as a potent stimulus to personal growth and fosters a variety of possibilities for change in the therapist himself.

(Aponte and Winter 1987: 94, original emphasis)

Aponte and Winter (p. 95) suggest that the catalyst for such change is embedded in various elements of therapeutic engagement with clients. Whilst they are primarily writing about, and for, family therapists, I think a number of their headings are meaningful for therapists in general and I have elaborated them in my own words.

- **Role structure**   The structure of the professional role provides emotional protection and allows therapists to reveal aspects of themselves with minimal risk.
- **Motivation**   For therapists who strive to attain standards of excellence in their practice, this drive can serve as a powerful motivator for them to address and deal with psychological and emotional difficulties or deficiencies that may appear to limit their effectiveness.
- **Courage**   Facing the needs of clients may engender courage in the therapist that is not demanded to the same extent or intensity in other relationships. The committed and courageous therapist will not duck the difficult issues about him or herself that are brought to the surface by interactions with clients who frequently seem to veer with unnerving accuracy towards our sensitive and tender spots (what a student of mine once called our 'crumple buttons').
- **Vantage point**   The therapeutic environment provides opportunities for the therapist to observe their own patterns of response and behaviour without undue threat. The focus of change is the client, not the counsellor, who thereby may feel released to examine aspects of self within a climate that is conducive to self-examination without requiring self-exposure. As Cashdan (1988: 163) has observed, 'our patients hold up mirrors to us. If we are willing to look into them, we sometimes get a clearer picture of who we are as human beings'.
- **Vicarious change**   In helping the client to engage in constructive change the therapist may, sometimes consciously, sometimes unconsciously, trigger change in themselves. An example of this process which I am on occasion aware of is when, in the process of exhorting a client to look after themselves better, I have the uneasy sense

of asking my client to take their medicine without having swallowed my own dose. Sometimes this will spur me on to effect changes in my immediate circumstances that ensure I am better addressing my own self-nurturing needs.

- **Special relationships**   As therapists we are privileged to have the opportunity to construct significant relationships with a range of unique individuals and such encounters provide us with opportunities for substantial development and learning.

To the above list of components suggested by Aponte and Winter, I would add one other, which is **Feedback**. Research conducted by Skovholt and Rønnestad (1992) over a period of ten years with one hundred qualified therapists in the United States has indicated that clients' feedback to therapists is a primary contributor to the evolving professional self. Therapists who include in their repertoire of interventions that of asking their clients for feedback – not just on how the therapy is progressing but on how they, the counsellor, are coming across in the relationship – create for themselves significant opportunities for learning about the self.

These developments of self that can take place through engagement with clients take us into the realm of meeting our own needs in the process of attending to the needs of others (Horton and Varma 1997). Therapists rightly need to be alert to the dangers that this brings and I have dealt with this subject more fully in Chapter 8. However, I do believe that the legitimate satisfaction of the therapist's needs can greatly enhance professional competence and commitment and that this then has a positive knock-on effect for clients. Burton (1972: 2) has expressed this process well in proferring the view that 'psychotherapy succeeds best when the therapist himself participates deeply in the process as a human being. When some of his growth needs are met, the therapy prospers; when they are not met, the therapy languishes'. Indeed, Burton goes as far as to suggest that the satisfaction of the therapist's (legitimate) needs expressed within his or her role are 'as important, if not more important than the client's for the simple reason that the unconscious takes over in extreme therapist dissatisfaction and punishes or even eliminates the client' (ibid.).

Immediacy – a catalyst of change

Immediacy is the name sometimes given to feedback that occurs in moments of direct, mutual dialogue between counsellor and client

(Carkhuff 1969a, 1969b; Carkhuff and Anthony 1979; Egan 1997; Patterson 1974). Patterson (1974) equates immediacy with genuineness and makes what I consider to be a useful distinction between immediacy and other forms of dialogue within the therapeutic relationship: 'Immediacy, while involving the relationship of the client to the therapist, is not a transference relationship. It involves the therapist as he really is, rather than simply, or mainly, as a representative of some other important figure in the client's experience' (p. 85).

Using immediacy is an important way that counsellors can make themselves available to clients. In essence immediacy is about how to be transparent with the client without becoming startlingly naked. In being immediate, hopefully, I am not self-disclosing in a way that will make the client stare at me or look away in embarrassment. Rather I am inviting the client to see further into him or herself through what I am revealing of myself. When I use an immediate response effectively the client will momentarily switch attention to me and then it will bounce back in such a way that they are able to receive and hold it.

It can be confusing for trainee and novice counsellors to work out which aspects of self are legitimate to express and which are not and this difficulty frequently surfaces around immediacy and self-disclosure – when to do it; when not to do it; how much and which bits to disclose? Students are often not helped by mixed messages handed on by the course, through its tutors and course materials. As Kottler (1986: 52) has observed, in training 'there is always a theme of "stifle yourself", juxtaposed with encouragement to be authentic'.

An important lesson for novice counsellors to learn is that only part of self-disclosure is in the conscious control of the counsellor. As Yalom (1980: 411) has observed 'the effective therapist cannot remain detached, passive and hidden. Therapist self-disclosure is integral to the therapeutic process'. The therapist will constantly 'give themselves away' by the merest flicker of expression, movement, voice-tone, change in breathing, heart-beat, physical arousal, skin colouring, etc. The experiences that bring people into counselling have often also developed their skills of vigilance and sensitivity. Their physical or emotional well-being, and even survival, may have been previously determined by their ability to read accurately the signs displayed in the attitudes and behaviours of more powerful 'significant others' and then take avoidant or compliant action accordingly. This legacy will live on in the counselling relationship. My client will perceive things about me that I am not consciously choosing to disclose (for instance, if I am scared or embarrassed by what they are telling me) and as they come to know me they will come to know, at some level, whenever I am being incongruent. I have learnt it is best to 'come clean' even when this leaves me feeling vulnerable and exposed. It takes a great deal of effort and energy on my part to try *not* to let the client see what is going on for me. I have found that it is more productive to direct my energy into helping the client work out what impact my direct or indirect self-disclosure is having on them, rather than invest my energy in trying to conceal myself.

Counselling trainees, early on, frequently make the mistake of thinking of self-disclosure only in terms of what the counsellor reveals of a personal nature about themselves to the client. I seldom find it useful to self-disclose in this way. The danger is that the focus of the client's attention thereby shifts from them to me and they may then become more interested in my story than their own. When I have made errors in the past in disclosing personal material to clients, some of the negative effects arising from this have been: burdening the client with information they would rather not have; making them feel inadequate compared to me (where I let someone know I had had a similar difficulty to their own and had overcome it – I had mistakenly intended to inspire hope and optimism); startling the client and thereby seeming inconsistent in my way of being with them; annoying them by obtruding into their time and space; suddenly making them see me as a 'real' person whilst they still needed to construct me as someone else; frightening them into thinking I might die (when I let someone know I had recovered from an illness about which they had a phobia – again it was an ill-conceived attempt at modelling and reframing). I now use intentional personal self-disclosure with the utmost caution and only when I am pretty sure that my own motives are not suspect and reasonably certain that the client will welcome the initiative.

There is a second form of self-disclosure that is more closely related to immediacy. Rather than personal self-disclosure, this might be called *relational* self-disclosure. Here I agree with Yalom (1980: 414) who has commented: 'I feel it is often important to reveal my immediate here-and-now feelings to the patient. I rarely find it necessary or particularly helpful to reveal many details of my personal past and current life'. Jourard (1971: 19) has defined disclosure as meaning 'to unveil, to make manifest, or to show' and self-disclosure as 'the act of making yourself manifest, showing yourself so others can perceive you'. Thus relational self-disclosure can be taken to mean the therapist making themselves manifest within the therapeutic relationship.

This type of disclosure arises from my felt responses within the relationship with my client. These may be thoughts, feelings, images, fantasies, echoes or resonances, bodily sensations, lapses or increases in energy that can normally be trusted as having some relevance and significance because they arise from the meeting between us and not from something I choose to bring into that meeting. I normally find it useful to disclose something arising from my response (not necessarily the thing itself, which may be too raw and unprocessed) to my client when this occurs. Self-disclosure of this nature will often foster increased reflexivity in the client rather than distracting them, as the therapist's personal self-disclosure is wont to do. Paradoxically, a decrease in the frequency of personal self-disclosure by the counsellor or trainee can bring about an increase in intimacy where it is replaced with relational self-disclosure and immediacy used in this manner.

Immediacy is frequently about catching the client off their guard – in the best sense of the phrase – in so far as the therapist momentarily circumvents established defences and catches the client unawares in an opportunity for real engagement that they may not have been able to muster for themselves. Here are a few of examples of immediate interventions that I have made with clients and how they have responded.

1 VAL: I feel that it is hard for you to let me be close today.
   CLIENT: I don't want to keep you at a distance but it's not safe to let you any closer. I'm frightened I will contaminate you. I feel disgusting.
   VAL: I won't come closer than feels OK for you – but I do want you to know that I feel good in your presence.

2 VAL: We ended badly last week and I was concerned that you might not come back. I feel like we have had a row.
   CLIENT: I didn't think I would come back. I thought we were getting on OK until last week and then I felt like you didn't understand me at all.
   VAL: You sound hurt. I'm glad you came back, even though it was hard, so that we can talk about what happened.

3 VAL: I feel like we're not really connecting today and that makes me feel as if I am not helping you in the best way that I can.
   CLIENT: I don't know why I'm talking like this. It's not what I wanted to talk about. I think I'm avoiding what really hurts because it's so painful and if I let it out I'm frightened about how I'll cope later. It's such a long time before I see you again.
   VAL: In a way you're trying to look after yourself by keeping me away from your feelings. If you let them out it would be so

anguishing that you might feel overwhelmed and then I wouldn't be around to help. I know it's hard to have only one session a week. I feel that too.

4   [This client has been telling me about a suicide attempt made that morning and his resistance to taking steps to look after himself between now and the next session. We are at the end of the session.]

CLIENT: I can't see any point in going on. It's been like this for months and nothing changes. It's so painful and I just want to get out of it.

VAL: This is bloody hard for me too. I don't know if I will see you again [My client sees I am tearful].

CLIENT: It helps a bit to hear you say that. It makes the impact of what I might do more real. ... [Long pause and the client weeps.] ... You *will* see me next week. I don't want to say it – but I promise.

5   VAL: I feel like I want to gather you up in my arms and comfort you.

CLIENT: You don't know what it means to me when you say that. I want to be held so much and it really makes me believe that you care for me, although I can't understand why you do.

You may notice in the examples above that whilst I am revealing some of my own feelings and perceptions to the client, I am not demanding anything in return. To do so, I think, is a corruption of immediacy in that it asks the client to attend to my needs rather than their own. No matter how powerful our feelings may be when we are moved by our clients it is absolutely fundamental to our role as helpers that we can contain those feelings and find ways of using them as invitations to the client to succour and sustain themselves, rather than as a means of requiring *them* to look after *us*.

The illustrations given also highlight the importance of timing and context. These examples are recorded with little or no context and some may seem stark or startling. The key question to bear in mind in being immediate with clients is: 'what can the relationship bear?' Immediacy is intensely challenging and asks a great deal of the client by way of a return investment in the relationship. It should only be embarked upon when the counsellor is reasonably sure that the relationship is sufficiently established and intact to tolerate the reverberations of the immediate intervention. It goes without saying that the counsellor also needs to be wholly committed to the relationship and its demands.

In example 2, above, I had knowingly 'instigated' the row to which I referred in the previous session. By this I mean that I had chosen to be immediate with my client in the knowledge that it would 'ruffle his feathers', but trusted that the relationship was sufficiently established to contain this and that he sensed that I cared about him. My client was someone who intellectualised a great deal and appeared mainly to use the counselling sessions as an opportunity to lecture me on his own belief system. One day I dared to say that I had found myself switching off when he 'climbed on to his soapbox'. He was clearly nonplussed by this and his response indicated that he felt I wasn't understanding or supporting him. I tried to explain that I had said this because I was interested in hearing about him as a person, rather than as an orator, but I clearly bungled it as we ended up having an argument. He went away disgruntled and I felt scared in case he didn't come back. He did in fact return and in response to my immediacy he allowed me, for the first time, to get close to his feelings and to see and hear that he was upset. This event activated a turning point in the counselling in that it provided him with the new experience of sticking with, and working through, feelings of upset in a relationship. His more characteristic response would have been to withdraw and decide that the other person wasn't worth bothering with. The incident led to a much more congruent relationship between us in which feelings began to be acknowledged and talked about, as well as thoughts and ideas. He stopped keeping me at arm's length and as a result, at times, I felt that our relationship became very close.

If I am uncertain that the relationship can stand the strain of unrestrained immediacy, I can still move towards a more immediate encounter with my client in a less challenging and direct way through using self-involving statements. For instance, taking example 5 above, I have given below four levels of alternative response that move gradually nearer to the most immediate (level 5) one. I might have used any of these instead of the one given if I had felt that my client wouldn't have been able to benefit from such a direct meeting with me, or it was too early in the relationship to invite such powerful mutuality. By way of illustration I have given the client's response at each level. These are real examples.

Level I response

VAL: You haven't said as much, but I wonder if you are feeling quite vulnerable today.

CLIENT: I'm not in a good mood today. Things have been really difficult for the last few days.

Level 2 response

VAL: It seems hard for you to talk about your feelings today and yet I sense that you are upset.

CLIENT: I *am* upset but I don't know if I want to talk about it. Sometimes it's better to keep the lid on things. I know that's not true, but sometimes it's easier.

Level 3 response

VAL: I notice we're not talking about your feelings today and when that's happened before it's often when you have been very frightened or very sad. If you're feeling like that today I'd like to help if I can.

CLIENT: I was thinking all the way here that I wanted to tell you how I'm feeling. But when I got here I couldn't. I'm glad you noticed even though I couldn't tell you. I've just been trying to hold myself together.

Level 4 response

VAL: It's hard for me to listen to you talk like this when I feel that your words may be covering up a lot of sadness and loneliness. I know that sometimes it's difficult for you to let me see you're upset and to let yourself be comforted here.

CLIENT: I know from past experience that I do feel comforted if I can express my feelings here. I want to, but it's so painful and I find it so hard to believe that anybody could really care about me.

Level 5 response

VAL: I feel like I want to gather you up in my arms and comfort you.

CLIENT: You don't know what it means to me when you say that. I want to be held so much and it really helps me to believe that you care for me, although I can't understand why you do.

The technique of wondering or thinking aloud (as in the level 1 response) is the least threatening and direct for the client who can, if they wish, choose to deflect it, ignore it, allow it to drop into the space between us, or make an indirect response (as the client does here). The level 2 response is more direct, yet is still tentative and allows the client plenty of room to determine the level of her own response. Even if she chooses not to take up my offer to talk about her distress she knows that I have sensed it and this may help her to feel cared for. The level 3 response is a more robust challenge for the client to own her feelings as it brings in 'evidence' from previous sessions. Coupled with the challenge, though, is an increased offer of support. In the level 4 response I am putting my cards more clearly on the table. This is potentially more threatening for the client because it lets her know that I have 'seen through' the resistance to displaying her real feelings. However it also lets her know that I understand and accept that it is hard for her to reveal her feelings and the implicit offer of support is stepped up with the more emotive word 'comfort'.

COUNTERPOINT

Counselling can be a dangerous occupation (Breakwell 1989). Counsellors need to have in place structures, safeguards and procedures that ensure that, as far as possible, they are protected from abuse, exploitation, or the acting out of destructive fantasies by disturbed clients. Similarly they need to make sure that, whatever intake and assessment procedures they employ, they take on for counselling, certainly in an out-patient setting, only those individuals who give a reasonable indication that they are psychologically minded and can make appropriate use of a counselling relationship and process (Lemma 1996; Palmer and McMahon 1997). Good and regular supervision is one such important mechanism for safeguarding counsellors as well as clients.

In particular, counsellors need to pay attention to issues relating to the client's boundaries and sense of self and be wary of taking on individuals who have such poor ego boundaries that a fragile sense of self may disintegrate to a point where boundaries between self and other are no longer discernible and capable of being respected. Therapists have been persecuted, stalked and even killed (Hewson 1996) by seriously disturbed clients. Therapy for some may only be safely proffered in an environment that provides security and protection for both client and therapist, for instance within the confines of a secure psychiatric unit where the risk of the client acting out destructive fantasies against the therapist is reduced by institutional safeguards that serve to protect and preserve the physical welfare and anonymity of the therapist. The use of self is also, and crucially, about therapists knowing and respecting their own limits as well as those of their clients.

Chapter 3

The use of self in research

> [T]he standard approach to psychological research submerges individual uniqueness in order to uncover empirical generalizations.
>
> (Howard 1986)

This chapter considers some of the issues surrounding the use of self in research and looks firstly at the individual therapist's contribution to research – both as the focus of research studies and when operating in the role of practitioner-researcher. The second part of the chapter introduces and outlines a research study I have recently undertaken that explores the therapist's use of self. Data and findings from the study are presented in Chapter 4.

RESEARCH AND THE INDIVIDUAL THERAPIST

Traditional experimental research has de-emphasised the role played by the self of the counsellor in psychotherapy process and outcome. Within reductionist research individual therapist characteristics have normally been viewed as variables to be eliminated in clinical trials. The dominant research paradigm has favoured the quantifiable study of comparable treatment interventions with homogeneous populations (Barlow *et al.* 1984; Frank 1982; Lambert 1989). This is despite the growing body of evidence that points towards the person of the therapist as possibly the most crucially determining factor in psychotherapy process and outcome research (Luborsky *et al.* 1985, Shapiro *et al.* 1989).

Lambert (1989) posits a number of reasons for the apparent reluctance of some members of the research community to take on board the significance of the individual therapist's contribution. He considers a central factor to be 'the threat that such research poses to the reputation, morale and even the livelihood of the practitioner' (p. 482). Lambert suggests that clinicians who might agree to take part in studies on individual therapist effectiveness would run the risk of compromising themselves professionally by offering themselves and their work up to the scrutiny of others. He proposes that even in confidential studies where therapists were to be guaranteed anonymity, dilemmas would arise for the practitioner who happened to discover hitherto unacknowledged weaknesses and deficits in his or her practice when compared with the work of other therapists studied. He concludes that 'such a highly threatening proposition is not likely to produce much cooperation from practitioners, administrators or researchers' (ibid.). Frank (1982) takes a similar line to that adopted by Lambert and proposes that research studies which purported to look at the relationship between individual practitioner qualities and outcomes could be extremely threatening, both to the self-esteem and the financial security of those found wanting in therapeutic effectiveness.

If, as Lambert and Frank assert, human nature dictates that individual counselling practitioners are likely to eschew evaluative studies of their own practice in order to protect their own interests (lamentable though this is in a profession that purports to value openness and accountability), perhaps a place to start is with encouraging therapists to reflect more openly about their work within a research climate that promotes open disclosure rather than secrecy. As a move towards this I have included in Chapters 5, 6 and 7 data gleaned from a survey sent to 200 qualified and experienced counsellors and psychotherapists on the topic of unorthodox practice and the therapeutic use of self. In the survey I invited therapists, anonymously, to record something of their own experience of progressive or innovative practice and any learning they had gained from this that had subsequently made an impact on their professional growth and development.

Findings from the study are reviewed in chapters which follow, however two facts about the responses to the survey were immediately striking and appear relevant to mention here. First, although these were all therapists whom I knew and had a professional connection with, the response rate was relatively low. From 195 questionnaires (five envelopes were returned unopened because the addressee had moved away and these are excluded from the analysis) 61 responses were received (a return rate of 31 per cent). However, of those therapists who did respond, well over half (37, i.e. 61 per cent), chose to identify themselves even though questionnaires were administered so that respondents could send their replies back anonymously. Furthermore, 12 of the therapists who identified themselves invited me to contact them further if I wished to interview them or ask them more about their experience of progressive and innovative work. It is perhaps significant to note, then, that in this study asking counsellors about their experience of unorthodox practice the majority of those contacted did not respond, yet the majority of those who did respond chose to reveal their identities. This may indicate that there are at least a small number of practitioners who are willing to identify themselves to a researcher, in confidence, in order to reflect openly on unorthodox procedures in their own practice that have impacted on their use of self.

PRACTITIONER OR RESEARCHER – OR BOTH?

Whenever I pause to review what seem to have been the important influences on my development as a counsellor I think of the valuable skills and perspectives I have adopted from my teachers and supervisors; I think of the hugely formative experiences I have undergone in learning from my clients and supervisees; and I think of the wisdom of experienced practitioners that I have heard about from their books and writings and have stored away to be raided from time to time. It slightly dismays me to realise how little of my learning appears to have derived from reading the research of others. I'm not sure why this is, but I realise that I am not alone in this position. Studies have confirmed just how low the rates of utilisation of psychotherapy research to inform the practice of experienced therapists are when compared with the learning gained from interpersonal encounters with clients (Morrow-Bradley and Elliott 1986; Norcross and Prochaska 1986; Skovholt and Rønnestad 1992; Trepper 1990).

In my own case I suspect that procrastination plays its part. I also know that much of what is set forth in learned journals I find to be inaccessible in that it is written in the language of academic psychology, a language that I find largely incomprehensible and devoid of warmth and energy. Esoteric language does not reach out to meet me as a fellow and fallible practitioner. I suspect, with Howard (1996: 105), that often 'journal articles build power, status and funds more than real, useful, relevant knowledge'. Rarely, it seems to me, do the people who record their conclusions about what is significant in psychotherapy process and outcome give the impression that they have any clients themselves. Whilst I am aware that the vast body of research literature has but minimally impacted on my own development as a counsellor, I am equally struck by the hugely significant influence that the small number of research studies I have engaged in with my own clients have had on my practice and professional development. One of these studies constitutes the subject matter of the following chapter.

The deployment of objective researchers having no previous connection with the subjects of their clinical trials is the norm in experimental research. Even research that purports to explore the impact of personal characteristics (clients' or counsellors') on the counselling process has usually been undertaken by objective researchers who study the counselling interaction from the sidelines. For the counsellor to attempt to research their own practice has, in the past, been seen by those who exclusively favour experimental research as dangerously subjective and biased, almost as if there is something faintly tainted or corrupt about a counsellor holding the dual role of practitioner and researcher. I am glad to report that this seems now to be changing and that the practitioner-researcher is slowly coming to be accepted as an invited and even welcome guest at the parade of research dignitaries rather than being tolerated as a somewhat shady and disreputable interloper.

If the individual therapist has infrequently featured as the focus of research studies, it appears, in turn, that he or she is often reluctant to undertake the role of researcher. Pleas for practitioners to engage more fully in personal research and scholarship have been made by a number of authors (e.g. Barlow *et al.* 1984; Clarkson 1998; Dryden 1991; Howard 1986; Lambert 1989; McLeod 1997b; Mahrer 1989; Ross 1996; Shipton 1996; Wilson and Barkham 1994). Ross provides what I consider to be a compelling rationale for this:

> Research and scholarship engender humility in us. This is a function of knowing just how fragile are the foundations of our profession. We then behave with real vulnerability in our relationships with clients. Indeed, our ethic demands that we do our best for the client, a best that can only be demonstrated by a concern for questioning assumptions and refining techniques and theories.
>
> (Ross 1996: 552)

Some of the apparent indifference to research and evaluation that is displayed by clinicians may mask resistance that has its roots in fear. Asking clients to reveal their experiences of being counselled by us may be exposing, but this is no reason for us not to do it. Shipton (1996: 541) wonders whether this fear 'also unconsciously promotes the production of certain kinds of questionnaires and other research tools which bring forth only bland, equivocal information which is hard to make use of but which is not a threat to established traditions' (p. 541). Yet for those who are courageous enough to use research as a means of making themselves known to others, rather than as something to hide behind, the rewards may be substantial. For as King (1996: 188) has emphasised, the fundamental payoff for the counsellor in undertaking research is that 'in learning about the other, we learn about the self'.

The long-standing schism between those who practise as counsellors and those who research and study the activities of counselling has been well documented (Andrews 1991; Barlow *et al.* 1984; Bergin and Strupp 1972; Butler and Strupp 1986; Cohen *et al.* 1986; Dryden 1980, 1996; Goldfried and Pradawer 1982; Goldstein 1982; Herron and Rouslin 1984; Howard 1986; McLeod 1994, 1996b, 1997b; Mahrer 1989; Morrow-Bradley and Elliott 1986; Ogles *et al.* 1996; Schön 1983, 1987: Strupp 1982, 1989; Treacher 1983; Watkins and Schneider 1991; Woolsey 1986). Watkins and Schneider (1991: 291) have expressed the somewhat fatalistic view that 'at some level, irresolvable polarities probably exist between counseling research and practice as basic enterprises', while Goldstein (1982) has captured the spirit of this dichotomy by referring to it as an unconsummated marriage between the two.

Whilst not speaking exclusively of psychotherapy, Schön has succinctly summarised this bifurcation as it occurs throughout the professions.

> Researchers are supposed to provide the basic and applied science from which to derive techniques for diagnosing and solving the problems of practice. Practitioners are supposed to furnish researchers with problems for study and with tests of the utility of research results. The researcher's role is distinct from, and usually considered superior to, the role of practitioner.
>
> (Schön 1983: 26)

Frank (1989b) contends that the failure of traditional experimental research to deliver clear evidence of the differential effectiveness of competing schools and treatment approaches lies in its search to establish facts 'whereas psychotherapy transpires in the realm of meaning' (p. 144). He argues that unlike facts, meanings cannot be confirmed or disconfirmed by the objective criteria of the scientific method. Since traditional scientific methods can deal only with facts, the slippage that occurs between the essentially different activities of mining for facts and delving for meanings may account for the relatively disappointing findings of psychotherapy research using conventional methods.

Mahrer (1989: 188) has made an impassioned plea for psychotherapy research to return to its roots and once again value the contributions that individual psychotherapists can make to 'the discovery of knowledge and the framing of data-generated hypotheses'. He recommends that 'the meaning of research be extended to include the thoughtful, penetrating, analytic, scholarly inquiry of psychotherapy by psychotherapists' (ibid.). Similarly, Wilson and Barkham (1994: 64) suggest that therapists should learn to shift from 'a limited range of explanations' founded on theoretical learning and assumptions and base their interventions on learning derived from conducting open-minded 'practice-based mini-research projects'.

Traditional experimental research, based as it is on a positivist world view (Ashworth 1997), has promoted a double standard in the profession. Whilst uncertainty, creative confusion and the toleration of not knowing lie at the heart of counselling and psychotherapy, the positivist research paradigm, with its emphasis on scientific laws of cause and effect and its belief in an unequivocal underlying reality, has regarded such concepts with suspicion or as factors to be eradicated. Here the urge to know the answer and to arrive at conclusions that are deemed objectively valid, verifiable and open to replication has been paramount. This drive to know is exemplified through the oft mooted but essentially elusive question, 'is psychotherapy effective?' – a question which seems to me about as useful as asking 'is public transport effective?' Phenomenologists, taking a non-positivist stance, are more likely to ask: 'how can we hope to know a final truth about an activity that has at its heart the impenetrable mysteries of the human condition and which has the primary purpose of uncovering each individual's unique and subjective truth about their own experience?'

LEARNING FROM RESEARCH

Howard (1986) has taken an original and somewhat radical stance on the practitioner–researcher divide by turning it on its head and suggesting that experienced clinicians, by dint of their role, are the true torch bearers of research. He argues that therapists naturally and automatically undertake this task as they practise their craft and do so in ways that may be intrinsically more significant and valid than are the experimental trials conducted by scientist-researchers.

[C]linicians have self-consciously immersed themselves in the domain of human psychological functioning. Purposely seeking feedback to improve further their insight and skills in this area (e.g. through supervision), clinicians possess highly sophisticated private research skills that they constantly practice and refine through the daily challenges of clinical practice. . . . I believe that overall the quality of knowledge garnered through clinical acumen is at least as valid as the knowledge of clinical phenomena obtained via public research. The tools of public research, such as psychological tests, research designs, and statistics, are quite different from the methods of private research (e.g. intuitive sensing of patterns, hunches, interpretations, etc.). Consequently they yield quite different (and therefore noncomparable) types of knowledge.

(Howard 1986: 84)

Barlow and colleagues (1984: 23), writing on a similar tack, suggest that the resistance that practitioners have traditionally expressed towards the idea of undertaking research is not resistance to the idea *per se*, 'but rather the inability to develop the tools to implement the idea'. The traditional experimental research paradigm with its complex statistical procedures has proved unpopular, unworkable, or downright irrelevant to the majority of problems and questions that clinicians encounter in their everyday practice. As Goldstein (1982) remarks, whilst such procedures have been 'high in precision' they have remained 'low in psychological significance' (p. 320). The problem is further compounded when practitioners perceive researchers as primarily interested in methodology and theoretical formulations and only marginally interested in the practical application of research findings to clinical contexts (Toukmanian 1996). At its worst, Goldfried and Pradawer (1982) suggest that the extreme outcrop of this research mentality constitutes 'a sophisticated form of autism' (p. 32).

I first learned about the value of researching my counselling practice on my initial training course. I was fortunate enough to undertake a diploma course where students were required to complete a research project designed to explore and evaluate their own counselling work. To undertake such a piece of research was a revelation to me. Although my own project (Wosket 1989) was rough hewn, certainly naïve in conception and over-ambitious in its execution (this was my first attempt at any form of research), it none the less provided me with the most important and valuable learning of my entire training. It is this learning that grounded me as a counsellor and, although it occurred some years ago now, it is learning that I fall back on time and time again when I need to re-find my footing or remind myself of what is the most effective help I can offer to my clients.

In many ways undertaking this early piece of research formed a rite of passage. I gained my first powerful experience of countertransference not in a counselling interaction, but in a research interview where I reacted punitively to a research participant who pushed one of my defensive buttons by, as I thought, questioning my level of competence and expertise. I feel embarrassed, even now, to confess that I switched the tape recorder off while I took the time to justify and explain myself. Even while doing this I was conscious of thinking '*What* are you doing? This is not OK' – but somehow the urge to defend myself overrode my efforts to remain objective and stay in the researcher role. My immediate feelings of shame and confusion alerted me that something was going on that was more about me than my respondent but it was only later that I realised that all this was about familiar feelings of needing to justify and protect myself when feeling criticised or put down by older men. Then it took only another small step to make the further uncomfortable connection that in those few moments with my interviewee I had replayed the enduring dynamic between myself and my father. It was as a direct consequence of experiencing personal disruptions such as this, as a researcher, that I stopped toying with short bursts of counselling and took the plunge to enter long term therapy to work on some of my underlying issues that had risen to the surface whilst I undertook the study.

Whilst such experiences put me painfully in touch with my ability to blunder, deceive and defend myself, undertaking the research also gave my confidence as a counsellor a great boost. Here I had actual 'evidence' (albeit of the 'soft' rather than the 'hard' variety) of what had worked and not worked for four of my clients. Not only that, but I now had material about my use of self that I could call upon in the future. If this tiny sample of individuals had found certain things about me helpful and others unhelpful, and as there seemed to be some consistency in their views, I might begin to build my own schema of factors that seemed to be most effective with clients *and* which derived from my own personal style of working. Being able to name and categorise some of these factors meant that I could begin to utilise and refine them in a more conscious and intentional manner.

Whilst small scale research studies by counsellors into their own practice will always be blemished and flawed, most notably by the limitations of small samples and researcher subjectivity, I would contend that such flaws do not, in themselves, necessarily invalidate the research. In saying this I am influenced by the line of reasoning developed by Robyn Dawes (1994). In a chapter entitled 'Psychotherapy: the myth of expertise', Dawes discusses the landmark review of outcome research studies conducted by Lambert and colleagues (1986) in which the authors suggest that the body of research that has failed to provide conclusive evidence of the effectiveness of trained professional therapists should be viewed with caution because the studies concerned contain flaws. Dawes disputes the implication that studies are rendered invalid if they contain flaws in the following words:

> But *all* studies are 'flawed in several respects'. Psychology is a difficult field in which to conduct a good study, let alone one without any flaws at all. Are we to ignore what all these admittedly flawed studies indicate in common? Ignoring them would make sense only if they were all generally flawed in the *same* respect, but they aren't. Without such common flaws, it is extremely improbable that all the separate and unrelated flaws would lead to the same conclusion.
>
> (Dawes 1994: 57–8)

Dawes' line of reasoning is adopted by Orlinsky and colleagues who, in their (1994) major review of process and outcome studies, state: 'all the studies reviewed suffer from methodological flaws, some more than others; but all studies suffer from some flaws' (p. 365). Like Dawes, they assert that the problem is overcome when a number of studies, flawed though they are, suggest similar findings. These are valid points and ones that are encouraging for small scale practitioner-researchers who cannot hope to undertake perfectly flawless clinical studies. The presence of a flaw does not invalidate a piece of research, as long as the major part of the study is sound. A knot in a piece of oak or pine does not lessen its value and may well add interest to its appearance and texture. Flaws become a problem only when the researcher claims that the study is flawless when it is not. It is the deception that renders the work invalid.

Furthermore, as small scale practitioner-researchers are unlikely to claim that their studies are open to replication or their findings generalisable beyond their own immediate field of learning, it is erroneous to judge any such research as if it were purporting to show evidence of universal truth. Validity, as I see it, does not only mean that research findings should be generalisable, in a macro sense, to the wider professional community. The notion of validity can apply in a micro sense when the researcher-practitioner considers how she or he can generalise their findings from a small scale inquiry, research study, evaluation or case study, to the rest of their clinical work. Such a perspective on validity forms the *raison d'être* for what Mahrer (1988, 1996b) calls 'discovery-oriented' research. This is an approach to psychotherapy research that starts with the identification of 'good moments' (Mahrer and Nadler 1986) in the case work of individual therapists and builds on these to construct a schema of effective practice which can then be consciously utilised by the therapist to enhance their work and even to inform the wider research community. Rice (1992) similarly emphasises that clinicians can make thoughtful and significant contributions to theory 'by recognising productive incidents in their own practice, studying them in detail, and sharing them with other clinicians and researchers' (p. 18).

I would contend that if findings from a sufficient body of comparable studies produced by practitioner-researchers were to be pooled they might well, collectively, provide evidence of emerging patterns and themes and thereby contribute important knowledge to the field of psychotherapy research. As Butler and Strupp (1986) have suggested the 'systematic collection and observation of a number of . . . case studies allows meaningful comparisons of therapeutic process across patients, therapists, and outcomes which may lead to the identification of regular patterns and principles of interaction in the therapeutic context' (p. 38).

The myth that objective, large sample research studies have an exclusive claim on the tag of validity has deterred many practitioners from attempting to research and evaluate their own work in any systematic way. Clarkson (1995: 136) has warned of the dangers of the exclusive and unblemished counselling relationship creating 'a false and entirely artificial, hermetically sealed incubator' which is divorced from the realities and 'vicissitudes of real life'. I think there is a similar danger of artificiality and abstraction when counselling research gets hived off into sterile laboratory-like conditions and divorced from the context from which it derives its meaning, that is the clinical setting. As Frank (1982) has usefully observed in discussing the limitations of traditional approaches to outcome research: 'since therapy does not occur in a social vacuum, many of the determinants of outcome lie outside the patient–therapist dyad, and therefore, no matter how sophisticated the focus on it, important sources of variance will be missed' (p. 288). One such important source of variance that is often missed in experimental research is multicultural variance. Rarely are transcultural perspectives taken into account in the conduct of experimental research, yet, as Frank observes, 'differences in world view of different cultures would be expected severely to limit the cross-cultural generalizability of findings' (ibid.).

The danger of clinical invalidity mounts when analogue trials (those using student confederates or volunteer clients instead of real patients or clients) are undertaken in contrived environments and the findings from these are transposed to clinical settings without questioning their applicability. Whilst large numbers of subjects may be studied in experimental trials and the data gleaned may be comparatively free of contamination, in the process of 'purification' findings may lose much of their relevance to actual clinical practice and their appeal to practitioners is thereby greatly diminished. As House (1997) has asserted, 'one of the greatest dangers of predominantly or exclusively quantitative research is that we end up knowing the *price* (or numerical value) of everything, and the *value* (or essential quality) of nothing' (p. 201, original emphases).

A RESEARCH STUDY ON THE THERAPIST'S USE OF SELF

Recently I have come back to looking at the client's experience of counselling through an extended case study. The challenge and the paradox of this section and the chapter that follows is to say something of interest and relevance to other counsellors when, essentially, I am presenting the work of one counsellor with one client. This material is included as an example of the kind of small scale research study that the therapist can undertake in their own clinical setting. I strongly believe that such research can reinvigorate practice and provide a unique forum for the counsellor's ongoing personal and professional development, and not least for learning about the therapeutic use of self.

Research design and rationale

The following chapter tells the story of a counselling relationship that took place over eighteen months in which the client (called here Rachel) and the counsellor (myself) met weekly, apart from holiday breaks. The client and counsellor wrote separate structured accounts of the counselling sessions after they had taken place. These were not shown to each other during the course of the therapy. Thus different versions of the same story were recorded by the counsellor and the client. The story is one that was both spoken and written down. The spoken story occurred in the counselling sessions through the dialogue that took place between counsellor and client. The written story evolved as counsellor and client regularly recorded their experiences of the therapeutic process and their relationship within it by writing responses to certain prompts – the sentence stems that are given below. These stories came to interweave imperceptibly as that which was first written became spoken, and that which was first spoken was later written down and embellished further. While parts of the written story, as explained later, are incomplete, the spoken story reached a semblance of conclusion and completion – in so far are stories are ever really finished.

The study was born out of my awareness of a whole dimension of parallel process that exists within any therapeutic relationship yet is rarely made explicit or utilised by the therapist and client. Orlinsksy and Howard (1986: 484) have commented that 'psychotherapy clearly induces a self-reflective mode of experience in both the patient and the therapist'. This process of self-reflection occurs side by side with the overt work that is taking place in the therapy sessions along an unseen track that comprises the unspoken thoughts and feelings – the internal dialogue – of both participants. Cooper (1997) has astutely observed that for both psychotherapist and client engaged in the process of therapy the most important conversation that they have is likely to be the one they have with themselves. It is, then, 'the interpersonal sharing and processing of these two conversations that each has with themself that makes the relationship therapeutic and offers the possibility of growth' (p. 24). Rennie (1992, 1998) has called this component of the therapeutic process 'reflexivity'. By which he means (citing a definition by Lawson [1985]) a 'turning back on the self' (Rennie 1992: 225). Reflexivity is a concept that incorporates notions both of self-awareness (reflection on self) and agency (an active self).

Rennie (1992: 227) suggests that 'in the state of reflexivity, the person creates the unspoken, and the intentionality behind the spoken' and he proposes that research methods need to be designed which will give access to clients' reflexive processes in order to present their experience of therapy in its spoken and unspoken entirety. Successful attempts have been made to study the covert processes of therapy, notably through Interpersonal Process Recall (e.g. Barker 1985; Elliott 1986; Kagan 1967, 1984; Kagan and Kagan 1990; Rennie 1994a, 1994b), yet rarely has an extended series of ongoing counselling sessions been explored in this way or the covert process been called forth in a sustained and systematic manner in order to examine the influence it may have on what is overtly occurring between counsellor and client.

My contention, or to use Heron's (1996) term, my 'launching statement', was that this covert dialogue with the self might be of equal significance to the overt dialogue taking place between counsellor and client and that if it could be made more explicit through structured and systematic attention paid to it by both participants this might influence and enrich the therapy for both. As Rennie's (1994b) research into storytelling in psychotherapy has demonstrated 'the spoken story is often only an outcrop of a richer, inner story' (p. 240). More simply, though perhaps more ambitiously, I also wanted to check whether the assumptions I was making about what was helpful or hindering for her matched her own thoughts and feelings about this. In particular I hoped to find out more about my use of self as a counsellor and the impact this had on my client.

A belief I hold strongly is that qualitative research, at its best, can provide a positive and growthful learning experience for the respondent(s) as well as for the researcher. This is a view of research as reciprocity and it stands in opposition to the type of research where one person merely profits from, or at worst, exploits the other. The dominant experimental research paradigm has emphasised the importance of the objective neutrality of the researcher and of random samples of respondents. New paradigm research (Reason and Rowan 1981) on the other hand, with its phenomemological philosophy and qualitative methodologies, accepts as legitimate the dual role of researcher-practitioner and allows for subjectivity in both the role of researcher and in the selection of participants. Within this framework the client-participant can become a fully informed collaborator in the research endeavour who may well gain as much benefit from the experience as the counsellor-researcher (Goldman 1978; Mearns and McLeod 1984). Because new paradigm research is a collaborative activity respondents may be chosen rather than randomly selected:

> For practitioners seeking to carry out research into their own practice, it may be imperative to select clients not only with respect to their suitability for the research envisaged, but also with regard to the likely effect on their well-being and on the therapeutic alliance. . . . Full participatory involvement in most practice-based research can be an empowering experience for clients and their resilience should not be under-estimated. The open disclosures of therapeutic and research intention . . . are in contrast with the tradition of clinical observation and case-history write-up which has been widely used by psychotherapists from a variety of orientations.
>
> (Wilson and Barkham 1994: 57)

Orlinksy and Howard (1986) propose that the relevant question here is not whether the research activity alters the course of therapy (as it is bound to do this) but 'whether the inevitable alterations that research procedures induce in the process of observing a phenomenon are compatible or incompatible, facilitative or disruptive, to the general form and tendency of the phenomenon' (p. 484). My selection of the client for the present research study was gauged on a careful assessment of her suitability that included a consideration of how the research activity might intrude on the therapy. The design and methodology of the study were influenced by what I already knew of Rachel and were adapted to take account of her individual predilections.

Whilst I was interested in researching the theme of the individual counsellor's contribution to the process and outcome of a therapeutic encounter, I also wished to try to understand something of the individual client's contribution. My client and I would be researching our shared experience of our unique relationship together, although reflecting on it separately. King (1996) has stated, in promoting the notion of therapist-researcher reflexivity, that 'opening up the structures and operations that underlie our research and examining how we as researchers are an integral part of the data will amplify rather than restrict the voices of the participants, even when this openness is impeded by the researcher's unrecognised biases and assumptions' (p. 176). In this study I hoped that the voices of both client and counsellor would rise clearly and audibly above the scratches and hisses of what, inevitably, would prove to be an imperfect recording.

The interface between therapy and research

Attention has been drawn to the degree of complementarity that exists between the two activities of research and psychotherapy (Goldstein 1982; West 1998). In the present study complementarity is evident to the extent that the line drawn between what is research and what is counselling becomes indistinct. The research formed part of the therapeutic process and, in turn, appeared to stimulate movement and change for my client.

The ephemeral quality of counselling makes it almost impossible to trap its unique and intangible components in the way that an entomologist might use a killing jar to trap live insect specimens so that they can be mounted and observed. As Lewin has accurately remarked:

In this area there is so much that is difficult to describe because it is fleeting, rapidly shifting, only partially formed. In this area, we often know by immersion and intuition, which do not permit that extra degree of abstraction that makes it possible for us to know what we know and so describe what we know. This knowing by immersion and intuition and participation is an essential dynamic and determinative aspect of every psychotherapy in any depth.

(Lewin 1996: 17)

In this study, attempts to make a distinction between what is process and what is outcome become unnecessary. They are both facets of the same phenomenon. As Mair (1992: 144) has commented 'psychotherapy is a lengthy interaction in which it is difficult to separate process from outcome. A patient's active participation and self-relatedness may be seen as outcomes as much as processes, though they may influence further outcomes'.

The present study is designed so that the research becomes an integral part of the therapeutic work and complements that work, rather than co-exists as a separate and sidelined activity. Boundaries that have traditionally held firm between what is counselling and what is research are beginning to merge in qualitative research (Coyle 1998; Etherington 1996; Grafanaki 1996; King 1996). Grafanaki (1996) has pointed out similarities which exist between the nature and quality of the therapeutic alliance and the research alliance and has noted that a trusting relationship between the counsellor-researcher and their participants that mirrors the therapist–client relationship 'facilitates the gathering of data that are authentically grounded in participants' experience and are thus more complete and rich' (p. 331).

In this study the interface between counselling and research is explored through the use of data gathering methods within the counselling relationship that serve as a means of stimulating fresh awareness, cognitions and feelings for the client. Structured session-by-session reflections on the therapy by both counsellor and client provide a feedback loop into the counselling process and have an immediate impact on how it unfolds. Indeed, the research process appeared to stimulate additional therapeutic opportunities that would not have occurred if this process had not been going on in parallel with the counselling. I would go so far as to propose that what I have engaged in here might be termed a 'research-oriented' approach to counselling, in the sense that many of the client's disclosures and the counsellor's interventions are called forth by the act of research itself. Grafanaki (1996) has asserted that qualitative methods of data collection promote 'reflexivity, self-awareness and empowerment of the parties involved in the research, by giving voice to people to tell their stories in their own words. This sharing can be cathartic and therapeutic in itself' (p. 336). The data presented in the following chapter provide evidence of reciprocity through research in the manner described by Grafanaki.

The study was conducted in a spirit of enquiry that put the therapeutic needs of the client before the requirements of the research. My invitation to the client to take part in the study also included the option for her to suspend her writing or withdraw from the study at any point where she felt that the research activity interfered with the counselling process or she began to feel compelled to continue against her wishes. She did, in fact, opt to discontinue writing her reports after session 47. Prior to this she had recorded all the sessions except seven (sessions 26, 29, 32, 40, 43, 45 and 46). In all, 63 sessions of counselling took place and I wrote accounts of all of these.

Whilst I naturally felt some disappointment at the suspension of her part in the study, this was more than tempered by my relief that she had retained sufficient autonomy to exercise her own decision about her level of contribution. I took her decision as a mark of the robustness of the therapeutic alliance and of her increasing independence within the counselling relationship. Here was someone who, by her own admission, had spent much of her life compulsively pleasing others yet at some level I think she was allowing that I could manage my own feelings about her decision to stop writing. I was glad that she could release herself from the need to appease me by continuing to do something for me that had ceased to be manageable for her. The decision, perhaps, marked her ability to stop seeking my approval and indicated that she had worked through any compliance transference which the research process may have set up.

In terms of what was happening in the therapy at the time it was also entirely understandable that she should disengage from the research process at a point where, as it transpired, she had begun to embark on the most powerful and regressive period of the therapeutic work. It may well have been impossible (and might have been unhelpful too) during this period for her to detach sufficiently from her feelings to reflect on them. In terms of the ethics of research, clinical (i.e. the client's) interests were in conflict with my research interests at this point and in such instances ethical imperatives always carry the requirement that the matter be settled so that the therapeutic enterprise is not jeopardised by the research activity.

If we are to undertake meaningful and ethical research with actual clients in clinical settings we need to work within research contracts that do not bind our clients in ways that a counselling contract would not. Indeed a valid research contract should not demand that the requirements of the study in any way compromise the therapeutic requirements of the counselling contract. As the value and meaning of the study lie in the ongoing process rather than in neat or conclusive outcomes, I do not think that the client's decision to withdraw invalidates the data. In some ways the data have more value and significance because the study honours the client's self-determination about when and what to contribute. I hope in outlining the way this process was managed I have indicated that practitioners can undertake research that takes account of the vicissitudes of clinical practice and still remains meaningful and relevant. As Schön (1983: 308) advises, practitioners should be wary of exacerbating the dichotomous view of research as 'rigor or relevance' by being tempted 'to force practice situations into molds derived from research' when the practice situation calls for a more client-centred research paradigm. It is only as we are able to forge approaches to research design and methodology that dovetail comfortably with the values and practices of the clinician that we can hope to heal the long term breach of the researcher–practitioner divide.

Methodology of the study

It is becoming increasingly acceptable for choices about methodology to be guided by the personal convictions and values of the researcher (Wilson and Barkham 1994). My choice of methodology hinged on an existing prior relationship with my client as I had counselled her previously on two separate occasions (see background to the study in Chapter 4). I knew it would be asking a great deal from any client to write about each counselling session and it would have felt like a gross imposition to ask a new client 'cold' to do this. With Rachel I felt that our relationship was already substantial and intact enough to bear the weight of my asking. Indeed I formulated my precise methodology and research design only after she contacted me to ask if I would counsel her again, so in a very real sense this became a research study that assumed its particular shape and form in response to a unique counselling dyad.

In selecting a methodology I opted for a procedure using guided recall prompted by sentence stems that derived from a narrative research paradigm as elaborated by Toukmanian and Rennie (Rennie and Toukmanian 1992; Toukmanian 1996; Toukmanian and Rennie 1992).

Narrative research, according to Toukmanian 'is atheoretical and qualititative. It is concerned with the exploration of therapy participants'
experience of therapy' (Toukmanian 1996: 188) and is more interested
in discovery and meaning than in objective verification. Within this
paradigm psychotherapy 'is conceived of as a co-constructive process
that can be studied and understood only from the vantage point of client's
and/or therapist's experience of it' (ibid.). I decided to use a self-report
technique using sentence stems to stimulate recall for largely pragmatic
reasons. This strategy was designed to be minimally intrusive and
artificial and to require the least need to process or re-work the data. I
believed it was important, in order to capture the uniqueness and immediacy of the therapeutic encounter, to employ a methodology whereby
the data could stand alone and speak for itself as primary material upon
which I could then comment and make observations.

Both counsellor and client responded to similar sentence stem roots
which were reworded to take account of our different roles within the
relationship. The client was invited to respond flexibly to the sentence
stems as they were given and I encouraged her to use them selectively,
only where they seemed applicable, and to write more freely about her
experience if she felt that the prompts misdirected or constrained her in
what she wished to write. This allowed her to use the structure loosely
and creatively yet retained a framework which meant that there was the
possibility of comparability between what we had each written for each
session.

These are the sentence stems we used. The client's version is given
first, with the counsellor's given immediately beneath it.

1   **The most significant thing about the session for me was** ....
    The most significant thing about the session for me was ....
2   **Something that I found helpful was** ....
    Something I think my client found helpful was ....
3   **Something that I found unhelpful was** ....
    Something I think my client found unhelpful was ....
4   **Something I wanted from the session and didn't get was** ....
    **Something I think my client may have wanted from the session
    and didn't get was** ....
5   **My counsellor could have helped me to get this by** ....
    I could have helped her to get this by ....
6   **Something I would have liked to say but didn't was** ....
    **Something my client might have wanted to say but didn't
    was** ....

7   My counsellor could have helped me to say this by ....
    I could have helped her to say this by ....

8   I would describe my relationship with my counsellor in this
    session as ....
    I would describe my relationship with my client in this session
    as ....

9   An image I have in relation to the session is ....
    An image I have in relation to the session is ....

10 A theme of the session was ....
    A theme of the session was ....

11 Something else that occurs to me about the session or my
    counselling is ....
    Something else that occurs to me about the session or the
    counselling is ....

We agreed to write our accounts, wherever possible, within forty-eight hours of the session having taken place, as after this time short term memory is deemed to atrophy. Nothing of what we wrote was shown to each other during the course of the therapy. When the counselling ended the client was asked to choose whether she wanted to hand over what she had written to me. When the time came she agreed to do this and I made a copy of everything she had written to give back to her so that she retained her own record of the counselling.

Ethical issues and supervision

The complexities surrounding the ethical conduct of psychotherapy research have been well documented (e.g. Imber *et al.* 1986; McLeod 1994; Meara and Schmidt 1991; Shillito-Clarke 1996). The British Association for Counselling (BAC 1996b) has recognised these complexities in introducing a set of guidelines for the conduct of ethical counselling research. Such considerations are of paramount importance for, as Sanders and Liptrot (1994) have stated, 'unethical practice invalidates the practice of research because it abuses the relationship between the researcher and the participants which is at the centre of the work. If this relationship is lost, then all is lost' (p. 57). In order for clients' rights to be safeguarded, I believe that ethical research requires supervision from the counsellor-researcher's counselling supervisor who can monitor how the research may be impacting on the client and the therapy. This needs to happen in addition to any academic supervision the researcher may be getting from another source.

In preparing and doing the groundwork for the research study I spent a considerable amount of time discussing the project in supervision before asking my prospective client if she was willing to take part. Etherington (1996) has discussed the importance of supportive supervision for the counsellor-researcher and I was fortunate in having a counselling supervisor with a research mentality who was research active. If this had not been the case it would have been important for me to have access to another person who could supervise the research element of my work with this client and who could safely and fearlessly patrol with me the interface between counselling and research. I was able to raise a number of ethical issues with my supervisor, which are outlined below, confident in the knowledge that she could comfortably inhabit with me a research frame as well as the therapeutic frame.

- **Confidentiality of the material** The main issues discussed were in relation to the need to be clear with my client about how her material would be protected and ensuring that I gained her informed consent for using it in any published form. I subsequently contracted with my client that she could withdraw from the study at any point and she was assured that agreeing to take part did not automatically mean that she was giving her permission for me or others to have later access to her material.
- **Informed consent** McLeod (1996a) points out that it is good practice to invite research participants to read, and if necessary correct, draft material before it is published, not least so that they can ensure that their confidentiality has been safeguarded. I offered my client the opportunity (which she took up) of reading and approving the draft chapters of this book that dealt with the research study, prior to publication. Gaining informed consent also involved giving her the opportunity to comment on, and the right to change or remove, any of the sentence stem prompts on the semi-structured recall sheets.

Although I had initially intended to show my session reports to my client at the end of the therapy in the interests of maximising equality, my supervisor advised caution about this. She suggested that the client might feel burdened by reading private and personal information about me and my experience of the counselling (particularly where I had been having difficulties) and that this might unnecessarily interfere with or undermine the outcome of her therapy. I resolved the dilemma by explaining to her in advance why it might be difficult for her to read what I had written immediately after her counselling ended but emphasised that I would not deny her access to what I had written if she wished to see it at a later date.

This proved to be wise counsel by my supervisor. When I eventually sent drafts of this and the next chapter to Rachel for her to approve them before publication, part of what she wrote in her reply (written over two years after the counselling finished) was: 'reading your accounts of some of the sessions has made me realise how difficult it must have been for you to hear and see the depths of my despair session after session. I wish I had been more aware of your difficulties, but I was so locked into my own feelings I don't think it was possible at the time'. I would not have wanted her awareness of my difficulties to have blemished Rachel's experience of counselling at the point where we made an ending to our work together. Had I handed my session accounts over to her at the time, I now see that it is likely that this would have occurred.

- **Power issues**   I was concerned that as a person in distress and seeking help from someone in a position of relative power and authority, my client might feel some pressure to agree to my invitation to take part in the study. I presented the possibility of the research to her on the first occasion we met and asked her to think about my request for a week before giving me her decision, in the hope that the cool light of a week's reflection would allow her to make a more informed decision about this. I also assured her that I would still be available to counsel her whether or not she agreed to take part in the study (although I was aware that if she declined this would bring its own dynamic into the relationship). After she had agreed to take part I then said that I would like to charge her half of my normal fee for work with private clients in recognition of what would be a collaborative venture. (I had initially wanted to waive my fee entirely and then realised in discussion with my supervisor that she might then feel indebted to me to the point of feeling unable to exercise free choice about her level of involvement.)

My supervisor helped me to consider some issues that might arise at the interface of the therapy and research, in particular the dynamic for the client of being 'special and different' in being 'chosen' for this research. She invited me to think about how this might affect the counselling. Would the client be subject to elements of coercion or compliance? Might it set up a dynamic where the client became intent on pleasing me? Whilst I could not guarantee that the therapy would be free of such pressures, I was clear that I would, to the best of my ability, put the client's therapeutic needs before those of the research. Having thought this through in advance with my supervisor helped me to deal more clearly and cleanly with my client's decision to discontinue her session reports (as discussed above) when the issue arose. My supervisor also raised the important point of the need to have 'two endings' – one for the therapy and one to deal with any unfinished business in relation to the research. We would, in effect, need to take account of the dual relationship in which we had been engaged for eighteen months and have one ending as researcher and research participant, and one as therapist and client. I realised that it would be important to undertake the former first in order to prevent it unnecessarily intruding on the ending of the counselling relationship. Having described here how the research study was conceived and set up, in the next chapter I present a selection of the data and a discussion of issues arising from this.

Chapter 4

A research study into the use of self

Is it possible to conduct meaningful, scientific investigations into counselling and psychotherapy processes that recognise the uniqueness of individual clients and therapists?

(Martin 1992)

BACKGROUND TO THE STUDY

My client was a woman called Rachel, a lesbian in her late 50s who was divorced with two adult children, one of whom had a mental disability. She had suffered from severe depression for most of her adult life and, in her words, had an 'addictive personality'. Her addictions were to alcohol, prescription drugs (tranquillisers, sleeping tablets and anti-depressants) and to co-dependent relationships. She had suffered a severe psychological breakdown three years before I first met her which led to a stay of five months in a psychiatric hospital where she was given electroconvulsive therapy (ECT). She had also had two periods of treatment in an alcohol treatment centre. She had undergone a number of therapeutic experiences, including group psychotherapy and one-to-one counselling with a community psychiatric nurse. These interventions were behavioural in approach and she had found them of some help in the short term, mainly at a practical level.

I had counselled Rachel previously on two separate occasions while she was a student, studying for a part-time degree over six years. The first period of counselling lasted for six months (twenty-three sessions) and the second, which occurred two years later, for three months (ten sessions). On the first occasion she came to counselling in crisis following a number of difficult experiences, including the breakdown of an intense relationship with a lesbian partner, after which she had made a serious suicide attempt. On the second occasion she returned for counselling for a period of ten weeks prior to her final exams, suffering from acute anxiety and loss of confidence in her academic abilities. Eighteen months after she graduated she wrote to me asking if I would see her as a private client for some longer term counselling in which she hoped to address her underlying and long-standing problems. Influencing my decision to invite her to take part in the research study were my knowledge of the pre-existence of a good therapeutic alliance, established in the previous periods of counselling, and the fact that I knew she had an aptitude for writing.

ANALYSIS OF THE DATA

Data from the study were analysed selectively and thematically, following the process for thematic analysis outlined by Polkinghorne (1991). Several themes were selected as being pertinent to the scope and topic of the present volume. Themes were chosen which, in particular, reflected aspects of the use of self that are discussed elsewhere in this volume. These were: (i) **love, touch and sexuality**; (ii) **errors, mistakes and omissions made by the counsellor**; and (iii) **extratherapeutic factors occurring at the boundaries of the counselling work**. In addition to these three specific themes there is also discussion of two more general themes which appeared to feature strongly in both counsellor and client accounts. These are **therapy as narrative** and **the impact of the counselling relationship** on process and outcome.

In the presentation of data that follows, as well as highlighting what appear to have been significant events for the client, I have also included a section summarising my own learning. In particular I have recorded learning that I believe has since had an impact on the way that I work as a counsellor. In this study then, significant events are selected as 'windows into the process of change' (Elliott and Shapiro 1992: 164) for both client and counsellor in a way that takes account of the reciprocal nature of the research activity.

It will become clear that I have employed an entirely subjective selection of themes for the purposes of illustrating the thesis of this book. Some themes, as will be seen, overlap and could appear in more than one category. Where this happens they have been assigned to what appears to be the primary category. A fuller and more systematic category analysis would have allowed the data to be distributed into many more sub-categories. This is a preliminary impressionistic analysis and deals with only a fraction of the data presented in 103 session reports.

DISCUSSION

The discussion will present selected sections of session reports high-lighting the themes used for analysis. As space precludes discussion of every session report a sample of sessions is presented which display the main themes. Material under each heading is presented, for the main part, in chronological order to preserve a sense of how the therapeutic work unfolded.

Love, touch and sexuality

Rachel had suffered from neglectful parenting throughout her child-hood. From birth her father was frequently absent and her mother failed to provide her with emotional or physical affection. From the age of seven Rachel was called upon to act as mother's helper and substitute father to her three younger siblings. As an adult Rachel experienced a desperate craving for love and affection. This drove her into a series of dysfunctional and co-dependent relationships with individuals who either exploited her for their own needs or were eventually driven away by her own excessive neediness. She had a sense of feeling loved only when engaged in an intense physical and sexual relationship with another woman.

The theme of touch and sexuality is present in counselling interactions from session 1. Rachel writes that something she wanted from her counsellor and didn't get in the first session was 'a hug'. In her session 2 report she refers to her 'desperate need to be comforted'. Whilst I did not realise at the start of the therapy that she wanted physical contact, I sensed her neediness and saw it as an early indication that she might require me to stand in for a while as a mother figure. I wrote about the first session that: 'My sense is that I will need to be very tolerant and secure in the face of what might be Rachel's desperate need for a good mother'.

In her reflections on session 3 Rachel appears to begin to separate out the strands of her craving and make a distinction between sexual love and the non-sexual nurturing that she needs. She writes: 'what I didn't say was that my "child" wants to be physically held and comforted when she is expressing her pain. My felt need for physical contact with another human being is a constant aching void and because it feels so huge I don't feel able to ask for it and I think when I'm in a relationship this need for physical comfort gets confused with sexual desire'. Rachel thinks about her counsellor as a possible source of physical comfort yet is aware of the boundaries of the therapeutic relationship: 'I don't think that being physically comforted can be part of the counselling relationship – it would be too easy to misconstrue on the part of the client and could be damaging to both the client and the counsellor'.

It appears that I picked up something of what is unsaid between us here, as in my own reflections on session 3 I write that something my client might have wanted to say but didn't was 'I want you to love me'. This is mirrored in what Rachel writes about the risk involved in undergoing counselling: 'I feel frightened that at the end of it I shall still be alone and unloved and that the only way out will still be suicide'. These feelings find expression in an image first reported by Rachel after session 3. She writes that an image she has in relation to the session is 'of a small child in a very cold, dark place, curled up in a foetal position. She doesn't want to be there. She doesn't want to exist'. This is an image that arises again and again during the course of the therapy and eventually provides important clues about the direction in which her counselling needs to proceed.

Tensions around Rachel's needs for physical contact and comfort surface more clearly for both the client and counsellor in session 4. For a long time during the course of the therapy I struggled with my ambivalent feelings about touching her, without knowing what my ambivalence was about or that she was also struggling with this issue. In retrospect I can see that my ambivalence and confusion mirrored hers as she tussled with trying to separate the sexual from the non-sexual components of intimacy. With hindsight I now think that in the early stages of the work, before Rachel had sufficiently established her own boundaries between erotic and non-erotic touch, my wariness was around sensing that if I did touch her she might have a sexual response or the touch might trigger sexual fantasies that would have been troubling for her.

The dilemma I experienced here is captured by Bragan (1996) in what he writes about attunement between therapist and client:

> At the core level, attunement requires a sense of physical presence. Seeing the physical presence of the therapist may be sufficient, but not infrequently it also includes a pressing need for merging and for some physical contact. As the latter may come to be sexualised it can present a difficult problem for the therapist, being either a potential hazard or a potential disjunction, as the therapist is either drawn into sexual contact or adopts too distant a posture in order to be safe.
>
> (Bragan 1996: 25)

What I hadn't got straight at this stage is something that Gutheil and Gabbard (1993) have expressed very clearly in their exposition about therapist responses to clients' needs for physical nurturing:

> In attempting to delineate the appropriate role for the therapist vis-à-vis the patient's wishes and longings to be loved and held, it is useful to differentiate between 'libidinal demands', which cannot be gratified without entering into ethical transgressions and damaging enactments, and 'growth needs', which prevent growth if not gratified to some extent.
>
> (Gutheil and Gabbard 1993: 191)

Because I felt both drawn to offering to touch her as a way of helping her engage with and discharge her painful feelings from childhood and also wary about doing this, on occasion I acted incongruently. In session 4, for example, I responded from a countertransference feeling and provided an inauthentic hug when she asked me for one. I wrote: 'I felt not much use in the face of Rachel's immense feelings of loneliness and isolation. I responded to her request, at the end, for a hug even though I told my supervisor yesterday that I wouldn't touch her. I didn't know how to say no without devastating her'.

In session 9 I suggest some dialogue work with the child part of herself, which Rachel agrees to, even though she feels wary of the feelings this might access. I write that something I think Rachel may have wanted from this session and didn't get was for 'me to hold her while she cried'. Again I express my ambivalence about this: 'I felt I both wanted to and also wary'. Instead I settled for offering her a hug at end of the session, which this time felt more congruent and which she seemed glad to receive. Our relationship in this session appears to be moving towards a more reparative one, although one in which we are both helping one another. I describe the relationship as 'highly charged, careful, strong, nurturing, caring' and comment that 'I wanted to get it right for her so that she could feel her sadness and I struggled a bit with how to do this. Techniques such as "empty chair" don't come easily for me, although Rachel helped by letting me know in a previous session [from an earlier period of counselling] that this had been helpful in working through some stuff with her father'.

Rachel describes her sense of the relationship with her counsellor in this session as 'very enabling' and writes 'I have always been very self-reliant and find it difficult to ask other people for help. I was able to admit to her that although I knew I needed to get in touch with my painful feelings and I wanted to do so, I couldn't do it by myself. She was so gentle and encouraging, so supportive and kind and at the end offered me a hug which was very comforting. Every time I think about it it makes me cry. I don't think I allow people close enough to the real me, to allow them to be kind in that way'.

As the therapy proceeds and takes on a more regressive aspect with Rachel getting more and more in touch with her early childhood deprivation, the tensions around touch surface again. In my account of session 14 I write that something she may have wanted and didn't get was 'a hug (?) – or possibly for me to hold her while she wept'. In my ambivalence about touching her I am inconsistent in my behaviour towards her and this is reflected in Rachel's account of the session where she writes: 'I would describe my relationship with my counsellor in this session as less close than some of the recent sessions. I felt more self-conscious about being upset and crying and she didn't attempt to make any physical contact, like holding my hand [which I had done in a previous session]. It feels awful crying when she sits aloof from me and asks me questions which make me cry more. I know I have no right to expect her to comfort me, but I need it so badly'. Rachel appears more able to be congruent with herself than I am at this stage. While she is able to acknowledge that the relationship here is not giving her what she needs, I make the assumption that it is, and describe it as 'intense, nurturing, raw (I think for her), comforting, understanding, close, almost parental'. Ironically, I now think my last adjective is accurate – except that in this session where I imagined I was being the nurturing parent, I was actually being the withholding parent.

Instances such as this that show a dislocation between the counsellor's perception of what is happening and the client's experience can provide valuable insights into the helpful and hindering components of therapy. In discovery oriented research Elliott and Shapiro (1992) have pointed out that 'the traditional view of differences in perspective as error variance is not useful and results in the loss of important information about the nature of the different perspectives on therapy process' (p. 182). Differences in experience and perspective, as in this case, can promote significant learning for the therapist and therefore enhance clinical relevance and validity rather than lessen it. The learning about touch that I gained from my work with Rachel is summarised later in the chapter.

In some ways issues around touch seem to come to a head in session 33. Rachel is very honest in her session account about her feelings: 'what I need is a loving closeness, which again is inappropriate in my counselling relationship. Whilst I was able to shed a few tears with

Val – it was incredibly hard to just sit there and let Val watch me. What I wanted was to be held, to have my hair stroked and be comforted, whilst I sobbed out all the pain. . . . Deep down I still feel that without a close loving relationship my life is not worth living, and I feel that, if anything, I am moving further away from being able to achieve that'.

Yet, further on in her account, there is the glimmer of the hope of some resolution of her dilemma as Rachel reviews the counselling relationship and what it means to her at this stage: 'I would describe my relationship with my counsellor in this session as a close, but professional one. I felt that Val was a detached observer, which is what she's supposed to be, but it wasn't what I wanted. I was allowing her to see parts of me that very few, if any, others have been allowed to see and it was extremely hard to do it, even though I have learned to trust her more than anyone else. This seems to be tied up with my belief that before I can expose my inner most self to someone I have to be in a close physical and emotional relationship with them. I guess my counselling relationship is challenging that assumption and could make it possible for me to change my attitude'.

Though Rachel may have experienced me as detached and professional this was, in actuality, a difficult time for me too as I also felt despondent and distressed in the face of her enormous despair. Supervision was very important here in providing containment for me – both in the sense of giving emotional support and also in holding me to my task within the counselling process. I record in my report after session 33 that 'I cried about her in [my] supervision session when I spoke about her desire not to wake up from the ECT'. (When Rachel had been given ECT in the psychiatric hospital she had hoped that it would kill her.) I also write that some helpful and sustaining things my supervisor said to me were: 'There is an extraordinary level of empathy between you. When *you* thought "Is this helping; is there any point; will things ever be different for her?" that exactly matched what *she* was feeling. Remember you are standing in for a part of her she hasn't yet found. She is projecting on to you what she will eventually learn that she can give herself. Through you she will take that back, but she needs you to show it to her first – that is care, respect, understanding, being special. She will know at some level that she is special to you and will come to value herself as special'.

Though I don't offer her physical comfort at this time, the image I have of the counselling session (33) is of 'cradling a lost child' and I think my supervisor helped me here to see that emotionally, at least, I was holding and stroking her in the way that she craved. By the following session I have regained my sense of balance and write: 'I think she is feeling suicidal, but will keep going. I'm glad I have spoken about my concerns with my supervisor. It gives me the courage to allow her to do this work – even though it's hard for me to see her so distraught. I feel like I can hold her very strongly'.

By session 45, when Rachel is more intensely in contact with, and working through, her experiences of childhood neglect I am beginning to use touch therapeutically with her and have lost my sense of wariness about this. In this session I sat by her and put my arm around her shoulder as she expressed the distress of her three-year-old self feeling unloved and abandoned. I remark that 'I don't usually touch her but this felt right as a way of offering comfort and making up for the lack of comfort from her mother'. With the benefit of hindsight and Rachel's accounts to help me make sense of the process, I think that by this time I had become more confident that my touch would help her to gain access to her inner world of painful childhood experiences and assist her in releasing feelings, rather than distract her from these and move her into feelings and fantasies about her counsellor. In this session she had responded to my touch by taking my hand and holding it and said that she had felt 'cuddled' (a word that, perhaps significantly, has associations of childhood comfort).

Errors, mistakes and omissions made by the counsellor

A number of mistakes, errors and omissions made by the counsellor are revealed in Rachel's session reports, most frequently in response to the sentence prompt which invited her to state something she wanted from the session and didn't get. The following is an example that serves to illustrate how the counsellor may be 'guided' by their shadow (Page 1999) in using themselves in ways that appear to be errors, yet subsequently prove to carry therapeutic potential.

Two incidents of 'failing' Rachel came close together and appeared very significant – both in terms of where they occurred in the therapy and in the use that Rachel and I made of them. I had to cancel the session following session 17, at very short notice, because I was suddenly unwell. When she came for the re-scheduled meeting I couldn't see her as I had made a wrong entry in my diary and mistaken the date of her appointment. I had to send her away and arrange to see her the following day. When she arrived the next evening she brought me a plant – a rare and exotic bloom in a beautiful pot. She told me that it had been raised with care from seed and had an unusual flower. Furthermore, she said it required careful tending, had to be placed in a sunny position and needed to be watered every day or it would not thrive. I felt that the giving of the gift told me something about Rachel's need to be tenderly cared for and not forgotten and probably served as a displacement of her angry feelings about my having messed up her last two sessions. When I said to her that I imagined she might be angry with me she told me that she had needed to manage some very painful feelings on her own and was able to admit that she had felt let down by me.

Rachel writes about the event and its impact at some length, firstly in terms of the therapeutic relationship: 'I would describe my relationship with my counsellor in this session as more difficult than usual, because it was difficult for me to be completely honest about how I'd felt when my session was cancelled and then the date for the following session was mixed up and I had to return the following day. Val suggested I might have felt angry, which I denied, but I did say I had felt let down. I *had* felt quite angry, but because I understood the very valid reasons I thought anger was unreasonable. I usually try and avoid expressing any anger I feel directly to the person involved, partly through fear of the consequences and partly because I find anger hard to justify'. Further on she writes about how she coped 'after feeling that Val wasn't there when I'd really needed her. It would have been very easy for me to sink into depression as I had a lot of panic and anxiety feelings, plus quite a severe loss of self-confidence. I did in fact take responsibility for myself – I did what I felt able to do and took care of myself when I needed to. Both Val and I were very pleased that I'd been able to cope in this way and the fact that I made a conscious decision to look after myself is a new experience and one which worked for me'.

Normally I am punctilious in correctly entering appointments in my diary. I cannot remember another occasion where I entered an appointment wrongly or missed two counselling sessions in a row. It strikes me as fascinating that I let Rachel down not once, but twice, at a time when she was able to turn this into a positive and growthful experience for herself. This was the first occasion that Rachel was able to express negative feelings in her therapy and, indeed, the incident and our discussion about it seemed to liberate her angry feelings and lead, in later sessions, to the expression of a deep and intense anger that had been bottled up for years. If the therapy had progressed smoothly and to plan at this stage, I doubt whether my intentional strategies would have provided her with such a tangible opportunity for movement and change as did my unintentional blunders.

Extratherapeutic factors occurring at the boundaries of the counselling work

On many occasions Rachel writes about significant events, feelings and thoughts that she experiences outside of or around the edges of the therapy. Often, writing about these significant factors in her session reports appears to form a kind of rehearsal prior to telling me about them. The amount of rehearsal time Rachel needs before disclosing seems to depend on the 'weightiness' of the item and how she feels about it. Those things that she feels most ashamed of, or troubled about, appear to require the greatest incubation time. This accords with observations made by Rennie (1992) about client reflexivity and change. Rennie's research on this subject has shown that for a client the 'reflexive moment is a "safety zone": It is there that a course of action can be contemplated' (p. 227). His studies have uncovered the important role played by client reflexivity in determining the course and momentum of therapeutic change. He contends that reflexivity is 'the form of consciousness in which a decision may be reached about a contemplated action and in which the decision may be converted to action. The operative word, however, is *may*: It is in the indeterminacy of reflexivity that the individual has choices, and hence the possibility of control over change' (ibid. pp. 227–8, original emphasis). A couple of examples of Rachel's process of reflexivity are outlined here to illustrate how significant material was incubated and how it made an impact on the counsellor.

In relation to session 3, Rachel writes that something she would like to have said but didn't is that she is still having problems with alcohol and that she drank half a bottle of spirits after the previous session 'to dull the pain that I'd brought to the surface'. She suggests that I could have helped her to talk about this if I had asked her what repercussions the counselling sessions were having in her life and how she deals with the pain that is stirred up between sessions. Whilst I failed to address this issue with Rachel in the way that she needed me to do at the time, it is intriguing that I recorded the following fantasy in my report of session 5, which may indicate that the issue found its way into the room anyway: 'For a while I found myself wondering if she had been drinking. I imagined (I think) a smell of alcohol as it disappeared and wasn't there when I leaned closer to her as she was drawing. I wonder why I thought this. I have no reason to believe she had been drinking as she came straight from work'. With the benefit of Rachel's session accounts to throw light on what was happening here I can see that my fantasy was very relevant. Rather than dismissing it as imagination, it

would have been profitable (and more congruent) to have shared my
thought with Rachel, for instance by saying: 'I find myself wondering
about your alcohol consumption and I'm not sure why'. I have since
learned to take greater note of my 'hallucinatory' experiences and to
share something of these with my clients when they occur.

McLeod (1997a: 79) has proposed that 'writing can provide a safe
place to express potentially shameful experience' and this appears to
have been true for Rachel. Through her session accounts it is sometimes possible to track Rachel's movement towards disclosure and to
see how this links to her changing sense of self. In her report of session
20, for example, Rachel mentions that there are 'some things' that she
feels 'guilty about' and couldn't disclose in the session. However she
states her intention to disclose at a future date: 'I think I will ask Val to
encourage and support me to do it in one of the next few sessions'. Her
reference here is unusually oblique in that she does not name the 'things'
and it is almost as if she is using the reflective writing space as a place
to experiment with the possibility of disclosure, even to herself. Because they are not named in her session report the 'things' stay hidden
and safely stored for the time being. In the next session Rachel did let
me know, right at the end of that session, that she was withholding
some experiences that she felt ashamed of and would like to tell me
about in the future.

Rachel finally discloses her experiences, which are of sexual transgressions, in session 25. In her account of this session Rachel makes
sense of her reluctance to disclose: 'The most significant thing about
the session for me was that I finally managed to talk about times in my
life when I acted in ways I am ashamed of. As I am such a private
person I haven't talked to anyone about them or admitted to anyone
anything which I thought was or could be unacceptable behaviour. . . .
I think I have always tried to be a paragon of virtue, even being unable
to admit to mistakes I've made in all areas of my life. I suppose I
thought if people knew the real me they would reject me – rejection is
one thing I have been afraid of all my life, and I would do anything to
avoid that possibility'. She links her ability to disclose to the quality of
the therapeutic relationship, which she describes 'as one of great trust,
or I wouldn't have been able to tell her such personal, shameful (for
me) details' and she indicates that being able to disclose in this way is
significant in the process of relinquishing her false self: 'A theme of the
session was revelation of the deeper, more secret side of me, and also
the confirmation that for most of my life I have acted out the identity I
thought I should have – with disastrous consequences for me'.

In her account of session 5 Rachel introduces another important theme that she has been reflecting on, but has yet to raise in her therapy: 'Something I would like to say but didn't was that I have a growing feeling that I might have been sexually abused as a child'. She records her confusion and uncertainty about this: 'I have no conscious recollection of any sexual abuse which makes me wonder if I am jumping to conclusions because sexual abuse is so common and can result in similar consequences to mine'. Rachel considers the possibility of sexual abuse again in her report of session 9. She sees it as something that would make sense of her current predicament: 'Something I would have liked to say but didn't was to ask my counsellor if she thinks I may have been sexually abused as a child. I still have this vague, anxious feeling that maybe I did, but perhaps in a way I would find the pain of that more acceptable than the more abstract, invisible pain of emotional deprivation'. After incubating the sense that she may have been abused for a number of sessions, Rachel moves towards a clearer intention to disclose, expressed in her session 11 report: 'I think this is something I must bring up myself'. She eventually discloses her feeling that she might have been abused as a child in session 13, and writes about this that: 'I felt comfortable with seeing this as a possibility and not actively attempting to resurrect memories. I feel relieved that it is out in the open, but I still feel great reluctance to actually address it. However, I am determined this time in counselling to explore every avenue necessary to release emotional pain which has been locked inside me for so long and which has had such damaging effects on me'.

Rachel returns again to the possibility that she might have been sexually abused in her reflections on session 34. This is a session where she records that she is feeling so deeply depressed that she might 'commit suicide'. She writes about her struggle to release trapped feelings and links this to the possibility of abuse. 'Something I wanted from the session and didn't get was to be able to let go more with my emotions. I felt very self-controlled, there are so many barriers stopping me from expressing myself freely. I want very much to sweep them out of the way, because it feels as if there is something important to my psychological health hidden behind these barriers, and I think it may be to do with my fear of being sexually abused. I still have no conscious recollection of this occurring, just the sense (intuitive) that I have been'. Further on she writes that she would like to have talked about this 'but I suppose I'm frightened to, in case Val thinks I'm making it up – especially as I still have no conscious recollection of anything happening'. Despite her reservations Rachel does bring the subject up again in the next session and it leads us into a new and important phase of her counselling.

Although at this time I am unaware that Rachel is again contemplating the possibility of childhood sexual abuse I have a sense of her having suffered a profoundly damaging experience early in her life and offer her my image of 'a deep and painful wound which is being opened up to let the air get to it and clean it out'. This image resonates with Rachel and she writes: 'It was also helpful when Val said the image she had of my pain was of a very deep and damaging wound which needed to be exposed and cleaned out. That was an exact picture of what I was feeling, and it strengthened my conviction that Val does know how I feel and what my life has been like'. Rachel indicates that she has a sense of how the wound might be opened up and healed: 'the only way I know is by regressing me back to my childhood', although at this point it does not seem to her to be a viable option: 'but I don't think I would be able to let this happen. I want to but the barriers feel very solid and strong'.

In session 36 Rachel tells me that she has been feeling again like the image of the curled up foetus in a dark, lonely and frightening place. In the previous session she had told me that the sense of having been abused was present for her again. I begin to suspect that her image and the issue of abuse might be linked in indicating some very early, possibly pre-verbal, trauma and record that: 'I wondered aloud about the possibility of an attempted abortion or of picking up feelings of not being wanted while still in the womb'. I note Rachel's response: 'she said it felt like we might be on the right track and that the feeling of constriction in her chest was suddenly much stronger and had moved up into her throat – as if something wanted to come out'. At the same time that Rachel is recording her thoughts about regressive work I write that: 'I am wondering about encouraging her to go back to this feeling/incident/trauma and re-experience it to run it out'.

Rachel records in her account of the session (36) that something she found helpful was 'the suggestion from Val that my feelings of emotional deprivation could possibly stem from pre-birth (in the womb) experiences – a possible abortion attempt as I was conceived before my mother was married in [date], a time when conception before marriage was a great stigma and brought shame upon the whole family. We discussed asking my mother about it, but I felt I couldn't as she is so frail and vulnerable now. We also talked about not being wanted after I was born and the journey from [country] by sea back to the U.K. when I was six months old, and how frightened and apprehensive my mother

would have felt about seeing her family again. It helped to have a
feasible reason for the feelings I've had recently – it makes some sense
out of a time of confusion for me. I've found it very difficult not having
a clear idea of what was causing my intense distress'. Later in her
session report she further reflects that 'most probably my father didn't
want me either as he could have felt forced to marry my mother after
she became pregnant. If I had felt that neither my mother or father
wanted me I guess I could have blamed myself for the awful relationship they had, and felt that I didn't deserve to be loved myself'. Perhaps
it is significant that while beginning to contemplate the full extent of
the parental abandonment she suffered, Rachel records that she would
describe her relationship with her counsellor in this session as 'the
closest yet' and observes: 'I also felt a great warmth and sense that Val
cares about me and I was pleased that I could make her smile with
some of the things I said'. It is conceivable that her sense of feeling
securely held and cared for in the counselling relationship helped her to
face her worst fears in terms of the extreme form that her neglectful
parenting may have taken.

By session 39 we have contracted to do some regressive work to try
to locate and discharge Rachel's early feelings of abandonment. This was
clearly a significant session which Rachel wrote about at some length.
Her own words convey the tenor and the impact of the experience she
underwent:

> The most significant thing about the session for me was allowing
> myself to experience and investigate my feelings of emotional pain
> with Val's gentle encouragement and questioning. I experienced a
> great deal of fear whilst I was doing this and felt reluctance to face
> whatever would or might be revealed. Val emphasised that nothing
> could hurt me, that it was safe and OK to express whatever I
> needed to, but I still felt very strong barriers preventing me from
> letting go – it felt as though I was in some sort of emotional straight-
> jacket. Even so, I did manage to describe what it looked like – a
> thick metal spring, coiled very tightly and I felt I had to contain it
> and not allow it to spring apart or I would fall apart. This caused
> actual physical pain and tension in the upper part of my chest – the
> pain felt unbearable and as if it has always been there even though
> I have tried to push it as far away as possible.
>
> When I examined the pain it felt as though I had been totally
> abandoned, that I was reaching out to make contact with a person
> but there was no-one there. I felt intense isolation, that I was totally

unloved and unwanted. I was in a place that was cold and dark and silent and I couldn't move or speak. I felt I was very small – Val suggested I could possibly be a foetus – which seemed to make sense of why I couldn't move, see or speak. I felt I didn't want to be born if there was going to be no-one there for me – I felt I'd rather be dead.

The image I recorded of this session sums up what I felt I witnessed in the work that Rachel did – 'a silently howling baby in a womb'. Yet I was concerned not to direct Rachel into something that was not real for her and wrote: 'I hope we are on the right lines and I haven't suggested possibilities to her that aren't true. (I don't think I have – we are taking an "as if" perspective)'. Rachel's account indicates that the process was managed in such a way that she could feel in control: 'Something I found helpful was Val saying that I could come out of whatever came up at any time, that I only had to say I didn't want to continue and we would stop'. She writes that she experienced her relationship with her counsellor in this session 'as one in which I felt treated with gentleness, sensitivity and supportiveness and I felt a great deal of trust in her and even though it was extremely difficult I did feel a sense of security, that she was there for me and wouldn't let me down'.

Counsellor and client accounts of this session indicate that it constitutes a significant event, or critical incident, in the therapeutic process. Elliott and Shapiro (1992) define significant events as 'portions of therapy sessions . . . in which clients experience a meaningful degree of help or change' (p. 164). The value of uncovering significant events in therapy lies in the fact that they 'represent important general therapeutic factors but in a more concentrated form' (ibid.) than is found elsewhere in the therapy.

Clues to the nature and relevance of this event are provided in something that Rice and Greenberg (1990) have written about 'the interpersonal experiential learning dimension' (p. 406) of therapy. By this they mean experiential learning which takes place for the client through and in the relationship with the therapist and which has a cumulative impact. Such learning can be experienced by the client as 'extremely affirming, enabling them to respect themselves [and] begin to let go of artificially imposed criteria, and make their own unique changes' (ibid.). Though this learning builds gradually throughout the therapeutic process it can be substantially augmented by 'powerful relationship events that take place within a single session' (ibid. p. 407). The work described above provides an example of this kind of session, the characteristics of which Rice and Greenberg describe in some detail:

As clinicians we have encountered moments when a client was starting to express, often with great difficulty, some intense present emotional experience such as fear of the future or despair about his/her live [sic]. . . . This seemed to be a time for the therapist to resonate empathically with the client's feelings, and to reflect them in their full intensity, without being scared, clearly and genuinely prizing the client. We found that when we were truly able to respond in this way at such times, clients were able to go deeper and deeper into their feelings until they seemed to 'touch rockbottom' and were able to start up again. Clients seemed to experience a sense of relief and wholeness. The effects seemed to be much more than catharsis. The client had taken the risk of entering deeply into a feared experience, and the therapist, rather than being shocked or frightened, was clearly resonating to it as shared human experience. This seems to break the sense of isolation and fragmentation.

(Rice and Greenberg 1990: 407)

The repercussions of the work which Rachel did in this session are evident in her subsequent session accounts as she begins to make links between her emotional responses in current relationships and her very early experience of feeling unloved. In session 41, for instance, Rachel had brought painful feelings resulting from a sense of having been rejected by a potential partner that left her acknowledging that 'the need I have to be the primary person in someone else's life is still very strong'. In the session some re-attribution of these feelings takes place and she writes that something she found helpful 'was Val asking me if the feelings about the current situation were at all like the feelings I'd described in my pre-natal experience, i.e. about not feeling as though I was really wanted. The feelings I would say were almost identical'. Further on she writes that a theme of the session was 'how my current fears of rejection are linked to very old fears about not being wanted by my parents and that all these feelings are much nearer the surface and that even though it feels very uncomfortable allowing myself to express them, that is the way to heal them'.

I have written at some length about how the issue of possible abuse was addressed in Rachel's therapy because I think it illustrates a dilemma that may arise when counsellor and client attempt to work with feelings that are very tangible but where the origin of these is, for whatever reason, partly or fully obscured. In working with Rachel on this issue I had the sense of needing to maintain a careful balance between responding to her cues and concerns with my own hunches and also respecting that her original experience might not be fully available to conscious memory. The taking of an 'as if' perspective allowed us to treat her feelings as authentic and work with those, rather than getting caught up with the requirement for her to remember exactly what had happened to her. Both she and I were concerned not to introduce false memories, yet Rachel's feeling of very early and profound distress was intensely real to both of us. Had we been overcautious and too fearful of the false memory demon I think we would have avoided doing work of a regressive nature that proved to be central to her healing process.

Therapy as narrative

My understanding of counselling or psychotherapy is that it is essentially a creative activity that involves processing the moment-to-moment unfolding of subjective meaning and experience as it occurs between two searching people – one who reaches for the truth of their experience and the other who bears witness to that truth as it is revealed and brought to life in the therapeutic relationship. During the middle period of her counselling Rachel talked in great detail, over many sessions, about the twenty-five years of her deeply unhappy marriage and the period of her emotional breakdown that followed its ending. During this time I felt that my role was very much one of 'bearing witness' to her experience and that as I did so she was able to reconstruct the reality of her life in a fundamental and deeply healing way. Rachel's process, I think, illustrates what Lynch (1997: 127) has designated as the primary work of counselling and psychotherapy, which is 'confronting the silence of oppression'. In elaborating this theme he asserts:

> In permitting and enabling clients to articulate their experience, therapy can potentially allow the telling of stories which have been suppressed. The therapeutic space may thus function as a liberating context in which the client moves from the oppressed isolation of their silence to a deeper connection with others around them.
>
> (Lynch 1997: 127–8)

In her account of session 19 Rachel reflects on what it is like for her to talk to me about this time in her life: 'This period of my life ended ten years ago and after re-experiencing the horror which was my life I can't believe just how awful it was or why I stayed for so long. I have never talked to anyone else about it in such detail, and I feel a real need for someone to hear my story in detail'.

Rachel begins to shift her perspective on her past and gain a different understanding of it. Douglass and Moustakas (1985: 40) have written about reflection as 'a process of creating and clarifying the meaning of experience in terms of self in relation to self and self in relation to others'. This process is mirrored clearly in Rachel's session accounts that deal with the retelling of her experience of her married life. She writes (session 17) that something that occurs to her is 'how disorientating it feels to look back on past experiences with clear, more objective eyes and to realise that things were actually not the way I had previously perceived them. It's as if I've seen things through a mist, only half seeing and understanding what was going on. Because I've always related to other people and not to myself, my own perspective on things is missing I think. Now that I am looking from my own perspective and allowing my own feelings to surface, everything looks different'.

The impact of the counselling relationship

Tangible change for Rachel, as reported in her session accounts, appears to begin as the relationship between client and counsellor strengthens and deepens. By session 7, for example, both counsellor's and client's reflections show a growing mutuality in the relationship. I describe our relationship as 'affirming, nurturing, gentle and humorous' and say about Rachel that 'I am very fond of her and feel privileged to work with her'. She, in turn, comments about the impact that the relationship is having on her: 'I would describe my relationship with my counsellor in this session as very much working together. When I am talking about how things are or how they were my counsellor reflects back to me the positive qualities she sees about me, and gradually I am taking these on board, broadening the way I see myself. Her obvious pleasure when I talked about being able to say what I really think instead of what I think people want to hear really warmed me. Each session now I think I can open up more and let her see more of the real me, and it feels very much as though we are a partnership'.

During the process of the therapy, as I have stated, I am working without knowing what Rachel is writing in her session reports. The session reports provide some interesting glimpses into how I am attempting to tailor the relationship to what my client needs and how she responds to this. As we proceed I am trying to pitch my interventions at the level that the relationship can tolerate. So, for example, in session 10 I am concerned that I might have been too immediate with her. I write that something I think she might have found unhelpful was that 'she might have felt I was being a bit "over the top" when I told her that I experienced her as special and valued her specialness in not wanting to compromise her own reality and fit in with "average" people'.

Yet in her account of the same session, rather than feeling constrained by my immediacy as I feared, Rachel is expressing a new found freedom within the relationship: 'I felt more able in this session to be me than in any previous sessions. Over many years I have become very expert in reading situations and adept in providing "the right answers". It feels absolutely great not to do that any more, to say what I really think and feel and have no worries whether it is "right" or "wrong" '. She goes on to describe the relationship with her counsellor 'as one of greater trust, an ability on my part to be able to be me and express myself honestly, openly without fear of being criticised or judged and finding when I did so that I can be amusing and that she could differentiate things about me that are "special". It is this that has uplifted me, changed my own perception of me, and made a significant difference to my confidence'.

Perhaps it is not merely coincidence that immediately after this session Rachel finds the courage to end an unhealthy and co-dependent relationship with an ex-lover. This gives her 'an initial sense of liberation' yet leads her to face a painful truth, as recorded in her account of the following session, where she writes: 'I think the most painful part of the session was when I admitted that if I thought someone loved me, I was so *grateful*. I would do anything for them. The way I have lived most of my life just seems so crap. At the moment there seems little motivation to go on living. I have changed so many things in my life already, now I've let go of all my co-dependent relationships – I have no false hopes, but no real hopes either. Life feels very, very empty'. The possibility arises that there may have been a link here between Rachel's sense of being valued in the therapeutic relationship and her ability to take a step which, though it leaves her facing great despair, is essentially a healthy one.

Endnote

Although this chapter is included to provide an account of how researching one's own work with clients can help the counsellor discover more about the therapeutic use of self, I have the sense that some readers may be left wondering how the therapy proceeded when Rachel discontinued writing her session accounts (after session 47). For those who are interested, this is my version (though checked for accuracy with my client) of how our story ended.

Jung has written:

> [I]n every adult there lurks a child – an eternal child, something that is always becoming, is never completed, and calls for unceasing care, attention and education. That is the part of the human personality which wants to develop and become whole.
>
> (Jung 1983: 194)

These words about the inner child seem to capture something of what occurred during the last phase of Rachel's counselling. There followed a number of powerful sessions in which she met, and then courageously stayed in contact with, the child inside her. She came to know a part of herself that had been split off for many years. 'Little Rachel' had been feared and despised as weak and vulnerable. Now Rachel learned to feel compassion for this child inside and to know that she could be a source of strength and creativity as well as carrying her vulnerable and frightened feelings. She helped Little Rachel to mourn the loss of the close and loving relationship she had desperately wanted and never had with her mother. Rachel came to realise that she had spent much of her life attempting to find the one exclusive relationship with another woman that would make up for her mother's neglect.

As we neared the end of the counselling Rachel embarked on a relationship with a new partner in which she was able to choose to remain separate and independent and in control of her own level of commitment and involvement. She developed a circle of friends with whom she experienced loving and rewarding relationships that were balanced and healthy. She told me that she had made a vow to herself to preserve her own separate identity above everything else as she now felt like a whole person for the first time in her life. In my account of session 58 I wrote down some words that she said to me to convey her sense of herself as we approached the end of our counselling relationship. She said: 'I imagine what I feel now is what most people feel like. I could never understand how anyone could be positive and enjoy life. Now I feel like this too and I never want to feel any different. I will safeguard this feeling and never let anyone take it away from me'.

LEARNING FOR THE COUNSELLOR

Feltham (1998b: 6) has observed that while many therapists from the time of Freud onwards have published case studies focusing on clinical diagnosis, observation and treatment, 'fewer have focussed on what may actually be learned from clients'. In this section I wish to highlight the learning I gained from my client through conducting the study. This is learning that has provided me with important guiding principles for subsequent work with other clients and that has been formative in helping me to develop my own approach and style of counselling.

Reading Rachel's extended accounts of her therapy was a moving and powerful experience for me. I learnt many valuable lessons in hearing from her about such things as: what she had needed and didn't get from me; what had worked for her and why it had worked; how at times I could have helped her to disclose and express her feelings more effectively; how our relationship impacted on the work, and the effect on her of when I made mistakes, omissions and errors. I have changed and refined the way I work as a counsellor in innumerable ways as a result of what Rachel has taught me. Much of this learning provided the seeds of my interest in the topics that are located elsewhere in this volume.

- **Learning about staying focused**   On several occasions Rachel wrote that she would have liked more help from me in linking one session to another and in helping her to keep going with work started in a previous session, particularly where this involved staying in contact with painful or difficult feelings, such as anger or abandonment. For example, she observes in her account of session 6 that I could have helped her to stay focused on difficult issues if I had asked her at the start of the session what she planned to do in it and then 'made' her 'stick to it'. I had been allowing Rachel to start each session with whatever she chose to start with as I was concerned not to be directive. Eventually I 'twigged' that she sometimes needed my help, for instance on one occasion I contracted clearly with her to undertake some sustained and committed work on her 'inner child' at a time when she was both very fearful of doing this work and also saw it as being fundamental to her healing process. Rachel's accounts have helped me to realise that some clients need direction from the counsellor in order to help them stay with difficult issues. As a result of this learning I now more frequently remind clients of the material they brought in a previous session and ask if they would like my help with sustaining the same focus.
- **Learning about touch**   I regret now that I didn't discuss touch more openly and explicitly with Rachel in order to negotiate the

safe and non-erotic use of touch with her. I think the way I handled this issue bordered, at times, on misuse of power, particularly when I was inconsistent in my use of touch and seemed sometimes to be offering physical support and at other times to be withdrawing it.

My experience of working with Rachel, and of having access to her written responses, provided me with important learning about the therapeutic use of touch. What I feel I didn't get right for Rachel was differentiating between when touch could have enhanced the therapy, in particular by helping her release trapped and painful feelings, and when it might have undermined the therapy by feeding her physical or sexual craving. If I had been more skilled and sensitive at the time I would have talked about this with her. Had I done so, I believe there is a good possibility that I could have negotiated the appropriate use of therapeutic touch with her and this may have helped her more easily and naturally to release and relieve many painful feelings.

I now negotiate with clients more clearly about the possibility of using touch with them and try to make any concerns I have very much more explicit. For instance, I would now tend to 'think aloud' with my client if I sensed that touch might be welcomed yet could also be confusing or difficult for them. I might say something like: 'I'm aware that I'm thinking about whether you would like me to touch you when you are upset and also that I'm concerned this might be difficult and confusing for you if you are unsure about how you'd respond. I know that sometimes physical feelings get mixed up with sexual feelings for you'. Had I done this with Rachel it would have been far more congruent and given her a clearer message about where I was coming from. The issue of the ethical use of touch in therapy is dealt with more fully in Chapter 6.

- **Learning about counsellor assisted disclosure**   Until she spoke about it in session 13, I had no inkling that Rachel was considering the possibility of having been sexually abused as a child. From reading her accounts of these sessions I have learned that it can often be helpful to check with the client whether there is anything else around that they might like to talk about. Even when counselling seems to be going well, I now tend to ask clients if they would like to tell me anything else and I have been struck by how often this question bears the fruit of further disclosure. Issues around counsellor assisted disclosure are discussed further in Chapter 5.
- **Learning about the client's hidden seam**   Rachel's session reports bear witness to a rich seam of information about how she

was experiencing the therapy and making use of it. Although she sometimes had difficulty answering all of the prompts on the report form each time and would leave some blank, she almost always completed the sentence stem that began: 'Something I would have liked to say but didn't was . . .'. Much of what she wrote was then brought to sessions and made explicit. It may well be that the experience of spending time in structured recall of the sessions enabled her to do this. Very often she would start a counselling session with the words 'When I was writing up the session I realised that there was something I avoided telling you. I'd like to try to talk about it in this session'. Rachel's process appears to accord with findings that Rennie (1992) has uncovered in his research into the unfolding of clients' reflexivity. He records his main finding as: 'that what the client says in therapy does not necessarily reflect what he or she is thinking . . . it appears to be more generally the case that a host of things are going on that are not expressed' (p. 229).

As a result of knowing about Rachel's covert 'track' I am now very much more aware that clients may well be telling me only a part of what concerns them as they speak. This has altered my attitude towards listening. Since working with Rachel it is almost as if I have become able to amplify the quality of my listening and I now try to be much more alert to picking up signals that my client is thinking about telling me something more. My interventions with clients are now as much geared to inviting them to reveal their concealed thoughts, feelings and responses as they are to working with the material that the client reveals in the here and now of the session. For instance, I will often explicitly invite the disclosure of covert material by saying something like: 'Is there anything else you'd like me to hear today so that you don't leave wishing you had said something more?'

- **Learning about how to use session time and the impact of extratherapeutic factors**   On several occasions in her session accounts Rachel records that she went off track at the start of a session and the whole session was taken up with talking about something other than she had intended to discuss. Sometimes she records that this was useful in opening up unforeseen issues, at other times it meant that more pressing or significant work was avoided or missed. When we went astray this was sometimes because I would respond to Rachel's opening comments in a way that assumed that this was the focus she wished to bring to the session.

I am now much clearer about checking out with clients what it is that they need to spend session time on. I have come to realise that clients can manage (as Rachel did) a great deal of their own process of change between sessions and that it is therefore helpful for me to clarify with them what they are able to get on with without my assistance. This leaves us to deal, in the session, with whatever the client most needs my help with. Miller and colleagues (1997) call this 'minding the client's world' and suggest that paying attention to and encouraging change that is occurring outside of therapy is equally, if not more important as an indicator of favourable progress, than focusing on in-session movement and insight. Now when a client comes and launches into telling me something that sounds like a problem I will frequently say: 'Is this something you need my help with, or can you manage it on your own?' I wish I had known to ask this question years ago as it amazes me how often my client will say: 'I think I'll be able to sort that out for myself'. In asking this I am also conveying to my clients that I think they are capable of taking charge of their own lives and this seems to me to be a respectful and helpful thing to do.

- **Learning about mistakes**   It is from my experience with Rachel that I have come to ask myself whether mistakes and errors are to be welcomed, rather than regarded as something to be avoided. Clarkson (1995) has written this about the therapeutic use of errors:

> Whenever there is a break or a threatened break in the working alliance, whether it happens near the beginning, the middle, or the end of psychotherapy, it always presents an opportunity for establishing important gains, and for revising or reworking fundamental psychotherapeutic issues. . . . It is a matter of holding the person within the area of rational goodwill while allowing the maximum buffeting from unconscious, environmental, or existential challenges.
>
> (Clarkson 1995: 49–50)

The kind of therapeutic opportunity which Clarkson describes seemed clearly to occur on the occasion where I missed being there for Rachel for two sessions after session 17 (as described above). My error enabled her to get in touch with an authentic part of herself that had been suppressed for many years. She responded to the existential challenge of the moment and rediscovered her angry self. This part of her, once brought to life, infused the subsequent therapeutic work and rippled outwards to impact on other relationships in her life in many important ways. Because Rachel and I always had such high regard for one another, I think it would have been difficult for her to find a way to be angry with me if I had not 'let her down' so tangibly. I have seen how useful this mistake was for Rachel and I now look out for the therapeutic opportunity revealed in mistakes, errors and gaffs I make with other clients, rather than berate myself for having made them. More about the imperfect therapist and the therapeutic use of failure is said in the next chapter.

- **Learning about the relationship** From Rachel I learned the supreme lesson that if the counselling relationship is intact then the process of therapy can pretty much take care of itself. Consequently, if the relationship falters I now know that this requires attention before anything else. Breaches need to be acknowledged, understood and repaired in order that the relationship can serve to contain and sustain the work that needs to take place. Whilst I always *thought* the relationship was crucial, I now *know* it to be so and this means that I can trust more easily that my relationship with my client, if it is good, will build up credits that will then carry us through the worst of times as well as the best.

ISSUES OF VALIDITY AND IMPLICATIONS FOR FURTHER RESEARCH

Trepper (1990) has argued that, amongst other important functions, the case study serves as a means by which practitioners can communicate with one another and in this sense 'is analogous to the all-important case conference' (p. 6). As research (Morrow-Bradley and Elliott 1986) suggests that professionals favour discussion with other therapists above scientific enquiry as a means of accessing information about clinical practice, case studies like the one presented here may be viewed as significant mechanisms by which such dialogue between therapists can take place.

Drawing upon a review conducted by Stiles (1993), McLeod (1994) has outlined a number of criteria for evaluating the validity of qualitative research. Those that appear especially pertinent to an evaluation of the current study are given below.

1   **Clarity and comprehensiveness of the description of research procedures employed** The requirement here is for the researcher

to give a great deal of detail about the way that the study was carried out, in particular how participants were selected, what happened to them and how the data were analysed.

2   **Adequacy of conceptualisation of data**   The reader should be able to follow the line of argument and evidence that leads from the data to any conclusions or findings.

3   **Credibility of the researcher (reflexivity)**   Reflexive (personal narrative) accounts written by the researcher should demonstrate integrity and cover such topics as: how informants were contacted; how issues of trust and rapport were dealt with; how mistakes, misconceptions and unexpected events were experienced and taken account of. Additionally, the researcher should be scrupulous in detailing how ethical issues were addressed – for instance, imbalances of power and transference issues in the relationship.

4   **Experiential authenticity of the material**   The extent to which the descriptive account seems real and authentic (has face validity). 'An essential test of experiential authenticity is the degree to which the research report is received as an accurate description by the actual informants' (McLeod 1994: 100).

5   **Use of triangulation**   This involves checking against other sources of information. It includes negotiation with informants and testimonial validity gained through submitting drafts or parts of the research to participants to ask for their comments.

6   **Catalytic validity**   The degree to which the research process enables or empowers participants (as opposed to disempowers or exploits them). This involves asking participants about the impact that taking part in the research has had on their lives and may, therefore, involve further contact or follow-up.

I hope that what I have so far written about this study in this and the previous chapter demonstrates that it meets the first three criteria. I will turn my attention, as I conclude this chapter, to the final three criteria given. In so doing, I will draw upon the experience of my client as research participant.

As I have already mentioned, the client's session reports are incomplete and there remains the possibility that the counsellor's accounts, particularly in regard to the later sessions, put a gloss on the work that may misrepresent the client's perspective. The danger of this was minimised by sending drafts of this chapter and the previous one to Rachel to ask her to comment on whether the material presented seems to provide a truthful and accurate account of her experience of events.

With her permission I include here several excerpts from the letter Rachel wrote to me when I sent the draft chapters to her. Her letter is written two years and three months after our last counselling session took place. (I had had no communication with her since then, apart from a brief letter requesting her preliminary and provisional written permission to include material from our counselling sessions in this book, sent on the advice of my editor at the time I submitted the proposal to the publisher.) She asked me to make only one amendment, which was to a date I had mistakenly given. Otherwise she wrote: 'As far as the content of the chapters is concerned, I am happy with what you have written. You describe it how it was – with an honesty I admire. . . . there is nothing I wish to add or change in the text'.

Rachel also tells me something in her letter of her current state of emotional health: 'Since my counselling with you ended, I have had a few short periods of depression and anxiety, but on the whole this has been the most stable and balanced period of my life'. She then writes something about the significance for her of the therapeutic relationship: 'I shall always remember your kindness, understanding and sensitivity towards me and the very special relationship we had which continues to sustain me. I feel whole, with an inner sense of security which I know will always be part of me. I think I am still consolidating the work you and I did and am gradually learning to do things differently by being the "real" me. On the whole, I deal with what life throws at me much more effectively and in less damaging ways for myself and hopefully, for others'.

Rachel then comments on her experience of taking part in the study: 'It has given me such pleasure to hear how the research has added to your approach to counselling. I'm delighted that I have been able to give you something tangible that will benefit others who come to you for counselling and other counsellors in training. I feel very privileged to have been involved in this research study as it has enabled our relationship to be a reciprocal one, which is important to me, and which I should imagine most counselling relationships are not'. I think her words are important in the way that they underscore the message I have been trying to promote here – that research conducted sensitively and ethically by counsellors in their own practice settings, far from being damaging or exploitative, can actually enhance the therapeutic experience of clients.

In presenting this study my hope is that other counsellors may feel stirred to attempt some comparable research of their own in order to begin to put to the test some of the assumptions that inform their clinical practice. Studies of this nature can be viewed as making important, if modest, contributions to what Schön (1983: 315) has termed 'repertoire-building research'. I agree with Goldman who argued, as far back as 1977, that we should remove from the shoulders of individual researchers the 'burden' of requiring every study to make a substantial and significant contribution to knowledge. As Goldman (1977: 367) asserts, 'this burden has often stood in the way of people doing practical little studies that could help them to understand the people and situations they work with and judge to what extent the interventions of counselors and others have made a difference'.

Through undertaking research studies like the one presented here, it begins to be possible for the individual practitioner to start to catalogue the 'common factors' in their own practice that appear to be most effective. Were a number of practitioner-researchers to undertake similar studies it would then become possible to compare these factors and start looking for common elements across unique counselling dyads. Such procedures might then lead to the creation of a body of knowledge about what seems to be effective in counselling and psychotherapy that arises from the experience of counsellors and clients in the real world of clinical practice to set against the conclusions reached by academic researchers conducting experiments in laboratory settings. And, without question, that would prove to be a most invigorating and informative comparison.

Chapter 5

The impaired therapist and the value of therapist failure

> Psychotherapy is one of those occupations in which we have perpetual opportunity for remorse and regret over what we did not understand earlier on when we had less experience and less insight, not just into our patients but into ourselves and our practices.
>
> (Lewin 1996)

This chapter and the two that come after it will follow the same format. I will present a discussion of issues related to the chapter title, informed by relevant literature and research studies, and present a number of my own perspectives with examples drawn from practice. Each chapter will then present a selection of data from a survey into unorthodox practice and the use of self carried out with trained and experienced counsellors and psychotherapists.

THE NOTION OF THE IMPAIRED THERAPIST

Whilst the vast majority of counsellors and psychotherapists are no doubt committed to achieving high standards of therapeutic intervention for their clients, it is clearly a fallacy to consider that this can always be achieved. As Kottler (1986: 59) has observed the unfortunate truth is 'we are all incompetent some of the time. We just cannot get through to some people because of our deficiencies and limitations'. Whilst it is true that all therapists fail some of the time, admissions of failure are not widely or publicly discussed (McLennan 1996). This seems unfortunate since, as Casement (1985: 225) has observed, whilst 'analysts and therapists do not so readily share their failures . . . more can be gained by all when some are prepared to do so'.

Unless we are willing to admit to our failures, omissions and errors, we are likely to defend against weaknesses in our practice by leaping to assessments of unhelped clients as being 'resistant', 'not ready to change', or 'not really suitable for counselling'. These things may be true for a small number of our clients but I think we are sometimes too ready to jump to justifications of negative outcomes in our practice by dismissing clients as inadequate when perhaps it is we who were not prepared to go that extra mile to meet them in the way that they needed to be met.

I believe it is an ethical requirement for therapists to consider their own part in dislocations of the therapeutic process when these occur. This means that we should listen up when clients seem to be trying to tell us that we have got things wrong. I agree with Casement (1985: 180) in considering it to be 'a tragic loss when patients offer corrective cues to a therapist, but find these thrown back unrecognised for what they are'. Whilst our failures and impairments at times no doubt limit our ability to work effectively with clients, I believe, paradoxically, that they can also liberate much of our naturally inherent helping capacity through, as Schön (1983: 299) has asserted, becoming 'a source of discovery rather than an occasion for self defence' (p. 299). Hobson (1985: 203) has suggested that the therapist's most important attitude and skill may indeed be 'to be willing and able to *recognize signs that he is wrong*, and to modify his approach in the light of such evidence' (original emphasis). Clarkson (1995) provides a rationale for the therapeutic potential of failure in arguing that not only is it inevitable that we will fail our clients, but it is also necessary to fail them as a form of immunisation to help them 'develop the robustness, resilience and recalcitrance necessary for the development of a sturdy self' (p. 136). Mistakes can be liberating, for as Kottler and Blau (1989) have pointed out, 'failure draws one's attention to a result in need of explanation; it is a call to creativity and further experimentation' (p. 65). The learning we can glean from, and the use we make of, our mistakes and deficiencies is the subject of this chapter.

In considering the notion of the impaired therapist we are skating on a thin crust. The thin crust of our imperfections supports important aspects of self such as our fallibility, humility and vulnerability. When we are fallible we are at our most human and when we are most human we are in touch with our greatest potential for helping clients. Carl Rogers explicitly links the notion of the imperfect therapist with the potential for healing.

> The therapist needs to recognize very clearly the fact that he or she is an imperfect person with flaws which make him vulnerable. I

think it is only as the therapist views himself as imperfect and flawed that he can see himself as helping another person. Some people who call themselves therapists are not healers, because they are too busy defending themselves.

(Rogers in Baldwin 1987: 51)

Beneath the thin crust of the therapist's healing impairments lie the treacherous waters of abusive and unethical practice. Walking here, we need to tread carefully and with great caution to avoid plunging into depths from which we, and our clients, are unlikely to emerge unscathed. Setting out across this thin ice may, however, be the only way of reaching some clients and providing for them the help that they need. Not to attempt the crossing may constitute damage by neglect which may in itself comprise a breach of professional ethics. Abuse happens not only by action, but also through inaction (Clarkson 1996). Therapist impairments are frequently discussed under the rubric of the wounded healer and I consider this notion further in Chapter 8 where I discuss the shadow side of the use of self in counselling.

As therapists gain experience, hopefully they come to learn that mistakes are unavoidable and indeed seem frequently to be evoked by the counselling process itself where they can provide profitable grist to the therapeutic mill. Many mistakes are unavoidable because the therapist cannot know in advance what the client needed instead of what was offered. Often it is the therapist's mistake or misunderstanding that reveals the client's need. So the wrong footing is not so much a mistake as what might be termed 'creative slippage' prompted by the client, which can have valuable therapeutic potential. I agree with Hobson (1985) that 'learning how to correct misunderstandings is one (and perhaps, *the*) most important therapeutic factor' (p. 16, original emphasis). Kottler and Blau (1989) have gone as far as to suggest that therapists who use their mistakes as the principal signposts in their work do not really need other way markers.

Therapists who operate strategically need not ever know which interventions will work in effecting client changes as long as they pay attention to what does not work or has not worked before. A prime example of a therapeutic approach that values failure as much as success is one in which the clinician does not expect or need to be right during initial helping efforts. A respect for process, a belief in the client's resources, faith that healing results from struggle and experimentation, allows a therapeutic stance of patience and tolerance for failure.

(Kottler and Blau 1989: 58)

Clarkson (1989: 91) cites the anonymous person who commented 'the only real mistake you can make as a counsellor is to die'. Clearly this is not meant to be taken as a literal truth as there are, of course, many ways that therapists can harm their clients and all of these are mistakes. There are also those events that may be experienced as errors and omissions by clients but which are, of necessity, part of the clinician's ethical and professional 'stock in trade' – for instance where the therapist is not around because of holiday breaks, or ruptures an 'exclusive' bond by counselling someone else the client is acquainted with, or calls in medical help when the client wants to be left to kill themselves. However the quotation from Clarkson serves as a useful prompt to remind us not to consign our presumed failures and omissions too readily to the scrap yard of discarded experience before examining them for what they may hold as learning potential for us and therapeutic potential for our clients. The essential paradox here is that if I do not fail the client in some way then I *am* failing them by denying them the recognition that I am fallible. Unless they see me as fallible they are likely to look to me as the source of all that they crave in terms of love and approval. It is only when the client experiences me as having let them down that they can begin to look within themselves for a source of self-nurturing and an internal locus of evaluation.

Novice counsellors are, understandably, particularly fearful of making mistakes. As a trainee I used to put a lot of energy and attention into trying to avoid making mistakes, usually by thinking hard about what to say next while the client was speaking. This was energy and attention taken away from what I should have been doing – which was listening to my client. It came as a major revelation to me when I realised that I didn't need to pre-plan my interventions. If I listened well the client's words would provide the catalyst and a response would emerge without being forced. Gradually I learned that too great a preoccupation with selecting the best technique or intervention took me away from my client, rather than bringing me into closer contact with her or him. Lomas has summed up the quality of this kind of attentive listening: 'It is not the concentration of conscious effort to perfect a technique or adhere to a theory, but the concentration that appears naturally when one person is interested in another's being' (Lomas 1981: 26).

The more I learned about listening, the more I realised what a demanding and complicated skill it is. Not only does it involve hearing the client's words and the message conveyed by their non-verbal communication, just as importantly it means listening to myself and the impact the client is having on me in that moment. I have now learned that I work at my most effective when I can disengage from distracting thoughts and conceptualisations and become as still and empty as possible with my client. As Hycner (1991) has remarked, there is a danger in the therapist being 'too "intelligent" [where] we have too many thoughts, too much going on within us, such that there is little room for being receptive to the new, the *uniqueness*, to the *otherness*' of the client (p. 99, original emphases).

By becoming empty I become most receptive and attentive. Paradoxically, when I am able to achieve this state of emptiness – which feels like a kind of suspension of outside interference – I find that I often become filled with stray thoughts, associations, hunches, words, images and bodily sensations. These feel very different to external distractions or daydreams arising out of disengagement from my client and I have learnt to welcome them as a kind of meta-communication from the client that may alert me to something than needs attention. When at my best, it seems as if I am able to become a sort of divining rod that picks up and resonates with the client's unexpressed distress or disturbance.

An example of what I mean is sitting with a client who is telling me about what she has been doing to fill her time recently. She is speaking calmly and unemotionally. I sit with her and feel like crying. If I do not say something to break (what feels like my own) tension and heaviness I know that I will not be able to stop tears coming. I look at her eyes instead of listening to her words and say: 'You look very sad and lost today. Your eyes are soft'. She replies: 'You are very perceptive. I was hoping you wouldn't notice'. Later in the session she tells me that she has been taking small amounts of tablets all day with the intention of building up to a lethal overdose. She had not intended to tell me this when she came to the session and had planned to continue taking the tablets after seeing me. By the end of the day she had hoped to be dead. Now that I have noticed she (albeit reluctantly) allows me to intervene and get some medical attention for her.

Sometimes listening is really hard because if I do this well I am taking the risk of allowing the client to get beyond the protective layers of my professional persona and under the skin of the real me. Carl Rogers has talked in an interview about the quality of good listening. 'I used to think that [to really listen acceptantly] was easy. It has taken me a long time to realize that for me, for most people, this is extremely hard. To listen acceptantly, no matter what is being voiced, is a rare thing' (Rogers in Baldwin 1987).

When 'active listening' is merely reduced to a set of microskills such as using minimal prompts, open postures, reflecting, paraphrasing and summarising it becomes a pale imitation of the experience of true listening and can suggest a dangerous simplification. Attentive listening is a highly charged and significant process and one in which the therapist engages with their whole being, rather than a matter of body posture and verbal acknowledgement. The quality of listening is important because it carries the potential of being received by the client as an authentic and healing response that can exorcise much previous mis-attending that the client may have experienced in their life. Teaching the skill of listening should not be divorced from the person of the trainee. Trainees and supervisees need to be helped to understand the impact that really listening will have on them and be prepared for this. More about this is said in Chapter 9.

Of course no counsellor can listen perfectly or hope to hear absolutely everything that is significant for the client. Listening is further complicated when we consider that the client will frequently expend energy on hiding or keeping things from the therapist. This may happen particularly in the early stages of any therapeutic relationship (and early stages can last for months). We may ask open and global questions: 'What is troubling you?' or invite full disclosure: 'You can tell me anything', secure in our own knowledge of being unshockable and bottomless containers for all that our clients may need to disgorge. Yet it is a grandiose assumption to believe that our clients will routinely respond fully and truthfully to all such invitations. This view is borne out by research undertaken by Angus and Rennie who conducted a study into therapists' collaborative and noncollaborative styles in working with clients' metaphors and reached the following conclusion:

> It is apparent that therapists cannot safely assume that the comfort and specialty of the therapy encounter is sufficient to prompt clients to be both comprehensive and honest in their discourse. Instead, it would be more prudent for therapists to assume that what clients say is only a partial representation of meaning; and to devise communication strategies to stimulate clients to more fully reveal covert processes.

> (Angus and Rennie 1988: 559)

Clients are often, and I think rightly, more cautious and circumspect than we might assume and will frequently keep things back unless, and until, they are sure that the therapist can be trusted with their most loaded and difficult confidences. The therapist's failure here lies not in the inability to force premature disclosure – it is up to the client when and what they divulge – but in making the mistake of not remaining open to the possibility that the client may well have further issues to disclose as the therapy proceeds and may need some help in making these disclosures. This error is seriously compounded if we make evaluative and presumptive statements to clients, such as: 'I think you are being very open with me'. It then becomes almost impossible for the client to come back with: 'No I'm not – I've been hiding things'.

I had been working for about a year with a client who had a great many difficult experiences and issues to talk about. Because she talked about a good number of these and because they seemed so substantial, I made the assumption that she was telling me all that I needed to know. One day she came, and looking very uncomfortable, said: 'There's something I haven't told you' and, with some encouragement, was able to let me know that she was severely bulimic and had been for a number of years. As we talked about how she felt about disclosing this to me at this stage in the counselling, it transpired that her reluctance to disclose was partly about protecting me: 'I feel really guilty about not telling you this before. I thought you might think you had failed me because I've been seeing you for a year and I haven't said anything about it'.

Like most errors and omissions, such incidents can hold therapeutic potential depending on how the therapist understands, responds and handles the situation. In terms of the transference relationship I believe that my client was letting me know that, like her mother, I *had* failed her in not noticing the eating problem. On the level of the real relationship between us she was, perhaps, saying: 'I feel safe and secure enough in this relationship to risk telling you my secret'. To her spoken words I replied: 'I wasn't thinking that I have failed you. In fact, I was thinking how good our relationship must be *now* for you to be able to tell me something so difficult'. This moved us on to talking about how we both felt that our relationship was strengthening and deepening and the importance of this for my client. Over the months that followed she divulged, at intervals, a number of other 'secrets' of similar magnitude as she came to believe that I could hear her and would not shame her.

As the relationship develops and the counsellor becomes more sure of the client's growing trust and confidence it can be fruitful for the therapist to make opportunities for further disclosure to occur. Direct questions such as: 'Is there anything I've missed?' (useful near the end of a session) or indirect ones: 'I'm wondering if there's anything else you might like to tell me', or even, 'there might be other things around that are more difficult to talk to me about' can often bear fruit.

IMPAIRMENT, PERSONAL COUNSELLING AND THE USE OF SELF

A number of authors (see, for instance, Corey 1996; Corey *et al.* 1993; Dryden 1991; Dryden and Feltham 1994; Dryden *et al.* 1995; Johns 1996, 1997; Mearns 1997a, 1997b; Wheeler 1991, 1996; Wilkins 1997) have recently debated the requirement of personal counselling for the counsellor as part of training and ongoing professional development. However this debate progresses it appears that at least one professional body, the British Association for Counselling, has placed itself firmly within the camp of those who advocate personal therapy (or its equivalent) and has set a minimum number of hours (currently forty) as a requirement for counsellors applying for Accreditation and Registration (BAC 1996a).

As arguments about the pros and cons of personal counselling for the counsellor have been well covered in these recent publications, I will not attempt to restate the issues at any length in this section. A point worth noting, however, is that a comprehensive review of the research evidence pertaining to the relationship between personal therapy and therapist effectiveness (Beutler *et al.* 1994) has concluded that results are inconclusive and fail to show a direct correlation between the two. This finding is confirmed by Wheeler (1991).

My own view is that personal counselling, or an equivalent activity (such as considerable time spent in a personal growth group), is a prerequisite for those counsellors who aspire to draw upon their own life experience and personal attributes to any significant degree in their work with clients. Personal growth work, as Aponte (1982: 20) advises, makes 'more of the therapist's self available as "raw material" for the work of therapy'. I am not convinced that compulsory personal counselling for trainees is a road down which we should go. My concern is that some trainees will 'go through the motions' and have their minimum number of hours of (costly) therapy at a time determined by their training, which may or may not be the time when they are most able, or inclined, to make best use of it. They may then resist seeking further counselling when other personal issues arise that require attention, having paid their money and done their forty hours. I have supervised therapists who work with students who are undertaking (often it seems like submitting to) a required number of counselling sessions while on a training course. Whilst some of these trainees appear to be making excellent use of their counselling to undertake in-depth personal work, others seem clearly resistant or are slow to find focus and depth.

I also think there is a real danger that in some training courses development of the self will get 'hived off' into the required number of personal counselling hours, rather than being seen as having a central and ongoing place in the training experience. As Mearns (1997a: 117) has argued 'it is extremely dangerous to divest personal development to the periphery of a counselling training course' and one way in which this can happen is for trainers to sideline personal development work through the assumption that it will be adequately attended to if students are in compulsory therapy for part, or all, of their training. I agree with Mearns that a supportive and challenging group experience can raise opportunities for personal growth, which individual counselling may miss: 'personal therapy is a poor place for raising issues, a reasonable context for working on them but not nearly as vibrant as a group context for experimenting with the developing Self' (Mearns 1997a: 119).

I do believe that students should be actively encouraged by their trainers to undergo the experience of individual counselling at some time and that this should be when it is most likely to enhance higher levels of functioning when they are with their clients. Frequently this will be at a point where the trainee has engaged in sufficient work on self-awareness (which can happen through all, and any, of group work, supervision, tutorials, the processing of turbulent life experience, personal reflection, reading and feedback from peers) to begin to know which parts of the self need to be further unblocked, developed or healed.

It only becomes safe for the counsellor to rely heavily on the use of self in their clinical practice if they have prepared the ground of their personal landscape well in advance in order to achieve emotional stability and a secure sense of self. I believe that this is more about clearing away heavy scrub than meticulously forking out every single weed. As discussed later in this chapter, impairments have the potential for enriching and freeing up the therapist's practice as well as for choking it. To pursue my analogy – gardeners who spend a great deal of their time sifting through soil to eradicate every tiny weed and its roots will have proportionally less time left for growing and tending their plants. Gardeners like myself, who favour functionality over aesthetics, find that it is more effective and less time consuming to pull out the large weeds and fork the small ones back in so that they can turn into green compost to feed the vegetables. Similarly, therapists who feel they have to root out every imperfection through exhaustive bouts of compulsive therapy may, paradoxically, be denuding their psyche of richly nurturing material that might, if merely brought to the surface and turned over, act as nourishment for themselves and their clients. I think over-weeding has occurred when characteristics such as self-doubt, spontaneity, tentativeness, trepidation, uncertainty, excitability, clumsiness, teasing and mischievousness are no longer apparent in the therapist's demeanour towards their clients. In essence, I believe we need the services of a counsellor or therapist principally to help us identify what needs eradication and what can be retained and then utilised *in awareness* to good effect in our work with clients.

What this comes down to is that we need to have sufficiently resolved our own issues not to have to keep parts of ourselves out of our interactions with clients, or shut aspects of ourselves down because we cannot bear to have them restimulated by the client's material. One important measure of how effectively I am able to work with clients is governed by how deeply I can allow myself to be touched (and therefore changed) by my clients. My client will be helped to the extent that I can be fully available to him or her as my authentic and whole self. If I need to block, dodge, duck and dive when faced with certain aspects of the client's story in order to protect myself, I will certainly be preventing the client from doing the therapeutic work that they need to do. Despite what my early training might have led me to believe, this means that I might need to be *more*, rather than *less*, emotional with my clients. I am suspicious of lack of emotion in counsellors as I think that access to our fluent and fluid feelings when we are with clients can provide them with a powerful source of energy and affirmation. What is equally important is that we are able to contain and make use of our feelings or that we have the sense and the grace to withdraw if we can't manage this. The undisciplined use of self may occur when counsellors have not sufficiently chewed over and digested their own personal material to prevent its being regurgitated on to their clients.

I once saw a young woman in a first session who wanted help with her grieving over the death of her father who had just died from cancer. A day or two beforehand my mother had told me that she needed to have surgery for a potentially serious illness. I had been 'too busy' at work to allow this news to sink in. Now it hit me when I was with my client and sufficiently opened up to my feelings. Instantly, I knew I could not speak with her about her father's death without suffering for my own mother. I knew that I would not be able to frame an even minimally empathic response without bursting into tears. I explained that I was not the best person to help her because of something that was occurring in my own life and, with her agreement, referred her to another counsellor. This experience taught me a lot about the importance of assiduously checking out my own emotional state rather than leaving it to it my clients to act as an emotional barometer for me.

If I have to draw a curtain over, or erect a barricade between myself and my feelings (as I would have had to do in this case), I am likely to appear detached and impassive to my clients, because this is what I am being towards myself. On occasion I have chosen to stay with and respond from my own raw feelings when I am reasonably sure that they arise from being in relationship with my client and are a legitimate expression of that relationship. With one very suicidal client whom I feared I would not see again I recall saying: 'I am not going to be able to say this to you without crying. And what I want to say to you is that I do not think you know how much you will be missed if you choose to kill yourself'. The client took this on the chin and in not ducking the impact of my feelings began to find some strength in himself to continue living.

HEALING IMPAIRMENTS

All therapists bring imperfect selves to their practice of therapy. The therapist's personal struggle involves sorting out those impairments that may be damaging and therefore need to be kept away from clients and dealt with elsewhere, from those that can be legitimately incorporated into the therapist's repertoire of helping interventions, because they may actually benefit clients. It is not just our therapists who can help us to identify what we might term our 'healing impairments'. As I hope I demonstrated in Chapter 4, our clients can become a primary source of such feedback if only we provide them with opportunities for so doing. The wonderful thing about receiving feedback from our clients is that they see us as new and unencumbered by the expectations, limitations or requirements heaped on us by those with whom we have, or have had, close relationships in other aspects of our lives. Counselling relationships can be liberating for therapists as well as for their clients. I think Brazier has put his finger on why this might be in saying:

> Although we are required by society to have a self-concept, what is most personal and satisfying are those moments where we do not have to be remembering who we are. These are situations where we find intimacy, spontaneity and concern for others and for the natural environment. One is perhaps most alive when one feels moved by another or in direct communion with nature and most real when one is engaged in some action of evident intrinsic value.
>
> (Brazier 1993: 85)

Buber (1937) has stated that 'all real living is meeting' (p. 11) and that 'a person makes his appearance by entering into relation with other persons' (p. 62). I am frequently struck by the sense that my clients give me the opportunity to meet them in ways that seem to allow me to be most truly myself and without expecting me to present myself in a constructed way that may be called forth by the other roles I assume in my life. If a sense of self emerges in relationship with others, as was discussed in Chapter 1, then counselling can be understood as a form of socialised relationship that enables the counsellor, as well as the client, to develop their self-concept. As Bragan (1996: 20) has pointed out, therapy 'is a relationship process which moves towards each bringing the best out of the other, when it is going well'. In doing counselling I come to know who I am.

In moments of real meeting with clients, which are characterised by what Buber (1937) terms the 'I–Thou' quality of relationship, I some-how feel that my client knows the essence of me in a way that has little to do with my role as a counsellor. At such times it seems that we have a deep knowledge of one another that goes a long way back. It is as if, in these moments of heightened connectivity, I am able to contact the core of my client that exists beyond, before, beneath or above any problems or 'symptoms' that she or he may be caught up in. In the best of these moments it is as if we are meeting in a space that is outside of time and place and which is rich and vibrant in its healing potential. Clarkson (1990, 1994b, 1995) refers to such moments of meeting as entering into the spiritual dimension of psychotherapy that is actualised within the transpersonal relationship between therapist and client. She describes it thus:

> The transpersonal relationship is . . . characterised paradoxically by a kind of intimacy and by an 'emptying of the ego' at the same time. It is rather as if the ego of even the personal unconscious of the psychotherapist is 'emptied out' of the therapeutic space, leaving

space for something numinous to be created in the 'between' of the relationship. . . . It implies a letting go of skills, of knowledge, of experience, of preconceptions, even of the desire to heal, to be present. It is essentially allowing 'passivity' and receptiveness for which preparation is always inadequate.

(Clarkson 1990: 159)

Such moments are difficult to convey in the usual language with which we discuss therapeutic mutuality. They are characterised by a sense of connection that feels more akin to telepathy than to verbal discourse, although dialogue often arises from the connection. At such times I may think the client's thoughts or he or she may have mine in a way that seems to echo these words of Welwood (1985: x): 'My experience has been that there really is only one mind . . . the client's awareness and mine are two ends of one continuum in our moments of real contact'. I was, by way of illustration, sitting in silence with a client who was absorbed in contemplating the significance of a great personal loss. After several minutes in which neither of us had spoken she looked up and met my gaze and said: 'I don't know. I'm just aware of how huge this all is and I don't really know what I'm feeling'. She was answering the question that I was thinking, but had not spoken from fear of intruding, which was: 'What are you feeling in that long silence?'

The sense of heightened connectivity may find expression in such silence and also in non-verbal responses. My client was recalling a traumatic childhood episode. At one point she felt trapped and could not speak, which was exactly how she had felt in the experience itself. She looked across at me with young eyes filled with shock and terror and I said: 'Do you need a hug?' Whilst she still could not speak, I took the flicker in her eyes as my response and I sat beside her and put my arms around her. Many long minutes later, when the experience had been fully re-lived and cleared, we processed what had happened. My client said: 'You seemed to be there with me and know exactly what I needed. I couldn't speak and yet I desperately wanted you to know that I needed a hug. I felt so trapped and alone and I couldn't go on and when I looked at you you knew what I was asking for, even though I couldn't say it'.

At other moments of meeting I may find myself saying words that are the client's, that she dreads my speaking and yet which demand to be heard. For instance, I said to one client: 'It is as if a vital part of you is shut down' and she replied: 'Those are precisely the words I had in my mind and I didn't want you to say them. It upsets me so much because I feel that I will never wake up from all this'. On another occasion my client was talking about how she had felt numb and desolate for years and desperately craved a feeling of contentment. She lapsed into silence and I said: 'It is as if contentment is a country you have only heard about from others and never visited'. She replied: 'That's exactly the image I was looking at in my mind. I was thinking it's like when someone tells you about a country they have been to that you'd like to visit, but it's unreal to you because you haven't been there yet'.

Kottler (1986: 41–2) has observed that 'being a therapist affords us the opportunity for continual spiritual, intellectual and emotional growth' and I know that counselling allows me to find and express aspects of myself that don't normally find expression in other parts of my life and relationships. An example is that through being and becoming a coun-sellor I have found that I am someone who is capable of being a calm, resourceful, courageous and humorous companion to another person when they are in a state of profound emotional distress or disturbance. It feels important for me to know that I am this person and I feel good about myself in knowing this. I therefore look for opportunities to develop these parts of myself and find these in the therapeutic work that I do. The work then becomes both a motivator and the satisfaction of a need, in this instance, to like and value myself.

Curiously, I have found that aspects of my personality can appear as deficits in some circumstances and as credits in others. For example, I sometimes get the feedback from students and colleagues, especially on first acquaintance, that they can experience me as aloof and enigmatic. A number of my clients, on the other hand, have commented on the way that I stand back from them and don't smother them and thereby give them plenty of space in which to wander around to discover their own thoughts and feelings about themselves and their experience. I suspect that they may be alluding to the same characteristic which is, perhaps, something to do with the balance (or imbalance) in my nature between introspection and relatedness. This is a balance which Hycner (1991) considers to be a desirable attribute for all counsellors and psy-chotherapists: 'the therapist must be introverted enough to have a highly developed self-awareness, yet be able to easily relate to other people' (p. 13).

There are other examples of my personal impairments that, paradoxic-ally, it seems I am sometimes able to turn to good therapeutic use. The word impairment has a number of definitions and here I am using the term to mean those things about myself that can sometimes be disabling in my relationships with myself and others. I give some of them here in the hope that this may stimulate other counsellors to consider how the dust of their personal fallibility may sometimes be transmuted into therapeutic gold.

As a child I learned to contain, subdue and hold safe inside me many of my thoughts, feelings, hopes and aspirations. To reveal them meant risking disapproval, disregard or ridicule, particularly from my father. This has certainly helped to form the part of me that is able to contain, hold and react calmly to my clients' most turbulent feelings and disclosures and to respect their hopes and aspirations. I am sure that it has also contributed to the part of me that can be withdrawn, and yet my ability to be detached can be helpful as a counsellor.

I don't easily become overwhelmed by feelings (the client's or my own). I can usually disconnect sufficiently from my emotions when I need the space to think. It seems to me that this is different from suppressing feelings (although I learnt how to do this too, as a child). An example would be that I can disconnect from my rage towards an abuser when listening to a client tell me about how they have been abused and when the client is not yet capable of feeling his or her own rage. At this stage the client needs me to be calm, thoughtful and containing, not consumed on their behalf with outrage that they are not yet able to experience for themselves. The place to vent my own rage and distress at what has been done to my client is with my supervisor or a trusted colleague. By doing this I do not burden the client with yet more responsibility for looking after the needs of another person.

Perhaps because as a child I yearned for closer and more intimate relationships, as a counsellor I am very alert and responsive to my clients' invitations to be close. Similarly I am keenly sensitive to being 'kept out' and I will sometimes say to a client: 'I feel there is a distance between us today and I would rather be close to you'. I have experienced saying this as helping clients to think about what is going on for them in taking up a more distant position with me – for instance with a client who said: 'I have to keep you at a distance today because if I let you get close you might see how much I'm hurting. I hate myself today and I don't want to talk about my feelings'.

I am not closely attached to my immediate family and, I think, separated from them psychologically and emotionally at a younger age than many people do. Thus by the time I was eighteen I was eager to leave home and did not re-connect closely with my family thereafter. Largely because of this I think I do not have difficulty ending with clients and helping them to move on. I do not hang on to clients when they are ready to finish. What I *do* have to watch is that I don't hurry endings and assume that all my clients can leave me as easily as I am able to let them go. Sometimes I have to remind myself, or have my supervisor remind me, that I need to allow a longer time for an ending with a client than I might personally have chosen. Not surprisingly perhaps, my experience as a client first alerted me to this pattern in myself. When I felt ready to finish a period of therapy that had lasted for two and a half years I one day announced to my therapist that I would like to leave in two or three weeks. I can still picture the look of dismay on her face and she was congruent enough to say that it was too soon for her. We settled on a compromise of six weeks which, I must confess, felt to me like dragging it out a bit.

I often experienced the misery of feeling misunderstood as a child and I know that, as a counsellor, I seek ardently and diligently to understand and to convey my understanding to my clients. This is because it still distresses me to feel misunderstood or to witness my client's experience of feeling misunderstood. I was a fairly solitary child and spent a lot of time by myself, creating my own fantasy worlds. I learnt that on my own I could make choices and decisions about what I liked and wanted, whereas around my parents I experienced a lot confusion about this. (My mother modelled indecisiveness, compliance and passivity; my father encouraged deference to his views and feelings.) As part of retreating to my own world of daydreams, I became fond of stories at an early age, both through reading and making up my own. I often felt as if I had more real and vibrant relationships with characters in books than with the adults who were around me in my own life. As a counsellor I have retained this absorption in stories (which I suppose is a form of inquisitiveness, with shades even of voyeurism or vicarious living). Because I find the narratives of my clients vivid and absorbing I have no difficulty listening attentively to them. I sense that I listen well and with interest. I remember details and themes and I naturally conjure up metaphors and images and offer these back to my clients in ways they frequently seem to find useful. It is as if I feed off their stories, enter into, and become a contributor to them. What started as an escapist activity for a sometimes lonely and confused child has now come to be an apparently constructive and certainly a personally satisfying part of my therapeutic repertoire.

I have given these personal examples here because I hope they might encourage other therapists to look again at their own personal histories and thereby begin to make more explicit the connection between personal characteristics and the potential for the therapeutic use of self.

I suspect we can easily overlook as 'personal baggage' the energy and creativity we can harness from our own psychological makeup and individual life experiences.

A number of writers have suggested that the therapist's living dynamics, including their own pathology, even when undisclosed to the client, feed into the counselling situation and influence not only the conduct of the therapy but also the kind of issues that clients bring and even which clients come to us for therapy (Clarkson 1995; Keith 1987; Searles 1958; Sedgwick 1994). There seems to be a mysterious process, akin to synchronicity, operating here in which disruptions in the therapist's personal life act as strong currents that funnel in those clients who can take strength from the therapist's particular and unique flaws and inflamed areas. Perhaps tenderness and compassion leach out from these damaged aspects of self and have a scent that attracts and hooks certain clients. Hycner (1991) puts it like this: 'it is the very nature of one's own difficulties which sensitize the therapist to the vulnerability of the other' (p. 12). Hillman (1979: 22) has described the therapist's wound as 'an opening in the walls, a passage through which we may become infected and also through which we affect others' and has suggested that healing comes from this 'unguarded side, from where we are foolish and vulnerable'. Whilst it can be painful to have our wounds and scars touched and reactivated by our clients it can also prove to be healing and beneficial to both client *and* counsellor.

To concretise this notion I will give another perspective from personal experience. In my twenties I suffered from a near fatal illness that left me unable to bear children. As a therapist, one issue I need to be vigorously alert to is how this thwarted biological drive may impact on my relationships with clients. What has certainly been a personal loss surprisingly often also seems, unless I am deceiving myself, to constitute a source of potential benefit to my clients.

For a long time I preferred not to notice or admit that I seem to attract more than I might, by chance, expect to receive as my allotted share of clients who have experienced smothering, neglectful or abusive mothering. More recently I recognise that it is almost as if a place in my psyche, created by the loss of potential motherhood, has opened up to receive those parts of my clients that, for a while, need to experience a good mother. I am also aware that within the transference I seem to be able to be many different kinds of chameleon mother. For my clients who need close and loving attachment I can offer this. For those who need a separate and releasing mother I can be this too. I can also, it seems, easily move through stages of mothering which may start with tender merging and advance towards growthful separation and tougher distancing. I believe that my ability to be the kind of mother some of my clients need me to be probably rests largely on the fact that I do not have my own experience of being a mother to fix its imprint on to them.

To have been a mother myself would undoubtedly have constrained to some extent the form in which I am able to appear as a mothering counsellor. I know this from the many counsellors I have supervised who are mothers and who show me how their own experience of being a mother is reactivated by the child in their clients. I, on the other hand, do not know what sort of mother I might have been and perhaps because of this I can experiment with different forms of mothering that are summoned up by what my clients seem to need and didn't get from their own mothers. I am also now more easily able to admit, without immediate disquiet, that the experience of being in a relationship with my client that mirrors a parent–child relationship is one that, to some degree, meets my own personal need. I hope I can always continue to question in myself whether this motivator remains on the right side of the functional/dysfunctional divide in the belief that functional motivators possess a reciprocal quality that is growth promoting for counsellor and client alike. For, as Bugental (1964) has remarked, 'in a truly synergic relationship that which contributes to the fulfilment of one of the participants is most fulfilling of the other also' (p. 274).

Trying to disentangle our healing impairments from those flaws in our nature that may harm our clients is an ongoing struggle for most therapists. Reading over what I have written about myself in the passages above, I have a horrible creeping suspicion that I may come across as sounding smug, superior and self-congratulatory. If this is so, I suspect that the internalised father within me has shown itself in a need to seek approval and admiration. I have an immediate urge to disown this part of myself. Yet I know that this part of me also creeps into my counselling relationships and is present whenever I find myself basking in the warm glow of my clients' praise and admiration. It is also the part of me that provides a home for the stubborn self who always likes to be right and won't easily admit to having made errors or misjudgements. Yet from this hails my determination to succeed as a counsellor, for I hate giving up and being proved wrong. Once on their side, my clients tend to have me stick with them for the duration. I am struggling here to find a way of expressing something that I think Feltham (1998a) has captured clearly and forcefully in writing about his search for sanity and authenticity through becoming a counsellor. He writes:

I realize that in counselling sessions I often vacate my everyday self, somehow becoming a reliable, objective other for the client. That part of me which is not fucked-up temporarily overrides that which is, it is fallibility available to the client, just as that part of them that is not fucked-up reaches out fumblingly to me and to a sensed sanity beyond our common social madness.

(Feltham 1998a: 89)

PART TWO: SOME THERAPISTS SPEAK ON THEIR MISTAKES, FAILURES AND IMPERFECTIONS

The final section of this chapter comprises data about mistakes, failures and impairments provided by counsellors and psychotherapists who responded to a postal survey. The mailing list for the survey comprised 200 therapists trained to at least diploma level and having a minimum of three years clinical experience. Approximately 25 per cent of those contacted were trained to masters level or above (including doctorate) and almost 50 per cent had an additional qualification in counselling supervision. Sixty-one responses were received. Open-ended question-naires were used to give participants the opportunity to respond as freely and fully as they wished to the research questions. Respondents were informed that their responses might be included in published material unless they specifically requested that they should not be. They were asked to ensure that identifying features of individuals were ex-punged in order to safeguard confidentiality and preserve the anonymity of clients.

Evaluation of the data comprised a thematic and impressionistic analysis in accordance with a phenomenological research methodology (Polkinghorne 1991). Participants reported experiences of 137 identified examples of unorthodox practice in relation to the use of self within the three primary categories to which they were invited to respond. The primary categories were 'rule breaking', 'working at the boundaries of counselling' and 'therapist failure'. The precise wording of question-naires is given on pages 127, 156 and 183. A thematic analysis of data within the three primary categories revealed sixteen sub-categories, as presented in Table 5.1.

Presented here is a selection of critical incidents and issues relating to unorthodox practice and the use of self reported by informants. The inclusion of this material is intended to provide evidence of the kinds of

Table 5.1 Categories of 137 experiences of unorthodox practice and the use of self

Category	n	%
Contact with clients outside counselling sessions (accidental or intentional)	29	21
Dual relationships with clients	27	20
Therapist mention of addressing own needs/agenda in work with clients	13	9
Using self-disclosure/immediacy with clients	10	7
Breaching professional or institutional directives in the interests of clients	7	5
Touching or holding clients	7	5
Being over-challenging or too confrontational with clients	7	5
Over-involvement with clients	6	4
Extending normal session time	6	4
Taking on clients unsuitable for counselling	5	4
Giving advice, direction or information	5	4
Taking action on behalf of clients	5	4
Using a counselling approach 'impurely' (e.g. person-centred with cognitive-behavioural)	5	4
Using spouse or partner to debrief client work	2	1
Effect on client work of therapist depletion (e.g. due to stress or illness)	2	1
Not charging fee	2	1

challenges and opportunities with which therapists are grappling in their day-to-day work in the hope that this will promote further discussion about such issues amongst practitioners and trainees. Data included in this section were provided by therapists in the postal survey who responded to the following question:

'What was your most significant learning *about yourself as a therapist* from a mistake, omission, failure or error in your practice? Please describe the experience and something you learned about yourself which you feel has had an impact on the way you work now as a counsellor or psychotherapist.'

Therapist 'failure' was defined for respondents as meaning: 'where you are aware of some feeling of responsibility for things having gone wrong, or you have made what you consider to be mistakes, omissions or errors'.

Seven experiences of touching or holding clients were mentioned in responses and several of these were regarded as instances of therapeutic failure. The following example provides evidence of how the difficulties surrounding the issue of touching clients can spark important and lasting learning for the counsellor:

My first piece of longish-term work was with a female client who had a history of 'looking after' males – father, siblings, friends, lovers – to the detriment of her own well-being. She also bore a remarkable resemblance to a girlfriend of mine from many years before. In our work I was very aware of wanting neither to relate to her as other males seemed to, nor to confuse our work with my history. At the time the solution seemed, to me, to lie in adopting a cautious and formal approach. In effect this meant that, at some level, I left the difficult emotional aspects of our relationship to her – just the usual male way of being in her life and exactly what I had wanted *not* to do!

But I was able to be my real, more open self to a sufficient extent to achieve therapeutic change with this client and be a different enough sort of experience for her. In our final session she asked for a hug after our forty hours together. I readily assented but her parting comment – 'I've felt all year this wasn't allowed' – left me plenty to think about and learn from.

Now I feel she taught me some invaluable lessons. (1) Not to try to solve difficulties in advance but simply to hold them in awareness as potentially problematic/informative aspects of a relationship. (2) I probably *will* get drawn into a re-enactment of the client's drama and the trick is to catch this and work with it so the client gains a different and therapeutic experience of the 'same old stuff' which informs instead of damaging. (3) Be explicitly clear about touch. I'm sure we could have had more physical contact quite safely, from which she might have learned that different ways of being with men were possible. I'm also sure we could have had only the very limited last hug we had but, if I'd been clear about that at the outset she would have understood it as being to do with 'counselling stuff' rather than because she was untouchable.

Finally, I think I also learned not to be too hard on myself about 'therapist failure' – *my* mistakes. Both the content and manner of her communication to me twelve months later made it clear that – whatever I didn't do quite as I would now wish – I did do plenty of things right.

This counsellor's philosophical endnote seems to underscore a message delivered by Kottler and Blau (1989) about the importance of keeping a balanced perspective on our mistakes and errors:

> Failure is a reminder of our fallibility; it thus fosters a sense of modesty and counteracts the tendency toward narcissism that is so prevalent in our profession. The therapist who occasionally fails, who accepts these lapses as indicative of an imperfect being who is trying very hard to grow, will maintain feelings of competence and yet become a model of self-acceptance.
>
> (Kottler and Blau 1989: 72–3)

The powerful personal and professional learning that may arise from mistakes is evident in a number of replies. An example is provided by a counsellor who writes about a misjudged decision to reply supportively to letters, and then tapes, sent to her by a (disabled) ex-client.

> The tapes would be long, unfocused and included chat and distressed clips and I realised soon that trying to continue a counselling relationship by tape was ineffective and frustrating. I had offered this service as a person to person response to her needs and from an ill-advised Rescuer position. It had not been negotiated, formulated, contained and I had not properly finished my contact initially.
>
> My supervisor gave me excellent help and support to recognise my mistakes and to end this relationship appropriately but painfully. I learned a lot about my 'rescuer' motivations through this experience. I started to examine closely my motivations to be a counsellor and started to question and probe into the ethics of helping others. I learned about my limitations and my responses to illness and disability – a need to make better. I learned about my feelings towards my mother who gave consistently to strangers without question and my guilt for not wanting to accompany her always. I learned the significance of clear endings no matter how painful/difficult so that a client can move on and commit to a new relationship/way of managing. Fundamentally it has helped me be clearer about my boundaries and thus safer for my clients.

Other counsellors in the survey reported that attempts to adopt an unusual or different way of working led to mistakes, errors and failure. The common theme in these experiences seems to be that the different way of working was adopted in response to the counsellor's needs or agenda rather than as a sensitive appraisal of what would be in the best interests of the client. This example is illustrative:

> [W]ith hindsight my experimentation with a new approach to counselling resulted in the client's real needs being overlooked. I had been working with a psychiatrist who introduced me to the 'Solution Focused Brief Therapy' (SFBT) method of counselling. ... The approach is condemned by some as superficial and cosmetic and [viewed] by others as a powerful way of motivating clients to search for, and use, their strengths instead of pathologising problems or digging too deep into past material.
>
> Enthused by the positive nature of working with clients in this manner I employed it with a new client who had been suffering a depressive episode and who had survived a very abusive marriage. Initially the client made great progress and the focus on strengths really paid dividends in a big way. Then, when meeting for our sixth session, the client reported a return of the thoughts and feelings experienced when we first started our work together and seemingly cosmetic gains were lost.
>
> I did feel a sense of failure in this particular case that I attribute to applying an approach more in line with my own needs than the client's. In some respects I made the client fit the model. The opportunity to experiment and try something new blinded me to the client's actual needs. The client's problems were in fact deeply rooted and long-standing, demanding a different counselling approach. The responsibility to access a way of working in line with the client's needs rested with me and in a way I abused the unequal power relationship. It could be said that I subjected the client to subtle manipulation and wasted time in offering the help she really needed.
>
> I learned from the encounter that counsellors do have responsibility towards the client, who may be vulnerable and ready to comply with whatever therapy is offered almost without question, to put their interests foremost and not to use them as subjects of naive experimentation. It also highlighted the immense power counsellors can wield and the impotence of many clients to exercise autonomy in such relationships. Finally it also exposed my lack of competence and patience in assessing the client's needs and the dangers of experimenting with a therapeutic approach (SFBT) without adequate training or expert supervision.

Rennie's (1994a) study into clients' resistance in therapy revealed the importance of counsellors being alert and sensitive to the client's

thoughts and feelings about a selected treatment approach. This counsellor's experience would appear to reinforce that message. Unless
the counsellor encourages the expression of such thoughts 'the power
differential in the counselling relationship makes it difficult for clients
to challenge the counsellor' (Rennie 1994a: 55) and the therapeutic
alliance may be seriously undermined, as in the case reported here. One
other counsellor records a rather different experience of being misled to
try an unfamiliar way of working in a mistaken belief that he was
thereby addressing the client's needs rather than his own:

> A client in an initial session responded to my brief resumé of my
> working approach with a request for something different in philo-
> sophy and structure. I had enough knowledge of and experience of
> this approach to agree. I now view this as a hopeless mistake! I
> think I was motivated by a misconceived idea of what it is to be
> client-led and by a subconscious wish to give away my power as a
> counsellor, a power which embarrassed me, as if it wasn't OK to
> have skills in my own way.
>
> Though I was able to work as requested the client was dissatis-
> fied and eventually ended our contract after politely making clear
> her view that I was not up to it. I guess now that she was testing
> boundaries at some level with her initial request – just as much as
> if she'd wanted to stay for 90 minutes instead of 50, or wanted to
> go for a drink together after our session. These are things I wouldn't
> accede to either then or now and I had failed to see that this request
> too demanded firmness and clarity and the safe containment that
> these can provide.
>
> I think what I learned from this incident is that all requests to
> vary the therapeutic frame require exploration rather than immedi-
> ate acting upon. I also learned greater respect for and confidence in
> my preferred approach through this attempt to pretend to be some-
> thing else. I have grown altogether more confident about saying
> 'no' during an initial session; I've always been clear that the client
> may assess me during this time and indeed I encourage this. I am
> now much clearer it is alright, indeed necessary, that I allow myself
> the same decision-making power.

I will conclude these accounts of therapists' errors and omissions
with the words of one respondent that reveal the freedom that can be
found in failure. These words come from a therapist who characteristic-
ally worked with great caution and who experienced a very traumatic

'falling from grace' in suddenly finding themselves embroiled in an unforeseen and inappropriate dual relationship, from which they then had to extricate themselves with some considerable difficulty:

> I 'know' that this was a once in a lifetime lesson and that I was forcing myself to face personal issues about guilt which rested in my unconscious but held me back at times in my therapeutic work – I was afraid I would get it wrong. Thus by getting it wrong big time I liberated myself to act more fearlessly in my therapeutic work.

What is striking about the powerful learning recorded in these responses is that it is situated within unique encounters with clients. This is learning that could not take place in the lecture hall, the skills training room, in discussion with a supervisor or through reading the research and teaching of others. It is learning about using the self that comes about when counsellors are able to experience themselves as fallible in the presence of their clients. And for many of these therapists it is clearly very precious learning that is to be welcomed and befriended. In an important way our errors and failures may thus become our allies and even our mentors if we allow ourselves to recognise them as such instead of turning them away as strangers to be shunned and avoided in a vain attempt to preserve a sense of omnipotence. For as Kottler and Blau (1989: 55) have accurately observed, no matter how hard we try, we cannot avoid failure 'for in our self-deception we are certain, eventually, to fail. Suppressing all the evidence does not make it disappear. It simply makes it more powerful and makes us more dedicated to its extinction'.

Chapter 6

Breaking the rules in counselling

> Psychotherapists do seem to be able to help people; perhaps because they often manage to outgrow the handicaps imposed by their training. Wherever two or three psychotherapists are gathered together, confessions gradually emerge about their deviations from orthodoxy.
>
> (Mair 1992)

I notice that these days in reading the literature on counselling and psychotherapy, I am more and more drawn to the 'rule-breakers' and those who confess to engaging in unorthodox and intuitive work which takes them beyond, and often away from, the confines of their original training (e.g. Thorne 1987, 1997; Davis 1997; Mearns 1992). I have come to believe that rules can limit therapeutic effectiveness even as they also importantly define the boundaries of safe practice. Paradoxically, I have sometimes experienced the breaking of rules as seeming to provide an increase in safety and containment for clients. I hope the material included in this chapter will illustrate how this may happen.

I intend to consider some aspects of rule breaking which may be of benefit to the client. I am using the term rule breaking in a colloquial and context specific, rather than strictly moral, sense. By rule breaking I mean where the therapist breaches the guidelines or dictates of accepted practice as established by their education and training, chosen therapeutic approach, or professional association, in favour of responses determined by more internally located standards of self-regulation. I am using the term subjectively in the knowledge that rules and conventions will vary among individual therapists and between schools of therapy depending on the social and historical cultures in which they operate.

Rule breaking often manifests as boundary transgression. In their review of the theory and research relating to patient–therapist boundary issues, Smith and Fitzpatrick (1995: 500) declare that 'boundaries are regularly transgressed by even the most competent of therapists, and such transgressions are not always to the detriment of the client'. These authors make an important distinction between boundary crossing and boundary violation and consider that while boundary crossing 'is a non pejorative term that describes departures from commonly accepted clinical practice that may or may not benefit the client', a boundary violation, in contrast, 'is a departure from accepted practice that places the client or the therapeutic process at serious risk' (ibid.). The (often difficult) task for the therapist is to accurately distinguish between the two in the daily exigencies of clinical practice. As Smith and Fitzpatrick rightly observe, 'given the individual differences among clients, fine adjustments are required in every case' (p. 505). In starting to consider ways in which this sensitive task might be accomplished, I will turn first to the subject of the therapeutic use of touch.

TO TOUCH OR NOT TO TOUCH

A great deal of attention in the counselling and psychotherapy literature has recently been directed to the issue of sexual contact between therapists and their clients. As the literature has been extensively reviewed elsewhere (see, for instance, Garrett 1994; Szymanska and Palmer 1997) I will confine my observations here to the less frequently discussed topic of non-erotic touch in therapy. First I wish to state that I do not condone the use of erotic touch or sexual contact with clients under any circumstances and I agree with those authors (e.g. Butler and Zelin 1977; Gabbard and Pope 1988; Hartmann 1997; Herlihy and Corey 1992; Hermansson 1997; Herron and Rouslin 1984; Holroyd and Brodsky 1980; Hunter and Struve 1998; Pope and Bouhoutsos 1986; Russell 1993, 1996; Rutter 1989) who view this as a serious abuse of power which parallels incest dynamics.

In the climate of minimal risk taking that seems currently to govern therapeutic procedures I have a real concern that perfectly appropriate and respectable responses to clients are regarded as suspect. This is apparent to the extent that often only guarded and circumspect interventions appear to be sanctioned by the profession and its stakeholders. There are signs that one of the first casualties to fall in this atmosphere characterised by watchful, self-conscious and low risk procedures may be that of touch (Hilton, V. 1997a). There is a real danger that over-cautious counsellors will jettison this essentially human response from their range of therapeutic strategies from fear of being accused of abusing or exploiting clients, or from having fallen prey to the widespread view that physical contact is frequently the precursor to sexual exploitation. Lamentably, as Hunter and Struve (1998) have noted, 'within the prevailing climate, most clinicians have resolved the cultural and professional tensions surrounding the issue of touch by adopting a one-word guideline: *Don't*' (p. 67, original emphasis).

Many counsellors have chosen not to touch clients, others do so rarely. This is fine if the decision stems from theoretical persuasion, personal style or preference, or soundly reasoned judgement. My concern, and one that is shared by others (e.g. Corey *et al.* 1993), is that counsellors and trainees may increasingly reject outright the possibility of touching clients for reasons approximating damage limitation rather than from a thoughtful consideration of therapeutic options in response to legitimate client need. Garrett (1994) has surveyed the research evidence on sexual contact and touch in psychotherapy and observed that in the current climate, in which motives are constantly under scrutiny, some therapists are becoming suspicious even of having warm feelings towards their clients and anxious about acknowledging these.

If we *are* to consider touching our clients, we need to carefully work out our own internal guidelines and rigorously question our own motives. To touch clients because I'm a 'touchy feely' person is not a good enough reason – I am likely to end up imposing my own preferences or gratifying my own needs at the expense of theirs. I do not often touch clients myself and whenever I do I endeavour to do so with discretion, caution and sensitivity *and always, and most importantly, with the client's permission*. The word endeavour is important in the previous sentence. At best we can only believe that permission is given when it appears to be so. In actuality, a degree of interpretation by the counsellor is normally involved in judging that permission to touch has been freely given by the client. Permissions are given or refused in a number of ways that are not only determined by verbal responses. The counsellor needs to be extremely sensitive to nuances of the client's non-verbal responses in relation to this issue and when in doubt, check them out carefully.

As a counsellor I am, indisputably, in a position of power and influence in relation to my clients and, because of this, I need to be keenly alert to compliant responses that are more to do with appeasing me or deferring to my judgement than with choices freely made. As Hunter and Struve (1998: 79) have pointed out 'touch increases intimacy in any relationship, and with increased intimacy, there is also increased vulnerability'. If I say to my client: 'Would you like a hug?' and he says 'OK' with even the tiniest inflection of dissent I need to be guided by the inflection and back off in order to check out his real wishes. If the client says nothing when I ask if he would like a hug yet I see his body relax or notice an almost imperceptible nod of the head I may have an affirmative response. I need to know myself and my client extremely well to trust such signals. If in doubt, it is imperative that I find ways of double-checking. It is less damaging for touch to be cautiously withheld by the counsellor when it is sought by the client than for the therapist to engage in touch that is imposed on the client without negotiation. This will almost certainly be experienced by the client as an invasion of boundaries and may well serve to reinforce previous boundary violations.

I try not to offer or to respond to a client's request to be touched if I have any sense of unease or feel that I cannot give this freely. It may seem churlish to refuse what it may have taken a great effort for the client to ask for, yet the client is likely to pick up the tension in a counsellor's touch that is not freely given. Frequently the counsellor's 'gut feelings' provide a clue that an incongruent communication will take place if the touch proceeds. This is what occurred at times in my relationship with Rachel (see Chapter 4). It is damn hard, but far more congruent for the counsellor to say: 'I'm not sure a hug is the best response I can give you now, even though you have asked me for one. I would prefer us to talk about what it is that you need because the hug might just cover that up rather than help us find out more about what that actually is'. An intervention such as this should be founded on sound clinical judgement rather than a defensive position wherein the therapist routinely resists any attempt by the client to initiate touch. Power differentials between therapist and client can be importantly ameliorated through reciprocity. A therapist who never accedes to a client's request for touch should not be initiating touch themselves, as in so doing they are clearly operating from their own agenda in a way that amounts to an abuse of power. Similarly, therapists who only ever touch same or different sex clients do well to consider the legitimacy of such decisions as set against the possibility of the misuse of power.

Despite the very real pitfalls surrounding the issue of touching clients, I would still contend that touching, holding or hugging a client can help them to feel valued, safe, comforted, understood, accompanied and restored in ways beyond those which verbal responses alone can convey. Sometimes my words will be clumsy, ill-chosen, only approximate to what the client is experiencing or not heard by them, when a touch of the hand might be experienced as compassionate resonance. Here is an example.

I am sitting with my client and it is our first session after a long, enforced break in which she has felt at her lowest. I struggle to make a verbal response – to find words to echo her despair and suicidal bleakness. She does her best to explain how she feels – she wants me to know. I do my best to reply to show that I have heard. What I say sounds trite and clumsy and I sit across from her as if divided by a deep pit into which my ineffectual words tumble and are lost. We both stumble in what we are trying to say. I say: 'I'm not making very good sense'. She says: 'Me neither'. A tense and miserable silence engulfs us both. We are near the end of the session and I yearn to make contact with her. I wonder if she feels the same and this prompts me to say: 'I'm wondering if you need or would like a hug'. She thinks about it and replies: 'I *do* need one . . . [she thinks some more] . . . I'd also like one'. I move a chair and sit beside her. I put my arms around her and she puts her arms round me and her head on my chest.

We sit very still and quiet for some minutes and I feel connected with her at last. From out of the hug she says: 'I'm trying to feel safe. I needed this. It helps me to feel that I might be worth valuing'. She comes out of the hug and looks at me and makes a small motion towards my hand. I offer it and she takes it. As I sit and hold her hand I feel very warm towards her and she seems to melt and soften and her tension dissipates. We talk about how hard it often is for her to try to explain how she feels. I tell her how difficult I find it sometimes to find the words to let her know that I have heard her and am listening. We talk about the hug and the holding of hands and speak of how touch can sometimes bypass the impasses that talking leads us into. We speak now of a feeling of closeness and connection that seems to transcend the need for explanation or the search for meaning. We are simply together and connected. We fall into a very different silence and sit quietly together holding hands. At times like this when I sit with her I can hardly bear it, because I can feel the torment that she is in. And yet, paradoxically, I experience a feeling of peace and calm as if we are resting somewhere together. And I know, at last, that I have understood and experienced something of what she feels.

When I showed the draft of this section to the client who features in the vignette above in order to ask her permission to use it, this sparked a conversation about touch in which she said the following. (These words were transcribed from memory immediately after we had spoken and later checked for accuracy with the client.)

I think you've captured the important bit about it being a process. I *did* stop and think about it like that. For me touching needs to be tentative and negotiated. I know it's alright for me to discuss it with you when it doesn't feel safe to be touched. It's helped me to distinguish between safe touch and unsafe touch and that helps in the process of erasing the memories from the past [this client had been sexually abused over an extended period of her childhood]. I know it's not you who is unsafe – it's the memories that are unsafe. And sometimes it really helps to experience the safety of touch, even when it feels risky. It's like I'm challenging myself to experience the safety and for the first time ever I'm having hugs because *I* want to, not because someone else thinks they're going to touch me when they feel like it.

The experience of being touched in counselling is very important for me because I can't learn about touch in the same way anywhere else. Outside counselling it would get mixed up with other things. Counselling is the only place where I can learn what it's like to give and receive touch without it getting lost in expectations and ties that might be there in family or partner relationships. It's important for me that it happens in a relationship where I can see it has an effect on you too. It wouldn't help me if you were detached, like you were doing something *to* me. I know that you're involved and receiving something back as well.

Touch and hugs mean different things to me at different times – things like safety, being at peace, or a feeling of containment. It reminds me that I'm worth feeling compassionate towards when I can't feel compassion for myself. It makes me feel real and gives me a sense of self – even when I don't feel that at other times. It gives me hope – a point to work from and something to come back to. No matter how bad things get, it feels like there is always a safe place in our relationship that I can come back to – even when it doesn't feel safe outside. When I let you touch me I also feel a warmth that I've never had before. A place inside me warms up.

My client's words, I think, illustrate well a process that has been outlined by Robert Hilton (1997c) where he argues that touch can provide a powerfully reparative experience for clients who have experienced deficits of nurturing touch in childhood. Hilton observes that children who naturally reach out for loving contact and receive discounting, punishing or abusive responses in return, will contract and shrink back and, if the response is repeatedly given, will withdraw and armour themselves against further pain by learning to repress and deny their natural yearning for loving physical contact. The contractions serve to 'establish a state of equilibrium, which functions to reduce anxiety' (p. 168) but the cost of warding off painful feelings of deprivation and loss in this way is that the child thereby creates a 'false self' that carries many repressed feelings.

Hilton likens the experience of the client with this kind of history who is touched by their therapist to a person suffering from frostbite who is placed in the warmth.

> Touching the patient adds warmth to the frozen and contracted areas of her body. This may help to bring her back to life but it will also revive the pain connected with why she had to contract in the beginning. Thus, touching, as it changes the equilibrium in the body, brings back the rage, sorrow, love, and fear that have lain buried in its frozenness. Touching, at times, appears to be cruel because it revives a hope that cannot be fulfilled, and yet not to touch may leave a person lost in her own frozen wasteland.
>
> (Hilton 1997c: 169)

Even though, as Hilton advises, touch may revive hope that cannot be fulfilled, the revival of hope leads to the possibility of mourning that which has been lost or never given. If the client remains defended against their childhood loss the possibility of healing through grieving is also lost. Therapeutic touch that melts the client's frozenness allows the client to re-experience feelings and sensations that may have been blocked or denied for many years. As Hilton suggests, 'this expression always has a regressive quality to it since it is unfinished business from the past. With our touch we are asking the child within the patient to respond once more to the world' (p. 170).

Hunter and Struve (1998) point out that the only guidelines currently in existence in relation to touch are those which contain prohibitions and state what therapists should *not* do – most notably engage in sexual conduct with clients. These authors have attempted to redress this omission by providing a set of guidelines for the ethical use of touch in psychotherapy that take as their rationale the need to set standards that avoid harm to clients and which also encourage counsellors to consider touch as a legitimate, and on occasion even necessary, component of the therapeutic relationship. They contend that the ethical use of touch has many positive functions. Amongst those they list are: the provision of real or symbolic contact; the provision of nurturance and containment; facilitation of the experiencing and resolution of feelings; and the restoration of touch as a healthy, natural and important dimension in relationships.

Guiding principles suggested by Hunter and Struve (1998: 138–46) to assess when it may be clinically appropriate to use touch in psychotherapy are summarised below:

- **The client wants to touch or be touched** this needs to be checked out through a process of information giving and negotiation which ensures that the client gives informed consent and is clear about their right to say 'no' to being touched at any time.

- **The purpose of the touch is made clear** through simple explanations given by the therapist, preferably at the contracting stage, so that the client has this information before the possibility of any touch arises.

- **The touch is clearly intended for the client's benefit** and not for the therapist's gratification.

- **The client understands concepts of empowerment and has demonstrated an ability to use those in therapy** this occurs through a dialogue with the therapist whereby the client is helped to understand that choices about who they are touched by, when, and in what way are their fundamental right.

- **The therapist has a solid knowledge base about the clinical impact of using touch** that they have achieved through clinical training, familiarity with the relevant research and literature, competency in the therapeutic use of touch, and a sound understanding of where the concept of touch fits into their own personal philosophy of counselling.

- **The boundaries governing the use of touch are clearly understood by both client and therapist** this is achieved through the therapist's clear communication that no touch will occur between the waist line and knees of any client nor anywhere on the chest of female clients in addition to whatever further prohibitions or limits the client may define.

- **Enough time remains in the therapy session to process the touch interaction** in a way that enables the client to make sense of, and resurface, from any unexpected or powerful feelings that the touch may have triggered.

- **The therapist–client relationship has sufficiently developed** to accommodate the level of intimacy provoked by touch and to ensure that this does not extend beyond that which the client can tolerate.
- **Touch can be offered to all types of clients** regardless of age, gender, cultural heritage, physical attributes and sexual orientation and is not restricted by demographic variables based on therapist selection. Where therapist and client are of different race or culture it is important for the therapist to be aware that different norms and assumptions about touch will be in operation and to check these out explicitly with the client before acting.
- **Consultation is available and used** and this happens regularly with a supervisor with whom the therapist can be scrupulously honest about their touch intentions, behaviours, anxieties and reactions.
- **The therapist is comfortable with touch** both in general and in specific situations with clients. Therapists as well as clients have the right to refuse touch and when this happens the counsellor then has a responsibility to discuss their decision with the client and any feelings it may have raised for the client.

As well as carefully and fully elaborating on the safe and ethical use of touch, Hunter and Struve (1998: 147–51) also take pains to outline when touch in counselling and psychotherapy is not clinically advisable. Counter-indications for the use of touch are given as: (i) where the focus of therapy has involved sexual material prior to touch; (ii) where a client is inclined towards violent behaviour or has a poor history of impulse control; (iii) where the touch occurs as a 'secret' between therapist and client; (iv) where the therapist doubts the client's ability to say no or to give informed consent; (v) where the therapist feels manipulated or coerced into touching the client; (vi) where the use of touch is clinically inappropriate, for example with a client experiencing a psychotic episode; (vii) where touch is used to replace rather than complement verbal therapy, so that, for example, processing of the touch experience does not take place; (viii) where the client does not want to touch or be touched – which may be known from the outset of therapy but may also happen subsequent to initial permission for touch having been granted; (ix) the therapist is not comfortable using touch.

I would defend the sensitive and carefully negotiated use of touch even with clients who have been sexually abused. As my client's comments above perhaps indicate, to experience non-intrusive, non-sexual touch from a counsellor can be healing and reassuring for a client who has come to equate touch with unwanted sexual arousal and the violation of boundaries. Exploring her or his responses to the therapist's non-threatening touch can help the client who has been abused begin to reclaim and re-establish personal boundaries that the abuse has robbed them of. As Hunter and Struve (1998) suggest, non-erotic touch may enhance ego strength in the client who has been abused by assisting her or him 'in the process of individuating from the neglectful or abusive world with which he has remained fused' (p. 131). Indeed they go further than this and propose that clients who have been sexually or physically abused may be restricted in their healing process where touch is not a therapeutic option.

Those who object to the use of touch in therapy frequently do so on the grounds that it provides specious reassurance that undermines, rather than enhances, the development of insight and change. The following observation is typical of this view: 'Rather than facilitating someone's inner exploration, it [i.e. the therapist's touch] is likely to put the person back in touch with the outer world, encouraging conscious ideas and daydreams about the counsellor's process as well as providing pathological gratification instead of deeper levels of emotional insight' (Delroy 1996: 98). Whilst there may be a danger of these things happening where touch is driven by the counsellor's need for gratification, or given through inexperience or ignorance of its likely impact on the client, well-timed and sensitively proffered touch that is given as an authentic and human response to the client's predicament, and as part of an intentional therapeutic procedure, can have the effect of encouraging movement, growth and healing.

A client who had been sexually abused in extreme ways over an extended period of her life spoke to me of her fears that physical touch that fell into the accepted range of 'normal' and non-sexual contact would 'not be enough to satisfy' her. Here is the conversation we had about this, with some commentary given in brackets.

CLIENT: I'm scared that holding hands or having someone's arm around me wouldn't be enough.

VAL: [There had been occasions in our counselling sessions when, with her permission, I had done both of these things.] How does it feel when I do that?

CLIENT: [Quizzically, and after a thoughtful pause] It feels OK.

VAL: [I remind her of a recent occasion where I sat beside her and held her hand at the end of a session that had comprised a particularly traumatic re-living of the abuse.] What was it like when we sat together and you reached over and took my hand?

CLIENT: It felt good – like we were acknowledging we'd come through something difficult together.

VAL: And was it enough for you?

CLIENT: Yes, it felt really good.

VAL: That's how it felt for me too – calm, peaceful and loving. And not at all sexual.

CLIENT: I'm confused. Suddenly all the guilt and bad feeling went when you said that. It just suddenly disappeared and I don't feel bad or abnormal any more.

As you may imagine that wasn't the last of my client's bad feelings about herself, but the dissonance she experienced in this session between the sexually aberrated person she had come to believe she was and her emergent self marked a critical incident in her therapeutic journey. The vignette suggests the transforming and healing potential of touch, when it is used with sensitivity and discretion in a way that the client, with the therapist's help, can make sense of and link to their own healing process. As a further aspect of rule breaking, I will consider next the topic of dual relationships in counselling.

DUAL RELATIONSHIPS

By dual relationships in therapy I refer to any prior, concurrent or sequential relationship that a counsellor has with a client, in addition to that of therapist and client. Dual relationships can be malign, benign or neutral and can occur unexpectedly or evolve in very subtle and gradual ways (Herlihy and Corey 1992). Attitudes towards dual relationships are likely to be strongly influenced by the counsellor's training and allegiance to a particular school of therapy. A psychodynamic counsellor would likely view with suspicion the possibility of meeting with a client outside the agreed parameters of the therapeutic frame (time, place, duration and frequency). A behavioural counsellor might, conversely, regard it as acceptable and even desirable practice to engage in a concurrent relationship with the client that is akin to teaching or mentoring by accompanying them on *in vivo* homework assignments like, for example, visiting the insect house of a zoo with them as a part of a programme of systematic desensitisation.

This example raises the issue of what is, and isn't, a dual relationship. The behavioural therapist would probably view between-session contact as an extension of their role, rather than as an alteration of that role, as might a bereavement counsellor who agrees to accompany their client on a visit to a grave to assist them in their process of mourning. A psychodynamic counsellor, on the other hand, would be more likely to construe any extra-session contact as unhelpful and a significant disruption of the therapeutic frame that could well serve to dissipate the transference relationship.

The most obvious danger inherent in dual relationships is that of the abuse of power whereby the client may be exploited or used by the counsellor to meet his or her own emotional, financial, sexual or other relational needs. A particular hazard arises where the therapist engages in sequential relationships with clients where, for instance, he or she develops a friendship with the client or becomes their supervisor or trainer. Such a shift in relationship will undoubtedly result in a modification of, and may well damage, the client's internalised image of the therapist. It is important for this image to be preserved during therapy for it is this that may hold and carry the client's hopes, demands and aspirations and thereby sustain them and the work in, and between, sessions. Clients who develop other relationships with their counsellors may feel disillusioned by seeing the counsellor as a person who is different to the one they have constructed for themselves in order to be able to engage with their own psychic material. At worst, much of the therapeutic work may be undone by the precipitate bursting of this particular bubble.

Even in the face of these very real hazards, some commentators suggest that we should refrain from indictments against dual relationships that are derived from generalised proscriptions rather than a careful consideration of individual cases. Life for beleaguered therapists may seem simpler when blanket bans are imposed as a response to ethical dilemmas, yet prohibitions have an uneasy habit of turning into taboos. And if the possibility of engaging in dual relationships with clients becomes a taboo we will move closer to a climate of 'incessant naive moralising' and 'hysterical paranoia' which is said to surround the subject in America (Hedges 1997: 221). In Hedges' view, this is a climate which has 'undermined the spontaneous, creative, and unique aspects of the personal relationship that is essential to the psychotherapeutic process' (ibid.).

It is worthy of note that a survey of ethical dilemmas encountered by members of the American Psychological Association carried out by Pope and Vetter (1992), uncovered the fact that a number of therapists appear to disagree with the prevailing view in that they find dual relationships useful 'to provide role modelling, nurturing, and a giving quality to therapy' (p. 400). The notion that dual roles may actually benefit clients has been expanded by Hedges (1997) through the presention of a number of factors in praise of dual relationships in therapy. Those which I find most persuasive are paraphrased below.

- Dual relating is frequently inevitable and offers many constructive possibilities.
- Dual relationships are only one way that exploitive therapists can take advantage of clients and to single out dual relationships for opprobrium may mean that other, often more subtly damaging, unethical practices go undetected.
- Metaphors are mixed when duality is equated, as it usually is, with toxicity.
- Too great an emphasis on professional roles and boundaries may serve 'to diminish personal connectedness, thereby fostering human alienation and endorsing a privileged role hierarchy' (p. 223).
- Power differentials in any relationship can empower as well as exploit and extensions of the therapist's role can be beneficial to clients as well as causing harm.
- Dual relationships can serve to democratise and humanise therapeutic relationships and divest them of unnecessary trappings of paternalism, hierarchy and mystery.
- Dual relationships are not in themselves a problem – unethical and incompetent practitioners are.
- Appropriate classification and mature discussion of dual relationships are needed in the profession, rather than naïve injunctions and blanket bans.
- Categorical prohibitions on dual relationships reinforce the idea that therapy can, and should, be separated from the person of the therapist.
- Some overlap of relationships is inevitable in therapy (e.g. where therapist and client experience chance encounters between sessions) and clinicians need to learn how to milk the therapeutic potential of such encounters, rather than operate as if they don't, or shouldn't, occur.
- Relationships evolve, move around and change unpredictably over time and such organic processes will naturally find a place in dual relationships that occur in therapy.
- Duality may enhance mutuality and provide opportunities for increased congruence, honesty, integrity and equal collaboration within the therapeutic relationship.

- Dual relationships provide opportunities for ordinary human relatedness that reduce the probability of persistent transferential distortions.

To the list provided by Hedges I would add one other, which is that dual relating may provide an appropriate response to multicultural imperatives in therapy. World views of different social and ethnic cultures will carry different notions of what constitute appropriate boundaries and roles within relationships and these differences need to be considered and affirmed by culturally accountable therapists.

Gutheil and Gabbard (1993) are amongst those who have sought to find a way through the labyrinth of dual relationships by considering boundary dimensions in relation to risk management. They contend that 'the specific impact of a particular boundary crossing can only be assessed by careful attention to clinical context' and note that 'a clear boundary violation from one ideological perspective may be standard professional practice from another' (Gutheil and Gabbard 1993: 191). Their view is echoed by Smith and Fitzpatrick (1995: 505) who observe that 'clinicians should avoid setting simplistic standards that may create barriers to therapeutic progress'. Gottlieb (1993) asserts that holier than thou proscriptions against dual relationships in psychotherapy are unhelpful and unrealistic: 'The rule that mental health professionals avoid dual relationships is aspirational in nature. It is a goal we strive to reach, but one which is impossible to avoid completely on a daily basis' (p. 41). Corey (1996) strikes a similarly realistic note in pointing out that 'interpersonal boundaries are not static but undergo redefinition over time' and therefore 'the challenge for practitioners is to learn how to manage boundary fluctuations and to deal effectively with overlapping roles' (p. 76).

Gutheil and Gabbard (1993) suggest a number of self-regulatory devices that a therapist might employ to check out whether they are in danger of indulging in a dual relationship or boundary transgression that is likely to run counter to the welfare of the client. First, they suggest that an important difference between a benign and a malignant boundary crossing may be whether or not it is considered by the therapist to be discussible and if it *is* then discussed – their contention being that 'clinical exploration of a violation often defuses its potential for harm' (p. 190). Second, they propose that a question therapists can ask themselves, as a useful orienting device when faced with a boundary issue, is: 'Is this what a therapist does?' (ibid.). Third, they review the research that indicates that role boundary violations by therapists are usually the result of a gradual process of deterioration rather than a sudden falling from grace, and they advise therapists who begin to indulge in even the mildest of deviations from normal practice, such as a slight increase in tendency to self-disclose, to rigorously scrutinise their own motives for so doing. Finally, they suggest that any deviation from usual roles, practices and boundaries should be carefully documented by the therapist and the reasons for this fully set down.

Decision-making models for avoiding exploitive dual relationships that are based on pragmatism rather than rigid injunctions have been put forward by a number of authors (Corey 1996; Gottlieb 1993; Herlihy and Corey 1992; Kitchener 1988). Gottlieb's process model employs the three dimensions of power, duration and termination as decision-making factors. Thus a long term therapeutic relationship that has had a clear power differential (where, for instance, it has accommodated a significant transference relationship), or which has ended without a proscription on further therapeutic contact in the future, would preclude any subsequent other relationship. A therapeutic relationship that has been short term, of minimal interpersonal influence and clearly terminated with no expectation on either side of further counselling in the future may, on the other hand, allow for a subsequent other relationship.

Herlihy and Corey (1992) suggest that any decision-making model should start with consideration of the question of whether the dual relationship is avoidable or unavoidable. Where it is avoidable, a risk–benefit assessment should be carried out to help the therapist determine whether to proceed with the dual relationship or to decline to enter it (in which case an explanation should be given to the other person and referral arranged if appropriate). Where the dual relationship proceeds because it is deemed to be unavoidable or has been assessed as having benefits which outweigh its risks, they recommend that the following steps be taken, each of which has built-in safeguards: (i) the informed consent of the client is secured; (ii) the counsellor seeks consultation with professional colleagues – including those who may hold different views; (iii) the counsellor embarks on a rigorous process of self-monitoring which includes detailed documentation in case notes of the rationale for, and evaluation of, the dual relationship, and (iv) the counsellor obtains regular and rigorous supervision of the work.

An example from my own practice may serve to illustrate the discussion at this point. One (certainly avoidable) dual relationship that I have consented to on a number of occasions with clients or ex-clients is that of acting as the client's referee. If a past or current client asks me to provide a reference for them because, say, they are applying for a job or a course of training, I would normally agree to do this on the following conditions: first, that I will acknowledge in the reference that I am, or have been, the person's counsellor (whilst not divulging any of the content of the therapy); and second, I will always give a copy of the reference to the client or ex-client so that they know exactly what I have said. To decline a client's request for a reference (unless there are compelling reasons to do so – such as excessive fragility of a person's mental or physical health) could, I believe, undermine the therapeutic work. It is possible that the client will construe my refusal as a message that I do not think they are capable of doing the job or course, or because I do not think highly enough of them to be able to construct a positive reference. When I agree to a client's request, I do this in the full knowledge that my having acted as the person's referee and the content of that reference may become material that then needs to be addressed in counselling sessions.

I recall one client with unreasonably low self-esteem asking me to act as her referee for a job application. I posted a copy of what I had written to her and she arrived for the next session, in her words, 'on a high'. She commented that on first reading what I had written she failed to recognise herself and thought 'can I really be this person?' What I had written had been my measured and considered opinion of her personal and professional attributes and included nothing that I did not think I had already said to her. However she appeared for the first time to be really registering my words, through seeing them written to another person. Even though she failed to secure the job, the writing of the reference served as a powerful, if in this case indirect, source of feedback that provided a tangible boost to her self-esteem.

In general, I believe that a number of the commonly accepted rules and guidelines about how to conduct therapy that are handed on by generations of counsellors and psychotherapists have their roots in unexamined assumptions and myths and should therefore be regarded with a healthy degree of scepticism. This particularly applies where the client's therapeutic needs appear to require a more original and creative response than conventional therapeutic lore might offer. In the next section I give a personal selection of these myths and assumptions and my reasons for considering that the wise counsellor will, on occasion, allow themselves to consider breaching, as well as observing, the rules and guidelines that have grown out of them.

MYTHS AND ASSUMPTIONS ABOUT RULE BREAKING

The maintenance of confidentiality between client and counsellor is paramount

Whilst the maintenance of confidentiality between client and counsellor is normally viewed as sacrosanct, on rare occasions clients may benefit from others knowing their story. For the client who has against their will been subject to an abusive secret relationship, for instance, the repetition of an exclusive and 'secret' pairing within the therapeutic dyad may replicate this in a way that can undermine progress. For such an individual, important stages in the process of counselling may be marked by their disclosing to trusted others, with the counsellor's encouragement, something of what their experience has been.

I believe there is sometimes a case for extending the parameters of confidentiality beyond the therapeutic dyad to a wider field of professionals when this may also mean that a safety net of support and understanding is thereby created for a vulnerable client. This sometimes happens in my own counselling setting (a student counselling service within a university college), particularly where a student is attempting to re-engage with their academic course after a period of absence or intercalation (taking time out). With the client's permission, it can be very helpful for the student's lecturers, programme adviser, resident tutors and the registrar to be informed of the student's situation so that they can offer help and support from an informed perspective. In such instances it is very important that who is to know what is carefully and precisely negotiated with the client in order that they remain secure in feeling that their personal issues and difficulties are being safeguarded and protected.

Boundaries such as time, place and duration of counselling are sacrosanct and should be consistently held at all times

On occasion I believe it is necessary to stretch or alter these to provide 'sufficiency' (Mearns 1992) for the client when not to do so would be experienced by the client as punitive, exploitive, neglectful or abusive. The concept of sufficiency as it relates to boundary management is dealt with fully in Chapter 7.

Clients who 'do the rounds' are manipulative or resistant to change and such behaviour should be challenged and not tolerated

It may be important for a client to 'shop around' before finding the person who they feel able to work with. We should be wary of pathologising people who may simply be exercising their right to choose a counsellor who they sense will best match their personal needs and preferences. Or it may be that someone needs to make a couple of false starts before taking the risk to really commit themselves to counselling. I have known of several occasions where someone has made a false start with more than one counsellor within the same service before going on to do some very committed and important work with the person they finally settle with. For some clients an important determinant in their healing process can be the feeling that they have had the chance to exercise some choice with regard to who they see for counselling. It is not uncommon for clients to have spent years searching for the therapist with whom they feel they can work, or in bringing themselves to the point of readiness to undertake the work. (Rachel's story in Chapter 4 provides an example of this.)

If nothing appears to be happening in the counselling things are getting cosy or collusive and the counsellor should intervene to get things moving

Some clients may need a long period spent 'testing' the counsellor before developing sufficient confidence to trust the counsellor or to really believe that she or he is going to stick by them. It is only after a long 'settling in' period that such clients are likely to start talking about what really concerns them. This is particularly true when clients have issues of shame and guilt. They will expect that the therapist would be as disgusted with them as they are with themselves if they disclosed their true feelings and behaviour. Clients like this will often need to experience a long period of stability and acceptance by their therapist before they can dare to reveal their shame.

Counsellors should avoid being inquisitive and should not ask direct questions – particularly 'why' questions

Our clients may need us to be interested enough to probe into their most difficult experiences in order for them to be able to disclose. Sometimes they are only able to 'tell' us about these by non-verbal responses to our direct questions that, perhaps, dare to name things they find unspeakable. For example, if a client has regressed to the point where they are dealing with events that occurred prior to their ability to speak articulately they may need us to ask very specific questions in an uncomplicated fashion, which they can then confirm or disconfirm by a sign or a mere 'yes' or 'no' (Hall and Lloyd 1993). As the client knows more about the meaning of their symptom or dysfunctional coping strategy than I do, I find that when I am puzzled and ask 'why do you think you do this?' the client often has an answer that makes really good sense – as the following example illustrates.

I was confused and confounded because while my client appeared to be making progress in his therapy and developing greater self esteem, his self-harming behaviour was also escalating. The better he felt about himself, the more often he went away from sessions to stub cigarettes out on his body and dig at his flesh with sharp objects. These were things that had been done to him as a child by a cruel and sadistic foster mother. We both felt wretched that he felt compelled to abuse himself in this way and we worked hard in sessions trying to understand what was going on. One day, having run out of hunches myself, I said to him 'you will know better than me the meaning of this, why do *you* think you do it?' In the session he replied 'it just feels right to do it, but I don't know why that is'.

He brought the subject up again in the next session and said: 'We were talking last week about the way I harm myself in the same way that my foster mother hurt me and you asked me why I do such horrible things to myself. I thought about your question a lot and the only thing I can think of is that perhaps if I can do it to myself too, it can't have been *that* bad'.

Counsellors shouldn't be directive or give advice

Sometimes the client needs our advice and ideas about how to look after themselves, for instance when we might find ourselves saying something like: 'You need to take especial care to look after yourself at the moment to make sure that you do not harm yourself, even "by accident", whilst you are feeling so vulnerable'. It would be downright irresponsible with the client who is feeling suicidal for the counsellor *not* to say something like: 'I would like you to tell a trusted friend or phone your doctor if you feel you can't cope and may take another overdose'.

In any case, I think we delude ourselves if we consider that we do not give advice and are never directive. I agree with Howard (1996: 85) who has asserted that 'a nondirective counsellor is a nonexistent counsellor'. All our responses are selective in that they filter out some things the client has said or intimated and focus on others. Our interventions are therefore inevitably directed towards certain aspects of what the client is presenting, whilst disregarding others. Even voice inflection, or the echoing of key words or phrases, directs our clients to certain areas of their experience more than to others.

A favourite device that gets around the prohibition on advice giving and allows us to slip suggestions in disingenuously, under the guise of a non-directive intervention, is that of wondering aloud: 'I'm just wondering what it would be like if you *did* choose to tell your mother about this'. I'm afraid I do this rather a lot and, to their credit, clients often see through it – like the person who said, as we finished and evaluated our work together: 'What I found most helpful was all the advice you gave me'.

Whilst I suspect that I do give thinly disguised advice to my clients more often than I generally like to admit, I have no reason to believe that I am alone in this. From what I know and observe of the clinical work undertaken by my colleagues, supervisees and students, a lot of counselling sessions are liberally sprinkled with veiled advice. The difference may be that students do it more transparently than experienced therapists and therefore lay themselves open to being pulled up more sharply under the observant eyes of their trainers and supervisors. It may simply be that the more experienced we become, the more adept we are at adorning our directive interventions with tentative and questioning devices that camouflage their real nature. Experience in this case may merely give us the skill of expert dissimulation.

Counsellors should not do things for clients which they can do for themselves – it disempowers them

Sometimes going just that one step further to assist the client can actually empower them to take more responsibility for themselves. I once lent a client who was in hospital a small sum of money, when she had none, to make a telephone call that resulted in an outcome that the client had been working towards for some time but had only then found the courage to act towards. On rare occasions I have ordered taxis for clients to take them safely home when the alternative would have been for them to walk home in the dark in a state of heightened fear, distress, or hyper-vigilance following a particularly emotionally charged session. To do so seems to me to be a legitimate extension of my duty to care for the client, rather than an inappropriate action on their behalf. Whenever I have done these things I have said to my client: 'I will ask you to pay me back next time we meet' so that they are clear that they will not be beholden to me for the gesture.

When I showed the draft of this section to a client to ask her permission to use these case examples she commented on the occasions when I had ordered taxis to take her home on dark winter evenings even though she lived within walking distance of where she saw me for counselling. She said: 'Going home in a taxi after those sessions felt like it kept the work safe and contained and somehow ended what we had been doing. Going home safely meant that I could leave my distress and not take it away with me to cry for days. You also helped me to learn about taking care of myself by making sure I got home safely. I started to learn to do this better for myself and not take as many risks and I stopped wandering around so much on my own at night in unsafe places'.

Clients who are manipulative and controlling need to be challenged and confronted with regard to changing their behaviour

The label 'manipulative' is often applied to clients who are deeply distressed and do not know how to ask, or dare not ask directly, for what they need from fear that it will be withheld or that they will be punished for asking. These are individuals who have not had their dependency needs adequately met in childhood. To label a client 'manipulative' is frequently a cop-out by the counsellor who is either not sufficiently skilled to hear what is screaming out for attention or who is unable to offer the sufficiency of care and commitment the client would need in order to have the courage to move towards a more direct expression of their needs.

Some of the underlying messages I have heard from 'manipulative' clients are:

- 'Will you still be there for me if I try to push you away?'
- 'Can I *really* trust you to stay around when I am not being good?'
- 'Do you care about me enough to know what I need even when I'm afraid to ask for it, from fear that you won't give it to me?'

- 'Will you change or stay the same, even when I change and am not straight with you?'
- 'Can I really put my faith in you when so many others have rejected and betrayed me?'
- 'Will you be the one I can dare to tell it to?'
- 'When I don't know how to tell you what it is like for me, will you be able to see and hear what it is like?'
- 'Will you be strong or stupid?'
- 'Are you as clever as I am?'
- 'Will you see through my ruse, and yet still care for me?'
- 'Even when it is clear that I am seeking attention will you pretend, with me, that I deserve your attention?'

We do our clients a gross disservice to take their words and actions at face value as those of scheming adults. These are the secret questions of the frightened and lonely child within who is beginning to sense a glimmer of hope and who has the wisdom to be cautious.

Counsellors should keep their own personal material out of their work with clients as it interferes with objectivity

I believe there is a danger that counsellors who are not open to allowing their own personal difficulties and losses to inform their practice may close down a vital part of themselves when they are with clients. One of the many facets of the self comprises those painful or disturbing experiences that may be unresolved and ongoing. Adopting a professional façade to block these off, as if they don't exist, can mean that part of me acts as if it is dead or numb when I am counselling, much as a dam separates the living river from the still and artificial lake. Miller and Baldwin (1987) have discussed this notion in relation to the archetype of the wounded healer: 'Denial and repression of one's brokenness and vulnerability by itself may rob a healer of psychic energy and contribute to burnout. The act of affirming common human brokenness and vulnerability can bring life-giving energy and healing to both healer and patient' (p. 149).

To illustrate – I worked with a young woman client to whom I increasingly felt very close. I was deeply and unusually affected by her story, which was one of parental neglect and abandonment. She, in turn, clearly began to feel very attached to me. It felt right for us to be very close when I was with her, yet between sessions I began to worry that I was getting too involved. I tried to be more detached and felt that in so doing I was becoming punitive, intolerant and distant when my client very evidently needed me to be close and loving. This was a horrible time in which I felt very incongruent and during which my client took an overdose that came about partly because she felt she didn't want to 'bother' me with how desperate she was feeling.

I discussed my feelings about this client with my supervisor on a number of occasions and one day when I was travelling home from one of these supervision sessions, it suddenly dawned on me that my 'motherless' client was exactly the same age as the child I had lost through miscarriage would have been had she survived. While this came as a shock – I recall sitting on the bus with tears streaming down my face for some minutes – it also came as a huge relief as I now more clearly understood the depth of my feelings for my client and why I had been defending against them by sometimes acting indifferently towards her. My reluctance to involve myself to the extent that she needed my involvement diminished. For the time that she needed a close and loving mother figure in her therapist, I was more freely able to provide this for her. Now, though, it was with the awareness that whilst she was *not* my daughter, she was a daughter I would have been proud to have. What my client seemed to need was one person by whom she could feel specially loved and admired and maybe my own personal history gave me an unusual capacity to be this person for her. She was gradually able to internalise my feelings towards her and begin to feel affection and pride in herself.

I strongly believe that we cannot work with such unconscious, complex and risky dynamics in ourselves without *very* good supervision (and personal counselling when we need it too). It would be dangerous bravado for me to delude myself that I can safely and in isolation monitor my client's welfare where I am working at the interface between her needs and mine. Having said this, I do believe that some clients can benefit from a depth of engagement that derives more from the therapist's living river of personal experience, including their flotsam and jetsam, than from a sanitised pool of pre-prepared clinical strategies and interventions.

PART TWO: SOME THERAPISTS SPEAK ON RULE BREAKING IN COUNSELLING

Data given in this final section were provided by therapists in the postal survey who responded to the following question:

'What was your most significant learning *about yourself as a therapist* from a breach of guidelines or "rules" in your practice? Please describe the experience and something you learned about yourself which you feel has had an impact on the way you work now as a counsellor or psychotherapist'.

Rule breaking was defined for respondents as: 'breaching the guidelines or "rules" of accepted practice as given or understood by your education and training, chosen therapeutic approach or professional association'.

The second largest category of instances related to unorthodox practice reported by therapists in the survey was that of dual relationships (27 instances, 20 per cent of experiences recorded, see Table 5.1). Therapists wrote about dual relationships when invited to record instances of rule breaking and also where they were asked to write about experiences of working at the boundaries of their practice (see Chapter 7). Respondents reported both positive and negative experiences of engaging in dual relationships with clients. This accords with a review of the literature on boundaries and dual relationships carried out by Gutheil and Gabbard (1993: 189) who concluded that 'crossing certain boundaries may at times be salutary, at times neutral, and at times harmful'. Sometimes counsellors mentioned that they had encountered both beneficial and damaging experiences of dual relationships. Several compared circumstances where a dual relationship might be acceptable and productive for clients, with where it would be likely to undermine the process and outcome of therapy.

For instance, one respondent who is both a university lecturer and a counsellor wrote about both positive and negative experiences of dual relationships. With 'rare exceptions' this counsellor reported that being both a tutor and a counsellor of students 'has not been problematic', but highlighted the need for effective and thorough contracting at the outset, including discussion about how to manage the dual relationship:

> In general terms I have found a need to contract *very* clearly regarding meetings and venues (privacy from other people), confidentiality (who can/should know), unexpected chance encounters (how we deal with bumping into each other). The consequence is that I believe I have become both clearer about boundaries (mine/ clients) and more flexible in my use/construction of them.

In contrast to the relatively untroubled process of managing dual relationships with students, this counsellor reported difficulties on 'the first and only' occasion where they had entered into a counselling relationship with a colleague within the same organisation. In this case the dual relationship appears to have led to a relaxation of the counsellor's normally rigorous standards of practice:

> The client had a confused presenting problem, poor sense of self, shifting focus, poor attendance/time keeping record and yet was singularly needy. The absence of clear boundaries in his life . . . disarmed me to a level of greater flexibility, loss of momentum (missed sessions) and reduced (sustained) challenge or immediacy.
>
> Proximity and lack of commitment seemed to pose me sufficient problems that I believe I was less effective than I'd like to be, less focused, and lacked the guts to actually call a halt. In the event, by default (and while I was on holiday) the client sought out another counsellor to whom they committed due to (his words) 1. paying; 2. having to travel; 3. distance (psychological) from the problem/work.

This counsellor records the learning gained from this experience: 'I am reminded of the need to pay attention to gut feeling and unease about the dual relationship – i.e. some "dual" relationships do not pose a problem, indeed some clients see them as beneficial ("You know me . . . I don't have to go over everything again . . . You know the context/ problems . . .") but if I perceive potential difficulties it may be wiser to *not* start rather than to try to unpick it later.'

One interesting perspective on dual relationships was provided by a counsellor who works with young people in a residential school where he also holds a pastoral role. He makes a distinction between counselling young people and counselling adults in considering when a dual relationship might be appropriate and when it definitely wouldn't be:

> Some clients are always in trouble with the teachers and I sometimes come across a client being told off by a member of staff. At other times, I see the client sitting in the school foyer where miscreants are sent or doing things they are not supposed to be doing in school – like having a cigarette in some corner. Not being a teacher, I do not get involved in disciplinary matters so when these clients see me on these occasions they know they will not be told off or given a bad time. In the long term, this helps me in my work as a counsellor because the clients feel that they are going to see someone safe.

Counsellors who never see their clients outside of the counselling room may develop a relationship with those clients as if in a cocoon and which may be considered a true 'counselling' relationship. In my case the relationships are almost 'normal' in that they are on-going and can have all the vicissitudes of an ordinary social relationship. I think this is beneficial with young people who need to know where they stand with adults before confiding in them. With my adult clients I have felt the opposite and have been careful to avoid places where I know I might meet them.

This counsellor's experience raises the question of whether different client populations require different responses to the management of dual relationships. In particular he implies that we cannot expect children to open up directly to a stranger, even if they are a counsellor, in the same way that an adult might. Given that proscriptions against talking to strangers (particularly those who appear to invite an unusual form of intimacy) are drummed into most children from an early age, it would not be surprising if children are sometimes suspicious or uneasy about seeing a counsellor. It may be, as this counsellor's experience suggests, that the issue of safety can sometimes override conventions about dual relationships in instances where the client might benefit from prior contact with the therapist.

Several respondents wrote about how rule breaking fitted with their own search for personal authenticity as a counsellor or psychotherapist. The following response is illustrative:

I agreed to see a woman who is a friend of my wife who was depressed and I agreed to see her without any payment. In part, I did this because I wanted to be able to respond out of my own wish to help, I think in order to experiment with the feeling of self-determination (versus the constraint of 'Big Brother' BAC and other professionals' views on these matters). I wanted perhaps to be in touch with that part of myself that does 'good' things in a generous spirit, not because money is involved. The experience reminded me that awful things don't happen just because you 'transgress' a professional guideline. Perhaps it taught me that experimenting with boundaries is not only not cavalier and dangerous (necessarily) but can be fruitful. In a small way, the experience helped me to reclaim myself, loosen up, and to see myself whether dual relationships or offering free counselling has or hasn't dire consequences.

Hermansson (1997: 134) has suggested that a narrow perspective on boundary control 'can rigidify the fluid and dynamic elements of counselling'. This therapist's decision to adopt a more relaxed approach to boundary management would appear to have been made in the spirit of keeping open a range of creative responses to clients. Hermansson also addresses the issue of the abuse of power which may be inherent in inflexible boundary management and his views are echoed by one respondent who voiced the belief that willingness to engage in unorthodox practice could lead to a levelling out of the power imbalance between client and counsellor: 'Overall, I feel that by sticking solely to orthodox practice we may deny our clients many opportunities. My unorthodox practice is essentially about being human first and a counsellor second. When I lose sight of that basic underpinning philosophy I can easily lapse into the "expert" role, which stops clients finding their own way'.

Several informants wrote about how their own personal history influences unorthodox responses to clients. Here is one respondent's experience of rule breaking:

> Suicide! I have a sense of 'wrongdoing' about some of my practice in this area. There isn't a rule that forbids my approach – at least not one I've been able to find – but I hear the sharp intakes of breath from colleagues when this issue is discussed.
>
> Around direct personal questions from clients my usual practice would be to explore what anxiety/fear/desire lay behind the question. Having explored this I *might* also answer the actual question if this seemed relevant to the therapeutic process. But I might not.
>
> The question 'Have *you* ever felt close to suicide . . . have *you* tried?' somehow seems to ask and require a more direct response. My rationale for this might be something like, it is one thing to clarify awareness around anxiety but when someone is hanging on a cliff top contemplating oblivion I would want simply to offer my hand to hold on to. And 'yes' seems a more honest response to existential crisis than 'I wonder what concerns you about my experience?'
>
> It intrigues me that almost all the suicidal clients I have worked with have asked me this question and that I continue to break this unwritten rule in responding to them very directly. I guess I have learned that I am prepared to break unwritten rules in a way I would not break written rules; that the feelings of risk involved don't outweigh the desirability of working this way; that there is

room for flexibility in my own 'rules' about direct questions and that I don't berate myself for some sort of theoretical inconsistency. Maybe the biggest learning is that there are intensely difficult areas of my past which are sufficiently resolved to be vitally useful to me and my clients.

A fascinating question raised by this counsellor's experience is: 'How come almost all of his suicidal clients ask him if he has ever felt suicidal?' Again here the notion of whether clients find their way to counsellors whose personal history in some way most matches their own is raised. The counsellor's experience also highlights the capacity that some therapists seem to have to override normal conventions, even their own, when circumstances or particular clients appear to require an unusual and more immediate response.

Another counsellor provides an example of responding flexibly to perceived client need in what is a more clearly unconventional manner. This counsellor writes about his work with a newly disabled (brain damaged and suffering memory loss), institutionalised client. The client experienced the environment of the institution as 'severely claustrophobic' and, the counsellor writes, 'desperately' wanted to leave. He continues:

> Although I suggested a program of activities to his key worker, jointly worked out with the client, little happened so I decided to follow a policy of 'outward bound' counselling – mainly as a response to his frustration, my frustration, and institutional inertia. So far we have joined the library, been for a few pints (with me not drinking) been swimming several times, had several arguments. Partly the activity focus was to create a new biography, a new past, some exciting experiences with which to re-invigorate his memory.

The counsellor reported that as a result of this work the client's memory was improving and he was starting to make more contact with the outside world. In terms of his own learning he records that he has learned 'to take more risks; to be more creative, be more fluid; to trust myself re. innovative work; that I need help sometimes and supervision can make a big difference; that there is no right way; that "being with" someone else is sometimes enough to move it on; that I have limits with respect to challenging work and it's OK to back off; that "sharing the load" isn't failing'.

This counsellor's experience immediately raises an important question about whether clients with different or special needs may sometimes require unusual and innovative responses from counsellors. Such responses may appear to contravene rules of conduct laid down in established codes of practice, yet in providing them the counsellor may well be moving closer to observing the true spirit and underlying philosophy of counselling. In this case the counsellor's errant actions are geared towards assisting the client to live his life more resourcefully and satisfactorily and these are the very aspirations cited as the overall aim of counselling in one such code (BAC 1998).

Whilst to respond to clients in innovative and progressive ways is an option open to most therapists, it is perhaps a path wisely taken only by some. While there are many counsellors who can come to feel confident and even 'at home' in adopting individual and innovative procedures with clients, there will always be others who do their best work staying within the confines of tried and tested techniques and strategies.

I will close this chapter with the words of two counsellors who voiced personal reservations about rule breaking. Their words might well echo the feelings of many therapists as they contemplate moving beyond what their initial training has taught them and into more innovative ways of working that are, perhaps, also less conventional. These words emphasise the importance of moving with caution (if moving at all) towards unorthodox practice and at a pace that fits with the personality of the therapist.

The first of these counsellors writes: 'I realise I am personally a "rule keeper" and therefore *anxious* about breaking rules and guidelines in a way which I sometimes feel to be too rigid or precious or "pussyfooting". In other words I sometime imagine clients to be more fragile than they actually are and therefore am *over* cautious'. Yet this counsellor has also come to experience that rule breaking can have a beneficial impact on therapeutic work: 'I think rules are very important in counselling and therapy – *but* sometimes the *unplanned* breaking of them can provide some very rich material for therapeutic work – *if* they are brought into the open by the therapist and/or client'.

The second counsellor took the trouble to write me a letter explaining why she had not sent a completed questionnaire back. She wrote: 'I felt there was little contribution I could make. . . . I suppose I don't take many risks which in itself could be a barrier to developing as a counsellor and in relationships in general'. This is a counsellor and supervisor I respect and whom I consider to be a skilled and sensitive practitioner. I think her words underline an important principle about the therapeutic use of self – that it is about working in ways that rest easily with what we know about ourselves, rather than moving into ways of working that would reflect how we might *like* to see ourselves if only we were different. Whenever we take the latter route we are requiring clients to bolster our need to be seen as something other than we truly are – a manoeuvre that, at the very least, is bound to provide poor modelling for those of our clients who are bent on uncovering more about *their* true selves.

Chapter 7

Working at the boundaries in counselling

> I think different therapists have different kinds of boundaries: Some can give a great deal and not really harm themselves, and others find it difficult to do that.
>
> (Rogers, in Baldwin 1987)

It has been stated, rightly in my view, that 'no therapy of a correct-ive nature can occur until clear and safe boundaries within which to hold the therapeutic relationship have been established' (Hunter and Struve 1998: 77). For the purposes of this discussion of working at the boundaries in counselling, I will take as a starting point Owen's (1997) concept of boundary as referring to 'the expectations of coun-sellors for appropriate behaviour that have been set by their professional body, their training and the professional literature, which explicitly or implicitly defines required and disallowed forms of involvement' (p. 163). In this chapter I will argue that the ethical use of self in therapy can accommodate an evolving understanding and management of boundaries. For the therapist who comes to rely on an enlightened use of self in their counselling practice, boundary management may increasingly come to mean a reliance on internalised and intuitive hold-ing structures that have less to do with observing externally set limits than with knowing oneself and what one is capable of containing and sustaining.

The breaching of boundaries is normally frowned upon in whatever one reads in the counselling and psychotherapy literature. A useful definition of boundary violation is offered by Hartmann (1997: 155) who states that 'a boundary violation occurs whenever the therapist acts on the basis of his or her own needs or desires rather than the client's needs and best interests'. Until recently the prevailing view amongst commentators appears to have been that set boundaries should be preserved at all cost in the interests of client welfare. Few writers and commentators appear to have been open to the possibility that boundary relaxations and extensions might, on occasion, prove therapeutically beneficial and provide a greater experience of safety for the client than would rigid boundary enactment.

Yet recent research on boundary issues in psychotherapy suggests that clinicians may be more open than is commonly acknowledged to flexible boundary management. In America, Johnston and Farber (1996) recently surveyed 500 randomly selected experienced therapists and from the 213 responses received concluded that, while clients infrequently challenged boundaries established by their therapists, where they did so 'psychotherapists accommodated their requests in most cases' (p. 391). They comment that this finding 'stands in opposition to the generally accepted image of the psychotherapist standing firm in the face of persistent attempts by the patient to challenge existing boundaries, and suggests a spirit of cooperation and good faith underemphasised in theoretical writings' (p. 397).

There are various forms of boundary ruptures and extensions and many of these are indeed potentially abusive, or at the very least, illinformed. I do not wish to encourage therapists to transgress boundaries in any way that would exploit, violate or prove damagingly invasive to clients. As Johnston and Farber (1996: 391) emphasise: 'effective management of boundaries is crucial, because treatment often requires partial dissolution of the separation between therapist and patient'. What I do wish to consider in this chapter is the question: 'What therapeutic opportunities might be afforded when a counsellor extends or moves beyond the boundaries normally governing their practice?'

My contention is that, on occasion, moving beyond the limits that we have come to impose on ourselves through our training and reading of the psychotherapy literature can liberate our therapeutic potential and provide a response that is more truly and lastingly helpful to the client than would be the case if we merely stayed within safe and familiar constraints. This view is supported by Feltham (1996b: 304) who has observed that 'it is easy to insist that absolutely non-negotiable boundaries always protect clients, but they may also inhibit creative manoeuvres in counselling in certain instances'. Owen (1997) goes a step further and considers that the overly rigid enactment of boundaries constitutes a misuse of power by therapists that can 'be seen as part of an authoritarian and potentially exploitative mystification which invents artificial concepts that are discriminatory, judgmental and dehumanising' (p. 168). Hermansson (1997: 135), writing on the same topic, has suggested that 'counsellor aloofness, often promoted by boundary rigidity, is in itself potentially abusive'.

I believe that therapists need to be client-responsive in their management of boundaries and acknowledge the reality that different clients will experience the tightening and loosening of boundaries in various ways and that these responses will impact differentially on the therapy. Hartmann (1997), indeed, has proposed boundary 'thickness' to be a measurable and major dimension of personality and something that needs to be taken into account in the appropriate matching of client and therapist. A client who has been subjected to inappropriately restrictive and constraining boundaries in their life may experience as reparative the relaxing of rigid boundaries by a therapist whose boundaries can be somewhat 'elastic' whilst still containing. For the client who needs a very structured and predictable environment in order to feel secure, any such stretching of boundaries is likely to be experienced as frightening and disorienting. For some clients strict restraint can be as damaging to the therapeutic alliance as over-accommodation can be for others.

In taking account of individual differences in making adjustments to boundary management, the therapist also needs to consider the cultural, social, historical and organisational frameworks which impact on their work with clients (Webb 1997). This is particularly important when counsellor and client come from different cultures and may well hold different world views. In such cases the counsellor needs to engage in culturally sensitive negotiation with clients to avoid imposing norms about boundary management that may derive from unexamined assumptions belonging to the dominant culture. In such instances resorting to guidelines given in professional codes of ethics and practice may offer only partial help in that, as Webb (1997: 179) has observed, such codes are 'culture-specific, and even principles which are commonly understood as more universal may require re-definition'.

Far from being unprofessional and unethical, flexible boundary management may demonstrate a professional and unsimplisitic attitude towards client care that conveys respect and the willingness to take account of individual client differences. Such a stance may indeed, as Johnston and Farber (1996) contend, 'withstand greater patient challenges and inadvertent lapses on the part of the therapist' (p. 399) than a more traditional and rigid attitude, and may thereby foster a more robust and enduring therapeutic mutuality.

TIME BOUNDARIES

Let us take the case of the fifty or sixty minute therapeutic hour. How did this time convention arise? Why has it come to be viewed as the appropriate time slot to be applied in an indiscriminate manner across virtually all counselling approaches? Barlow and colleagues (1984: 35) consider these questions and conclude that rather than holding some therapeutic significance, the fifty minute hour more likely prevails 'as the modal psychotherapeutic practice . . . for reasons of economics and convenience'. Herron and Rouslin (1984: 88) have echoed these sentiments and suggested that while 'it could probably be argued that the time spent with a particular patient ought to be variable from session to session, depending on patient needs . . . such variations would wreak havoc for many a therapist's schedule. So, a regular time is stipulated and expected'.

There is growing evidence that a prescriptive rationing of therapist availability can, in certain instances, be counter-therapeutic. This is most notably the case for clients who are dealing with abuse issues. Counsellors and others who work with survivors of abuse frequently stress the need for practitioners to be more fully and readily available to this client group than they might need to be with others, particularly when clients are in the throes of re-experiencing the abuse and may be suffering intrusive and distressing flashbacks (Draucker 1992; Gomez 1995; Goodwin 1994; Hall and Lloyd 1993; Olio and Cornell 1993). As Goodwin (1994) has intimated, for clients dealing with the aftermath of severe abuse, 'requests for increased therapy should be taken seriously, not dismissed as "borderline manipulation"' (p. 39).

I believe serious dangers of re-abusing clients exist where boundary obsessed therapists first encourage the restimulation of traumatic episodes through their interventions and then peremptorily bring the guillotine down on a session when the client may be left in a highly restimulated state. The client may be unable to detach as summarily from their own psychic material as the counsellor is able to detach from them when the clock decrees it, and may even be left terrified and bewildered in the grip of restimulated material. The confusion and isolation that such relived trauma naturally induces is likely to be intensified in what may be experienced by the client as sudden abandonment by a therapist who, only moments previously, had appeared to offer unconditional support and availability in helping them contact and make sense of the trauma.

It is not unknown for clients reliving the trauma of abuse to go into what resembles a full-blown psychosis, with auditory, tactile and visual hallucinations. This is a natural response to repressed trauma and needs to be allowed to run its course. In such circumstances a humane response from the counsellor who has encouraged such a client to contact their feelings and memories about the experience would be to stay with them to help them through it, even if this means extending usual time boundaries. This is not the same thing as allowing time boundaries to lapse in a loose way that is confusing and unsafe for clients. On rare occasions it may, though, mean negotiating a change of time boundary, even mid-session. When the possibility of this occurs the client needs to have a very clear message that boundaries are being held by the therapist, even when they are being extended. Survivors of abuse will have had their own personal boundaries transgressed and violated and deserve better than a therapist who is slipshod about time boundaries.

The demand that the client finishes a session when the therapist is ready, whether or not the client is in fit state to end, tends to arise most frequently with therapists who like to be in control. With such therapists 'holding the therapeutic frame' may become a euphemism for inflexibility and the playing of power games in which boundaries are imposed rather than explained and negotiated. With such a therapist the unfortunate client is left in no doubt as to who is boss.

Therapists of this ilk may use boundaries as an excuse for 'laying down the law' in a punitive fashion. Though it may be said in kindly tones and sugared words, the message given amounts to: 'You can only continue to come to see me *if* . . . you always come at this time/we stop exactly when your time is up/you don't miss any more appointments/ you always let me know in advance if you're not going to make it', etc., etc. Admonishing the client to be better behaved is a poor substitute for the willingness to listen and understand what is contributing to the client's difficulties in adhering to arrangements in the first place. It may be important (eventually) to help the client who persistently arrives late or hangs on desperately at the end to adhere to session times without demurring, but in my view this is of secondary importance to discovering what the client is trying to tell me by this behaviour. Because my client surely *is* trying to tell me something and will try to express it more and more loudly until I have the grace to unblock my ears and listen. If I don't learn to listen the client may well give up entirely and stop showing up at all – or, worse still, learn to 'behave properly' and thereby give up the hope of ever being heard.

I find little space in the protocols of accepted practice for allowing that some counsellors and clients might work more effectively in longer, or even shorter, time slots and that, on occasion, units of time might usefully be adjusted to match client need. Whilst I normally work in sixty minute sessions, I have sometimes negotiated with individual clients to work in sessions that vary from thirty minutes to five hours in length. In saying that I work in such varying time slots I am not suggesting that it is acceptable for sessions to slip into whatever form and length the counsellor deems is appropriate. On the contrary I am advocating that any deviation from the fifty/sixty minute norm is carefully negotiated with the client, as a flexible response to individual need. I have had both my shortest and my longest negotiated sessions with clients who have been sexually abused. One client could, at first, only feel safe in opening up this topic if it was agreed in advance that initially our sessions would only last for thirty minutes. For another, several sessions of up to five hours were agreed in advance to allow the client the time and safety needed for the full recall and clearing of a number of incidents of sadistic abuse in their somatic entirety.

BETWEEN SESSION CONNECTIONS

A similar myth to that which surrounds the sanctity of the therapeutic hour prevails about the management of between session contact. The dominant view suggests that this is to be avoided wherever possible in order not to disturb or rupture the therapeutic frame. Whilst I can see the importance of this in approaches that are predicated on therapist objectivity or detachment, as in the psychodynamic schools, where the development and working through of the transference may be seen as being enhanced by frustrating the client's demands for greater access to the therapist's world, I am far from convinced that it should be regarded as a universal rule to be applied without exception across all counselling modalities.

My experience tells me that sometimes clients need to feel a sense of holding or connection with their counsellor that extends beyond the counselling session. Some clients are able to 'internalise' the therapist sufficiently to feel that they remain attached between sessions. They may, for instance, be able to conjure up an image of the counsellor to give themselves a sense of warmth or security, or hold imaginary conversations with the counsellor at times of decision making or increased anxiety. Others, particularly those clients who have had early attachments in their lives disrupted, may thrive on more tangible symbols and signs of connection.

With one client we were approaching a long summer break at a time in her therapy where she felt extremely vulnerable and unsafe. At our last meeting before the break I gave her a small shell that had been on the shelf in my room for a long time and said that she might like to take it away with her. The shell was nothing in itself, yet immediately became precious by the significance invested in it by my client and her way of receiving it. She commented: 'And this has been in your room all the time I have been seeing you? That means it has heard everything'. The shell became important for her as a kind of 'transitional object' (Bowlby 1969; Winnicott 1965, 1986) which kept us attached and connected even at difficult times in our relationship and sometimes she would tell me about where it had been with her and what it had meant to her at different times. After one session in which we both felt that our relationship was troubled and disconnected she left me feeling distressed and angry and I was concerned that she would direct her anger inward and harm herself. She later told me that she had carried the shell around with her for the rest of that evening and managed not to harm herself. I believe that it helped her to reach beyond the immediate breach in our relationship and re-connect with the underlying alliance that was still unshaken and very strong.

Sometimes the between session connection may be more clearly related to the ongoing issues that the client is addressing and provide a way of carrying the therapeutic work forward. I have found this to be true particularly with clients who are able to write things down between sessions as a way of feeling that they are making a bridge to the counsellor. This can amount to a sense that they are continuing a conversation with the counsellor.

When a client intimates that they are writing between sessions, or thinking about this, it is important for the counsellor to discuss the meaning of this with the client and make a clear offer as to how what is being written might become a part of the therapeutic dialogue, if the client so wishes. The counsellor needs to be clear about what they are willing to contribute to this process – for example if letters are sent, will they be read and responded to or will they merely be held to be read (or not read) in the next session? This may vary from client to client. In general I will tell clients who are inclined to write that I will receive and read anything they might wish to write to me between sessions and that normally I will not reply but will bring the piece of writing to our next session so that we can talk about it then. This both lets the client know that their communication will be received and heard but does not give rise to hopes that I will be drawn into additional dialogue with them outside of agreed session time. In this way I am still holding a boundary that acknowledges that the client is separate from me and able to function without me, yet not cutting them off from further work that might proceed if I remain attentive in this way between sessions.

At times of crisis the counsellor may elect to have additional, between session, personal contact with a client. Again I believe that this can be helpful and appropriate if it is clearly contracted and well managed by the counsellor. Occasionally I will arrange for a client to 'check in' with me between sessions at, and for, a precise time, say fifteen minutes. These short meetings are less about doing therapy than about providing a brief, but sometimes crucial, moment of human contact that can act as an anchor point for a client who may need some additional stability and direction at times of increased turbulence. Yet I have known clients make extraordinarily good therapeutic use of a fifteen minute 'check in' session when it has been pre-planned and set up in advance. Recently a client came for a short check in session and said: 'Because we only have a short time I want to use it really well and not waste it'. She took the opportunity to be very immediate with me and talk about how she felt about our relationship and the difference it was making to other relationships in her life outside. And this happened with someone who normally struggled, in longer sessions, to find her focus and acknowledge gains she was making. The experience of the check in session subsequently provided a way for me to challenge her about using our longer scheduled sessions more productively.

Sometimes the client will initiate the between session contact and the therapist then has the difficult task of deciding whether this seems like a good idea in terms of advancing the therapy or whether it constitutes a plea for a change of relationship that could undermine the work. Of course some counsellors will take the easy option of avoiding these difficult decisions by deciding in advance that they will *never*, under *any* circumstances, engage in between session contact. This might make life comfortable for the counsellor but in so doing may deny the client the possibility of making themselves known in a different and authentic way to the therapist – a way that the structure and boundaries of the therapeutic hour may not have not provided for.

I once counselled a very suicidal, adolescent young woman who covered up her intense grief over her beloved father's premature death with seemingly impenetrable bitterness and hostility towards the world and everyone in it, myself included. By the time she came to see me this bitterness had solidified into what I can only liken to a casing of armour-like spines. Whenever I ventured too close the spines would shoot out and stab me and I had no choice but to recoil to lick my wounds in bewilderment and frustration. I never retreated quite out of sight and hovered at a safe distance until, as it seems, she must have decided that I wasn't as much of a threat to her psychic equilibrium as she might at first have feared. During one session, as I was preparing myself for the usual attack, out of the blue she said that she would like me to see her pet guinea pig and asked if I would come to her house to meet him. This was the only time she had ever come close to reaching out to me. I felt drawn to respond and agreed to her request. It was an enlightening visit. The spines disappeared as I sat on the sofa and watched her sitting on the floor cuddling and soothing her guinea pig and whispering loving words to him. I realised that she was showing me something that she couldn't easily put into words – that she was vulnerable and soft inside and could make loving contact with another living thing if it wasn't threatening or demanding. It helped enormously that I could recall this image of her with her guinea pig whenever she returned to savaging me in future sessions, which she frequently did. Eventually she found the courage to let me stay close and to matter to her even though she knew I would have to leave her after a year, when I was due to move away. Years later she again reached out to me out of the blue when I received a card from her at my new place of work inviting me to her engagement party (on this occasion I thanked her but declined) and telling me about her hopeful plans for the future.

For the counsellor who draws to any extent on the use of self in their work there can be a tension between their intuitive sense of how boundaries need to be managed with individual clients and the withholding injunctions they carry from their training. I have found Mearns' (1992) concept of 'sufficiency' helpful in managing this dilemma. In discussing the ubiquitous core conditions of client-centred therapy, namely empathy, unconditional positive regard and congruence, Mearns writes: 'I find it helpful to think in terms of the necessity of a fourth condition, namely that the therapeutic context be sufficient for the needs of the client . . . sufficiency in terms of length of sessions, frequency, the physical context, but also the fullness of the counsellor's commitment as experienced by the client' (p. 74). Mearns further clarifies his notion of sufficiency in a phrase that places commitment at the heart of the healing encounter: 'In a way, the problem of commitment becomes one of offering a sufficiency of context which is larger than the size of the prison the client has built around himself' (p. 74). LeShan (1996) has also helped me to get my thinking straighter on this issue by writing about the importance of the therapist providing an 'environment' (as opposed to simply a relationship) in which the client can grow, flourish and heal themself. The therapeutic environment needs to be created differently for each individual client and this will involve negotiation about boundaries, depth and pacing of the work, as well as tailoring the quality and intensity of the relationship to match the client's needs.

When I work with deeply damaged, disturbed or distressed clients I often find that I feel drawn to offer more in terms of time and commitment than to my clients who are in less obvious need. It is not unusual for counsellors to have this response to needy clients and we are taught to resist such impulses by our trainers and supervisors. The dangers of becoming over-involved with such clients are real and have been well documented. However, there is a twin danger, which is rarely mentioned, that we can be *under-involved* (Mearns 1992) with our clients.

Therapists who practise under-involvement are usually very rigid in their holding of boundaries and do this in an undifferentiated way with all their clients. Whatever the client's difficulties they will be given one, or at the most two, fifty or sixty minute sessions per week. Clients who express distress in or between sessions are said to be 'acting in' or 'acting out' by such therapists who are likely to hold on to the reins of their boundaries even more tightly in response. The client may learn to accommodate to this rigidity, as the child who cries for attention when it wakes and is fearful learns eventually to suppress its cries if the parent repeatedly ignores them. The client who cannot make do with the level of availability their therapist has prescribed is likely to make no progress, or leave therapy, or have a breakdown, or harm themselves. The last option may be a desperate bid to have the therapist hear that they can't manage on so little. The under-involved therapist is not likely to have their feathers ruffled by such behaviour and is apt to conclude that the client is difficult, resistant, borderline, manipulative or a hopeless case.

Certainly abuse of clients does take place when therapists over-extend their boundaries and exploit vulnerable people for their own needs. I believe abuse can also take place through neglect or insufficiency of attention. Whilst most people who are able to benefit from counselling can indeed profit from one or two sessions of therapy a week, there are a small minority of clients who are so deeply damaged or experience distress of such profundity that in order to contact and clear it they need extended holding and attention. This can happen through additional session time and/or containment provided in other ways, for instance through access to other professionals and places of safety provided by mental health services.

I saw one client I worked with for one hour a week for several months. Nothing much happened in the therapy, although she was a 'good' client and attended regularly. However a great deal was happening around and in between sessions, including several suicide attempts and numerous instances of self-harming. I talked things through with her and, as a result, offered her two hours of counselling a week. Again my client was not sufficiently held by this arrangement. Whilst she began to bring material with more 'heat' in it to our sessions, the various crises also escalated, normally occurring just before she was due to see me again. These culminated in a short stay in hospital where she had a psychiatric assessment with the recommendation that she continue with her counselling. I renegotiated with her after her discharge from hospital and we settled on meeting three times a week for sessions that each lasted for two hours. So for several months I saw her for six hours a week during which time she also had some support from mental health services that included providing her with a safe place to spend time between counselling sessions. Her disturbed behaviour between sessions decreased markedly and she began to make full and courageous use of our time together, bravely confronting her underlying difficulties which, as it turned out, arose from deeply brutalising childhood experiences.

Clearly there is a cost for counsellors in providing such sufficiency of care and attention for their clients. Therapists who choose to use themselves in this way need to ensure that the balance of their own well-being does not tip over into insupportable amounts of stress and exhaustion that their increased availability to clients may generate. I endeavoured to look after myself when working with this client by asking for the support I needed from my supervisor and colleagues and by allowing my caseload of other clients to reduce through not taking on new clients when others left. Even so I needed to check out with myself, as the months went by, that I was still gladly and freely offering to do this extended work with my client. Had there come a time when I felt resentful or ungiving, or that my client no longer seemed to be benefiting from this arrangement it would have been very important to stop doing it in this way to protect both her and myself. Supervision was important here as my supervisor clearly, repeatedly, and in many different ways, asked me 'how are you?' whenever we met during this period of work.

I realise that in advocating therapist flexibility in this way I am posing a dilemma for counsellors who cannot easily extend the limits on what they can provide because of firm restraints placed on their time and availability. Often the client's neediness will not manifest until the therapy is well under way. Appropriate back-up systems and places of safety to which the client can retreat are often difficult, if not imposs-ible, to access. There are no easy answers to such dilemmas and all therapists grapple with them. My intention is not to make those who cannot realistically extend their therapeutic provision feel guilty about this or experience some pressure to overreach themselves. I am offering an alternative perspective on the management of boundaries in the hope that those therapists who are able to consider more flexible responses to clients will not immediately suppress these as countertransference feelings which should not be entertained or acted upon. Again I would highlight the importance of supportive supervision in helping counsel-lors manage these issues. It can be a great relief for the counsellor to hear from their supervisor, following a sensitive exploration of the dilemma, 'you need not feel guilty about holding your boundaries, you are doing good work within the limits of what you are able to provide'.

CONNECTIONS AND BEGINNINGS

I have become intrigued by the way that clients come to choose their therapists and how many of them appear to form a significant connec-tion with us before even the first session of counselling starts.

As I have said, I counsel within a student counselling service and, until quite recently, I was also a resident tutor within the university college where I work. Here are some of the things that clients have said to me about how they made a connection with me before the therapy started.

- A first year student: 'When you stood up at the induction talk and identified yourself as the counsellor, I felt "here is someone I could have a good relationship with"'.
- A private client: 'My wife was at a summer school that you taught on and she thought you would be the right person to help me'.
- A student who first approached me when I was the resident tutor on call: 'I waited until I knew you were on duty before I phoned, because I'd seen you around and heard that you were a counsellor. I didn't feel I could tell any of the others'.

- A student who attended a workshop that I was helping to run: 'I saw you come into the room and you were wearing leggings with a yellow pattern. I used to have some yellow leggings that I really liked and I'd never seen anyone else wear any that colour. Then I noticed that you were left-handed, like my mum. I knew you were one of the counsellors and I asked someone: "Who's that?" '

These examples beg the question of what impact the client's choice of, and initial connection with, the counsellor may then make on the subsequent counselling. McLennan (1996: 394) has argued that the outcome of any case of counselling or psychotherapy may be largely determined 'at the precise point in time where the client in question is paired with the given counsellor or therapist, before they ever meet'. The reason for this, he suggests, is that the research on counsellor and client matching indicates that successful outcomes are largely determined by how closely the therapist's relationship style and intervention skills match what the client brings to the interaction.

There is some evidence in the literature on 'common factors' in therapy (see Chapter 1) that client motivation and commitment can be significant determinants of outcome and I suspect that a positive experience of choosing a counsellor may well provide an enhancement of these factors. In the light of such comments from clients it is interesting to postulate when the therapeutic work *actually* starts. Is it in the first session, or when the client first makes a contact or connection with the counsellor? Or is it when they first make a decision to seek counselling, or even at some point beyond the first session when trust is sufficiently established for the client to actually risk getting down to the real business that has brought them to counselling?

The client whose attention was initially engaged by my choice of leggings was in therapy with me for a year before she began to reveal what was really troubling her (although she had given a hint at our first meeting of something big beneath the surface and knowing this helped me to wait patiently while, for a long time, we seemed only to be treading water). What became apparent with this client was the absolutely fundamental importance of trust-building. Because she had learned to distrust most people I think she needed to manufacture the seeds that might lead eventually to trust-building through an imagined connection with me. Perhaps a connection such as left-handedness or a shared taste in leggings might, rather like a life-raft, be something to hang on to which could afford minimal safety and buoyancy to keep her afloat once she found herself pitched into the deep waters of her own psychological distress. It took a further twelve months of consistent and reliable care and attention from me for her to begin to feel that she might trust me enough to let me plunge into her turbulence with her. Interestingly, this person had had a previous experience of counselling in which she never did divulge the true nature of her difficulties. When we talked about this and why it might have been that she could eventually disclose to me but not to her previous counsellor, all she could say was: 'I don't know why but I just felt from the moment I met you that I would be able to tell you'.

I have come to believe that clients often instinctively choose (when a choice is possible) a counsellor who has the personal characteristics that will best provide what they need in order to feel helped. Elements of the counsellor's temperament and character then turn out to constitute a substantial aspect of what is offered as that help. This seems like a mysterious process that may well extend beyond identifiable elements of client and counsellor matching. Herron and Rouslin (1984) have reviewed the research on counsellor and client matching and concluded that whilst a workable client–therapist match has been demonstrated to be a significant determining factor in outcome, its precise ingredients remain elusive. On the occasions where clients appear to take an active part in productive matching, choice may come down more to intuition or 'sixth sense' which is more about choosing the person than it is about selecting a counsellor with particular skills or expertise.

CONNECTIONS AND ENDINGS

I have referred earlier in this chapter to the importance of the counsellor providing a helping environment for the client (LeShan 1996). Elements of that environment include the context of the therapy and, I would argue, aspects of the self of the therapist. Because we rarely see them again, often we do not know exactly what it was that we provided that was helpful for our clients. When we do get the opportunity to receive the perspective of a past client the experience can be illuminating.

I recently received a telephone message that said something like: 'Can you please phone Susan on this number. She wouldn't leave her last name. She says you counselled her some time ago and she wants to know what approach you used on her'. I didn't know who the message was from as I had counselled a number of people called Susan or Sue. A little apprehensively (was she wanting to call me to account in some manner for the way I had worked with her?) I returned the call. When I got back to her she said: 'Hello, it's Sue. You counselled me a few years ago and it was brilliant. You really sorted me out and now I'm getting on with my life, but my brother's got some problems and wants to see a counsellor. I wanted to ask you what approach you use, because I think he'd benefit from seeing someone who works in the same way'. I was perplexed as I couldn't think who this person was. I asked her to tell me her second name, which she did, and instantly I remembered her well. I was still baffled as the person speaking seemed to be referring to a different counselling experience than the one I recalled.

I remembered a very distressed young woman whom I had seen (I hesitate to say counselled) off and on over three years until she had left college about four years previously. My recollection was of a few fragmented and erratic meetings, several notes and letters and a couple of telephones calls. She had turned up at the counselling service on her first day at college to say that she had decided to leave and thought she should let someone know. A couple of days later she telephoned me from home to ask: 'do you think I can come back?' On her return I offered her ongoing counselling. Although her understanding of what comprised 'ongoing' was clearly different to mine, I think I had the sense to let her make use of me in a way that she could manage, rather than demand that she commit herself in the more usual way or be refused use of the counselling service.

What followed were three years wherein she would intermittently make appointments to see me, most of which she never attended. When she didn't attend I invariably received a note under my door, apologising for her non-arrival and telling me a little of how she was doing. On other occasions she would turn up at the reception room of the counselling service and ask to see me when I wasn't available, or would knock on my office door to ask if she could just have a few minutes with me. If I was free and could see her without feeling intruded upon I would sometimes agree. At other times I explained it wasn't possible and would make her a 'proper' appointment for a different time. She rarely kept these.

Part of Sue's story was that she had been confined against her will for a period of time on an acute psychiatric ward and had experienced a sequence of deeply intrusive medical interventions that had left her feeling both physically and emotionally violated. She experienced this period of her life as one of both abandonment and enforced restraint. I think she was very afraid of being 'confined' in a counselling relationship, whilst also seeking a secure attachment and a sense of ongoing connection with me. I do recall one very powerful session where we got close to her traumatic story only to know that she couldn't then find words to tell it. Instead, with my encouragement, she drew a picture of the hospital in which she had been confined. We sat in silence for a long time while she drew a meticulous picture – it seemed important for it to be as detailed and specific as she could remember. Once the picture was out on the paper she was able to find a few words to tell me about what she had endured and she also began to discover her anger about what had been done to her. Towards the end of the session I asked her what she wanted to do with the picture. Silently she started tearing it up. She tore each piece again and again until it was in the tiniest bits that couldn't be torn any smaller. Carefully and very precisely, one by one, she put them in the waste bin.

She didn't need to contact me for a quite a while after that session. We never had an ending and one summer I realised that she would have graduated and our connection had ended. Of course, despite her words on the telephone, *I* didn't 'sort her out'. She sorted herself out through the rather unorthodox but clearly therapeutic process and environment that we co-created. As Guggenbühl-Craig (1979: 90) has asserted in discussing the wounded-healer archetype in therapy, 'neither wounds nor diseases can heal without the curative action of the inner healer' and I believe that I offered Sue the conditions in which she could activate her own inner healer. The supremely important aspects of this, I believe, were that she found me consistent and caring and able to let her come and go.

I believe it is important for counsellors to be flexible in how they allow their clients to make an ending with them. Sometimes this means managing the balance between not allowing the client to duck an ending that may be difficult for them and trusting that the client knows best how they need to end. With one client who was very musically gifted we had a last session before a long break (which might well have turned out to be an ending) where she chose to play her flute for me. I felt very honoured and greatly moved during the hour in which I sat before her as she stood and played to me in an empty studio. I knew that she feared and avoided playing in public and yet she had rehearsed for many hours for her audience of one in order to achieve a flawless performance. Endings that are allowed to be as the client chooses can be therapeutically significant in themselves and give the counselling process one last giant step forward.

I worked for two years with a client who needed to clear away many abusive incidents from her relationship with her mother. As the work progressed, aspects of our ongoing relationship were clearly reparative for her and I was conscious at times of feeling very mothering towards her. Quite unexpectedly she came one day to announce that she wanted to have a break from counselling. Like most counsellors, I have had clients who say they want a break when what they really mean is that they wish to end and to avoid an ending. I asked her if she thought she would want to continue with her counselling at some point in the future and she replied that she wasn't sure. Normally with such a response I would encourage the client to see me for a few more sessions, at least, to give us the opportunity to explore what was happening *as if* we might be ending permanently. I had a gut feeling that I needed to trust my client and I let her go. However I did ask her to contact me again at some time in the future even if she decided not to continue with her counselling so that we could have an ending. She said she would do this and we finished the session without further reference to endings.

On discussing this experience with my supervisor she expressed some surprise that I had allowed such a long term client to leave in what seemed an abrupt way. All I could say in my defence was that it had felt intuitively right to do so and as I explored this feeling with the help of my supervisor I began to make links between our ending and her relationship with her mother. My client had been dominated and con-trolled within a symbiotic relationship with her mother until her late teens, when she had tried to separate and begin to live her own life. At the first overt signs of her wish to separate my client's mother had demanded that she suppress these or leave and not come back. My client left abruptly, leaving a breach that remained unhealed in that she was never invited or welcomed back by her mother. I began to realise how important it was that I had allowed my client the autonomy to separate and leave *and* that I had also invited her back. I did not hear from her for six months, at which point she sent me a Christmas card and said that she would be in touch. I dropped her a line in response saying how pleased I had been to hear from her and that I was looking forward to seeing her again when she felt ready to come. After a further six months she contacted me again to arrange to come for one session. This is all we had and we made an ending that felt complete. I think the year in which she didn't see me, yet stayed connected, and the experi-ence of choosing when to return and of being welcomed back probably turned out to be of equal, if not more, therapeutic significance than the actual counselling sessions she attended over the previous two years when we had met on a regular basis.

EXTRATHERAPEUTIC FACTORS AND CONNECTIONS

Mays and Franks (1985: 285) have written that 'considering the fact that therapy rarely occupies more than a few hours a week, it is surprising how little attention has been paid by outcome researchers to events occurring outside the consulting room'. The vignettes given above perhaps serve to illustrate the power and significance that extratherapeutic factors may exert on the counselling process. Of equal, or even more importance to that which occurs in the counselling room may be how the session is incubated, mused over, processed, stored and afterwards recalled by the client. The research study outlined in Chapter 4 provides evidence of the potential power and significance of reflective work that is undertaken by the client between counselling sessions. Wise counsellors know that it can be important to engage the client's between session ruminations, perhaps by asking such questions as: 'What has come to the surface (or stayed with you) from the last session?' If space is not created for this material to emerge, major critical incidents in the client's therapy may be missed or go unacknowledged by the counsellor. Engaging in research and evaluation with clients is one important way of accessing and bringing to the surface critical therapeutic incidents that happen between or around sessions, as the following example perhaps shows.

In a research study that I undertook (Wosket 1989) to investigate clients' perceptions of counselling, I interviewed a client (called here Angela) at the end of her counselling relationship with me that had lasted approximately six months. In the research interview I discovered a great deal about what had been going on for my client between our meetings that threw much light on the process she had experienced whilst in therapy. In the following excerpt we are talking about a time when her self-esteem was at its lowest ebb and how our relationship impacted on that.

VAL: We've talked quite a lot now about perceptions – is there anything else that comes up for you?
ANGELA: I don't know if I'd have liked a bit more of your perceptions of me. It's just one particular thing I'm thinking about. It's kind of like when you really feel in the pits and you kind of think you're not worth liking, but there's this person sitting listening and, kind of, *giving* to you. It was when you asked me in the session: 'Do you think *I* like you?' and I just answered you. And then I went

home and I was sitting in my normal thinking place ... and it suddenly dawned on me why you asked it – or why I perceived you'd asked it. It's quite an important issue really ... but it came to me afterwards. It just made me laugh – because I'd sat and told you that nobody would like me if they knew what was deep down [laughter] and the person who knows most about the deep down is *you*. So then I just laughed.

VAL: But it's interesting that I asked you, rather than said to you that 'I like you', and there was a difference there.

ANGELA: Yes ... yes. If you'd have said 'but I like you', it wouldn't have made me think. But for you to ask me: 'Do you think *I* like you?' makes me weigh it up. It's kind of like, yeah, I like these bits about me, and also by asking that it puts *me* into it. It's my perceptions of me as seen through you.

VAL: Mmm ... so it's more about you than it is about me?

ANGELA: Yeah, it's my perceptions of what goes on in the sessions. And if I've got the low self esteem, it's me who's got to build it up. So by you asking me the question it means I've got to look for the answers and then *I* can build it up – build up my self-esteem.

Post-counselling research interviews of this nature can provide extremely valuable insights into how clients use the counselling process and what works for them. Such revelations can, in turn, provide the counsellor with significant feedback that then helps them to incorporate useful exemplars of good practice into their developing repertoire of helping interventions.

Non-attending clients

The traditional view about clients who fail to attend pre-arranged counselling sessions, or who are late turning up, is that they are avoiding or resisting therapy in some way. This is obviously true in many instances, yet I think we should also be alert to the mis-attending client who, paradoxically, may be making *better* use of the therapeutic process by *not* attending their counselling session. Here the client may be expressing a new found autonomy or exerting a healthy independence from the therapist. Perhaps it is hard for us to allow that the client might be making better use of their time than by being with their counsellor. I think it is important that we open our eyes and ears to this possibility rather than immediately latching on to the obvious fact that the client is late, or failed to attend, and – however nicely – requiring them to account for their absence.

On one occasion my client who had attended sessions punctually for over a year arrived twenty minutes late for her session. I was worried because I knew that she had been feeling unsafe and vulnerable and I wondered whether I had been too challenging with her in the previous session. When she eventually arrived the small smile around her eyes helped me to hold in check the part of myself that was ready to leap on to her tardiness and demand (pleasantly of course) that she give an account of why she had let me suffer those long minutes of disquiet. My client did not apologise for her lateness but explained, with a whiff of quiet pride in her own resourcefulness, that she had spent the last half an hour phoning around to make contact with various support agencies in her home town so that she could prepare herself in advance for a visit home that we had both recognised would be difficult for her. In my response, instead of the misplaced ticking off she nearly received, she got an affirmation of her ability to begin to release herself from the position of being a victim of her experience and move to a place where she could start to fashion it differently.

Knowing that the counsellor is there and safeguarding their time is still likely to be important for the client who is late or fails to arrive. I have had the experience often enough of having clients who arrive five or ten minutes before their allotted time is up, and then show tangible relief (or surprise) that I am still waiting for them, to learn the importance of standing by my post for that hour. As I work in a student counselling service I have, over the years, become aware of the many attractive diversions that are likely to distract a student from the serious business of counselling. I have come to make allowances for these as a necessary and important part of engaging with constructive life events, rather than seeing them as narrowly manipulative devices to avoid facing the counsellor. One young woman arrived breathless and dishevelled ten minutes before her session was due to end. She announced: 'I'm sorry I'm so late. I went to a party yesterday and had a really late night and then slept in. I've just come to let you know I'm OK and then I'm going back to bed'. I said: 'OK, I'll see you next week. Have a good sleep' and she left. When she came the following week, instead of dwelling on her absence from the previous session, we talked about how good she was beginning to feel about, at long last, having an active social life after having spent many solitary, lonely and homesick evenings in her room.

PART TWO: SOME THERAPISTS SPEAK ON WORKING AT THE BOUNDARIES

Data included in the last section of this chapter were given by therapists in the postal survey who responded to the following question:

'What was your most significant learning *about yourself as a therapist* from an experience of working at the boundaries in your practice? Please describe the experience and something you learned about yourself which you feel has had an impact on the way you work now as a counsellor or psychotherapist'.

Working at the boundaries was defined for respondents as meaning any of the following: '(a) dual or consecutive relationships with clients – i.e. a client who was, or is, in another relationship with you apart from that of therapist and client; (b) where the therapeutic work spills over or moves beyond your normal "holding" structures; (c) where clients "choose" or connect with you before the therapy starts or re-connect after the ending; (d) any significant incidence of between session contact with clients or experience of events outside of the sessions which have had an impact on you and your clients'.

The largest category of experiences of unorthodox practice recorded by respondents was of contact with clients outside counselling sessions (29 instances, 21 per cent of the total), whether this occurred by accident or design. Several respondents made the point that extratherapeutic contact is unavoidable within the small networks and communities that counsellors often share with their clients. It therefore seems important that counsellors prepare themselves for this eventuality and learn how to 'milk' situations for their therapeutic potential as and when they arise, rather than treating them as embarrassing episodes that are best avoided. As one respondent put it: 'my role is not in a vacuum in the context I work. . . . The "avoid blurred boundaries at all costs" philosophy does not work for me. Working at them is more realistic in my practice'.

Another respondent identified the dilemma which exists for the counsellor who identifies themselves with a particular social group or population from which they also draw their clients and who is likely to experience accidental meetings with current or past clients on a regular basis:

The existence of dual relationships and overlapping connections between the client–therapist relationship and the community in which they both live and work is usually prohibited in the counselling/ psychotherapy field. This has presented me with a number of 'duality dilemmas' as a lesbian counsellor working with lesbian clients. Over the years I have devised professional, respectful ways of dealing with overlap between therapy and community – and been sorely challenged both professionally and personally in striving to ensure that the ethical principle of fidelity is upheld. There has been some bittersweet learning along the way, and always a deep respect for the integrity and confidentiality of the therapy relationship. . . . I now discuss the possibility of overlapping connections/ dual relationships at the outset of the therapeutic relationship.

The counsellor informed me, at the time of writing, that she was involved in collaborating with two colleagues to 'produce guidelines on the ethical management of dilemmas in dual relationships in lesbian client–lesbian counsellor, and gay client–gay counsellor relationships'. Innovative responses such as this to the real life exigencies thrown up by boundary dilemmas are to be applauded as pragmatic alternatives to the sometimes unrealistic and prescriptive directives that are laid down by professional bodies.

Hermansson (1997: 135) has asserted that 'effective counselling – reliant as it is especially on the notion of empathy – demands, in a qualified way, boundary crossing'. He develops his argument in proposing that 'the major loss that can occur as a consequence of boundary rigidity and excessive distancing can be to what is essentially the counsellor's most potent therapeutic tool, that of empathy. . . . To be empathic, a counsellor has to move across a boundary into the life space of the client' (ibid.: 140). In a very literal sense one counsellor in the survey appears to exemplify this line of reasoning. In contrast to the occurrence of unforeseen meetings, an example of a planned meeting with a client outside the normal boundaries of the therapeutic frame is provided by this counsellor who wrote about an occasion where they spent an entire day with a client:

> This experience was with a client with whom I had worked over a period of two years covering a range of issues, latterly a bereavement and there was a sense of us working towards our ending in the therapy too. My client asked if I would accompany her on a journey that she wished to make, a sort of pilgrimage, to visit

significant places that related to her son who had died. She felt strongly that she needed to do this yet knew she couldn't face it alone and wanted me to be a companion. I surprised myself by intuitively agreeing and being immediate in this. . . . The experience itself involved a day of being together in a variety of settings: in the car, having a meal, being quietly reflective, me facilitating specific memories/emotions at certain points during the day – tracking continually what my client needed and wanted in order to move through the day in a meaningful way.

The counsellor records the important learning that arose from this experience of boundary crossing and links it to the strengthening of a different sort of boundary – something that has developed alongside a growing sense of personal and professional authenticity:

I learned a lot about myself as a therapist that day which has led me to trust my intuitiveness much more and the process of therapy too. . . . I realised that I have internal boundaries that serve when the 'normal' therapeutic boundaries are expanded. I am sure that this was possible because of the length and solidity of our trusting relationship. . . . The most significant learning I think which has affected my work is a real sense of 'me' and 'me as therapist' being bonded which allows me to be more real in my work, more congruent and immediate with my clients.

This counsellor appears to have discovered that a different kind of boundary management can be invoked to hold and contain therapeutic work that moves beyond their normal holding structures. Altogether, six respondents wrote about decisions to extend their normal session time either as an experience of rule breaking or of working at the boundaries of counselling. One example follows which indicates that flexibility in managing time boundaries is one means by which counsellors can choose to be with their clients in personally determined ways in response to unique situations and dilemmas. This counsellor writes at some length about the subjective process he experienced while making decisions to extend session times for a client as an instance of working at the boundaries of counselling. He gives a clear sense of what 'reflection-in-action' (Schön 1983) may be like for the therapist caught up in this kind of dilemma.

This relates to a client I worked with about 4 years ago. By about the 4th or 5th session we had already had a couple of sessions that had spilled over the normal hour by about $^1/_2$ an hour or so. The sessions had been difficult and a lot of depressive feelings had been expressed. I hadn't felt able to conclude after an hour and let the client go. I was beginning to be concerned about this and came to the session thinking about intending to structure it more carefully and draw things to a close, but again, when the hour came, the client was in the process of expressing some complex and important ideas about the past event which seemed to be at the root of her issues.

Again I felt the conflict – my training telling me I should be finishing, but my self or some inner voice saying that wouldn't be appropriate/fair/caring/ethical. This session went on up to the 2 hour mark, and seemed to be reaching some sort of impasse. There didn't seem to be much more to say at that point but it still felt very difficult and I was concerned for the client's safety – she had expressed some suicidal thoughts which I took seriously. I shared this and she felt equally stuck. I'm not sure why, but at that point I suggested going for a walk, to which she agreed. This really seemed to help detach from the session content in a safe way. We talked about her feelings in the here and now, and then about the immediate environment as we walked. After about 20 minutes we returned to the counselling room and it did feel safe to conclude. We made a contract about not harming herself before talking to me in the next week.

This was the start of a long period of work with this client (about 18 months in total) during which we had a few more extended sessions, and did a lot of different work, but I think what I learned was to listen carefully to that inner voice and trust it more than I had. I'd sometimes felt that there would necessarily be dire (though unspecified) consequences if I transgressed the boundaries of the *hour*. I learned that sometimes clients are in such a dark place that (a) one hour won't do, and (b) they can benefit from seeing you as someone who really understands and really cares, and doesn't just turn that on for an hour. There are other ways of managing the dependency that then might be a risk.

Johnston and Farber (1996: 399) have concluded from their research into the maintenance of boundaries (including time boundaries) in psychotherapeutic practice that 'it is conceivable that to many patients the therapist's accommodation conveys respect, a professional approach to the task at hand, and an appreciation for the complexity and variety of tasks required in the course of psychotherapy'. In the above account the counsellor conveys a sense of working flexibly with a very depressed client who, in his judgement, required an unsual response that matched her apparent level of need.

The issue of extending time boundaries was also written about in relation to awareness displayed by a number of respondents of how therapeutic interventions are adjusted to meet the counsellor's needs as well as (or even instead of) the client's. One counsellor who wrote about time management revealed how she had resolved the tension between her own needs and those of her clients. This counsellor reported that despite having spent much time in supervision exploring the issue, she still frequently went over time with clients. However she had learned why this tended to happen: 'I give extra time as a sort of compensation for my perceived inadequacy [and] I want to "hold" the client longer to demonstrate my valuing of them'. The way she had evolved to manage the problem is described: 'I have moved to a more relaxed contracting agreement, where we agree to meet "for up to 90 minutes" (or whatever). This seems easier to manage and also affords the client a greater share in the decision about when to end. (I'm able to offer this because I see very few clients currently and have the flexibility to set my own timetable.)'

Several counsellors who responded to survey questions expanded on the idea of how doing therapy meets the counsellor's own needs through making links between the management (or mismanagement) of boundary issues and their own search for personal authenticity and, even, identity. One person wrote about a number of boundary issues with clients and supervisees, some of which were related to his struggle to separate from a professional identity which he had held in a previous career. He added: 'Having written all this, I realise that this all says more about me than clients. It, at some level, is about my own identity and my own search for individuation. It is when I am working at the edges of the "safe area" that I am able to be the greatest value to clients and at the same time learn more about myself'.

Another counsellor recorded the painful, but crucial, learning about self that arose from an experience of boundary mismanagement. This therapist had agreed to take a client on for counselling with whom they had had a previous, minimal, connection – but significantly one where there had been a power imbalance in favour of the therapist. The counsellor wrote: 'against my better judgement, even at the time, I took him on. It was a mistake. He idealised me and denigrated himself. He wanted to be like me, be me, be my friend, be valued by me, etc. After a year

I managed to finish with him and refer him. . . . I learned a lot about the importance of boundaries and my slight tendency to trivialise issues such as this. I kid myself "of course it won't matter – we can work it through". I let him persuade me it would be OK because I liked him and was flattered. There is no room for flattery in counselling and I have been pulled up sharp. I must value myself for who I am and not allow clients to do it for me'.

I will conclude the topic of working at the boundaries in counselling with the words of a counsellor who wrote fully and feelingly about her difficult but enlightening experience of trying to manage dual relationships in her work when she sees clients who belong to a community of which she is also a member. This counsellor highlights the importance of clear contracting at the outset of a counselling relationship where therapist and client are likely to encounter one another between sessions. In so doing she makes the point that the counsellor needs to create a fine balance between clarity about boundaries and an over-emphasis on them which might imbue the relationship with artificial and self-conscious constraint. She writes that she has learned that 'whilst contracting carefully the boundary issues – not making them such a "big thing" that they become intrusive to the relationship and give a staccato effect to the therapeutic process'. When the balance is well enough adjusted it can allow for moments of therapeutic meeting that, as this counsellor observes, move beyond externally imposed limits to a place of unconstrained mutuality. She records that a profound learning from her experience of working at the boundaries of counselling has been 'realising there are times when contact with a person is a truly spiritual encounter which somehow "in the moment" transcends the complexities of boundaries so that they melt as obstacles and belong only in the physical sense of the relationship'.

Chapter 8

The shadow side of the use of self in counselling

> The instrument of the therapist is his or her person, and if that person is corrupt, then the psychotherapy is bound to reflect that corruption.
>
> (Masson 1992)

One could be forgiven for thinking that current researchers and theorists, particularly those who profess allegiance to the behavioural, cognitive-behavioural and brief therapy schools of counselling, are bent on removing entirely, as far as is possible, the personhood of the counsellor from the therapeutic encounter. We are even now entering the era of counselling by computer (Bloom 1998; King *et al.* 1998; Lago 1996; Murphy and Mitchell 1998; Robson and Robson 1998; Sanders and Rosenfield 1998; Wessler and Wessler 1997).

As I come to the point of considering the shadow side of the use of self in counselling, I begin to wonder if this movement to de-personalise counselling is something to do with trying to sanitise the activity of therapy – to somehow clean it up and get rid of the mess and confusion that inevitably result when two people come together and struggle to express themselves clearly and helpfully to one another. Perhaps we have begun to shy away from claiming that what we contribute personally to the helping process may be something that makes a difference to the client because we are so familiar with the dire warnings in much of the psychotherapy literature about the dangers of therapist arrogance and narcissism (see, for instance, Brightman 1984; Eckler-Hart 1987; Goldberg 1986; Guggenbühl-Craig 1979; Guy 1987; Kottler 1986; Lomas 1981; Lowen 1985; Marmor 1953; Miller 1997; Page 1999; Pines 1982; Sharaf and Levinson 1964). What these writers share is an interest in contemplating the numerous ways in which therapists have the capacity to deceive themselves. Some of these are reviewed below.

The notion of the shadow to conceptualise the way that therapists deceive themselves is one that has come to popular attention through the work of Carl Jung, where it is considered to mean 'the "negative" side of the personality, the sum of all those unpleasant qualities we like to hide, together with the insufficiently developed functions and contents of the personal unconscious' (Jung 1983: 88). The greatest danger for therapists (and by implication for their clients) lies not in the having of a shadow side – we all do – but in the 'personal fallout' (Kottler 1986: 38) that happens when we are unaware of the existence of our shadow or are bent on ignoring it. Jung has revealed that 'everyone carries a shadow, and the less it is embodied in the individual's conscious life, the blacker and denser it is' (Jung 1983: 89).

In this chapter I intend to offer some reflections on those messier and less sanitised aspects of the use of self in therapy under the rubric of the counsellor's shadow. This will by no means constitute a full exposition on the shadow side of counselling and for a fuller treatment of the subject readers are referred to Page's (1999) book *The Shadow and the Counsellor* where the topic is explored in great depth. In his book Page traces in detail a developmental process by which the counsellor comes to incorporate their shadow within the authentic personal and professional self. He tracks this development through five identifiable stages that are termed: denying the shadow; recognising the shadow; confronting the shadow; incorporating the shadow, and learning to use the shadow as guide. Page's first stage concerns therapists who are still in a state of generalised denial of their shadow. He suggests this is common for beginning therapists who may have limited self-awareness coupled with a huge investment in preserving their sense of competence. As Page warns, any counsellors still in this state of denial who try 'to work beyond the strictures of their initial training are very vulnerable to their shadow intervening' (p. 57). He suggests that the use of self therefore involves an acknowledgement that innovative practice needs to be carefully adjusted to accommodate the gradual integration of the counsellor's shadow side. The following section follows Page's schema in turning first to a consideration of aspects of denial of the counsellor's shadow.

THERAPIST SELF-DECEPTION

A good overarching term for this is grandiosity. As therapists we may develop an inflated sense of self-importance as a means of protecting ourselves against feelings of worthlessness and the fear of failure. We may get caught up in fantasies of omnipotence because of our need to defend ourselves against the very substantial power that our clients seem to have, whether by dint of their personal machinations or the intransigence of their problems, to make us feel inadequate and useless. Research conducted by Eckler-Hart (1987) has indicated that 'success or failure in doing psychotherapy [is] often perceived as a more global success or failure as a person' by psychotherapists in training and that 'evaluation of one's abilities as a therapist is often experienced as complete evaluation of the self' (p. 686). Therapists who are unable to move forward from this position as they gain experience are likely to carry with them a need to be admired and seen as infallible, by clients and colleagues alike, in order to bolster a fragile sense of self-esteem that may derive, in no small measure, from an over-involvement of self in their professional role.

As he or she gains experience and wisdom, the task for the therapist is to negotiate a period of psychic adjustment, akin in some ways to a process of mourning (Brightman 1984), in order to relinquish the quest for omnipotence and learn to see themselves as vulnerable and ordinary. A sense of humility is the best companion the therapist can hope for in this journey towards the acceptance of fallibility. Fortunately those who we meet in the path of our professional work, as well as sometimes fuelling our self-delusions, are the people who can best help us engender a sense of humility.

I saw a young woman for an assessment session in the student counselling service in which I work. As I had a full case load of clients at the time, I referred her to another counsellor. This didn't work out for her as, I later discovered, she felt unable to form a close relationship with the counsellor. Instead, she continued to seek me out in numerous ways. She would regularly knock on my office door and ask if I could spare a few minutes, while other counsellors and the receptionists told me that she would frequently show up at the counselling service asking for me. At this time I was also a resident tutor and on the evenings and weekends when I was on call I was obliged to respond indiscriminately to requests for support and assistance from any student within the university college. For a period of some weeks, whenever my name was on the duty rota this young woman would telephone and ask for my support.

On one of these occasions she told me that she had so far been referred to six different helpers, none of whom she felt she could talk to. Again she insisted that she would be able to talk to me about her difficulties if I would only listen. Whilst I continued to insist that I was unable to take her on as a counselling client, I confess that a tiny of part of me was preening itself as a very small voice whispered: 'perhaps she sees something in you that she has not seen in the other counsellors'. During one meeting in response to an evening call out from her we were going over this for the umpteenth time, locked in the same stalemate where I declined to fall into counselling mode with her while she lamented 'but I can talk to you'. In desperation I said: 'Isn't there anyone else you can talk to except me?' Without a moment's hesitation she replied 'yes, I can talk to X [another member of the resident tutor team] but she's not a counsellor'. Then the penny dropped and I said: 'Is it because she is young?' She replied 'yes, everyone I've seen so far has been too old and it's easier for me to talk to someone nearer my own age'. I was knocked headlong from my pedestal. Not only did my grandiose fantasy of being an exceptionally gifted counsellor lie in tatters around me, but I realised that her keenness to seek me out was based on a misperception. I look young for my years and yet I was well over twice her age. I knew that X was a good fifteen years younger than me and I uneasily suspected that if she knew how old I actually was I would have been consigned to the scrap heap along with the other 'elderly' helpers. I retained a shred of personal dignity by not disclosing my true age to her and, instead, supported her in arranging to see a young counsellor in an external agency – with whom she finally settled.

Such encounters are excellent learning experiences in that they provide salutary reminders of our capacity for self-delusion. Skovholt and Rønnestad (1992) suggest that a 'series of humiliations' (p. 23) in which the grandiose professional self receives refreshing jolts of reality such as this are important in helping the therapist shift from a position of counsellor power to client power. As I move more proactively in my journey towards ordinary humanness, it can help me to consider how aspects of my fallible or impaired self become transmuted into my professional self (as discussed in Chapter 5) and to remind myself that they are simply flip sides of the same coins. For instance, whilst I know that I can be a calm and safe container for my clients I do well to remind myself that in my own life I am frequently anxious and unsettled; that my courageous and confrontational therapist persona often has to make way for a different self who is shy, self-doubting and over-cautious; that whilst I am adept at being other-focused as a therapist, I easily become self-absorbed and questioning in my personal life, and that the resilient and tenacious therapist who takes centre stage can all too quickly give way to the stubborn and obstinate doppelganger I am more familiar with, who constantly loiters in the wings. Contemplating myself in this way can be humbling and cause me to pause in my step whenever I find that I am climbing back up on to the pedestal on which my client is inviting me to assume a posture.

Guggenbühl-Craig (1979) has written about the therapist's shadow being manifested through the charlatan and false prophet that lurk within us all and which tend to come to prominence, fuelled by our clients' adulation, when we are feeling at our most omnipotent.

> The analyst often receives no warning from his patient when he is being unconsciously destructive. For the patient is himself oriented toward the charlatan and false prophet in the analyst and encourages these aspects. A therapist often has the impression that his work is going splendidly, the deeper he falls into his own shadow.
> (Guggenbühl-Craig 1979: 28)

Some years ago I was working with a client whose therapy appeared to be going well and to whom I happened to feel attracted. The problem was that at that time I had difficulty allowing myself to acknowledge such feelings as I thought they did not have a legitimate place in the counselling relationship. While I wasn't consciously aware of the attraction it lurked in the shadow to which I had confined it. Shadows have a habit of falling across lighted areas, which is what then occurred. At the start of one session I had occasion to ask the client for his telephone number so that I could contact him to arrange a future appointment. As I opened my diary to write the number down I said to him: 'You have the same area code as my telephone number'. Even as I found myself saying this it was as if I was jolted by an electric current. I had the disturbing sensation as of listening to another person speak and at the same time thinking 'did I really just say that?' In the same moment I knew that his telephone number was not even remotely similar to mine. I also as quickly knew that something had gone seriously amiss for me. I felt acutely uncomfortable and ashamed and far too confused and self-conscious to deal with the issue in any sensible fashion. Fortunately a vestige of my internal supervisor kicked in and I said something like: 'Oh no, it's quite different, I always have trouble remembering my own number' and the moment moved on without the client giving any tangible sign that he was troubled by my blunder.

As Page (1999: 58) has observed 'any thought, feeling or behaviour that is driven by unconscious forces also provides an opportunity for growth, a window through which the shadow is visible, if sometimes only for a moment'. And indeed, this proved to be a truly critical incident for me in my development as a counsellor, albeit one that I still feel uncomfortable recounting. I felt so ashamed that I did not even tell my supervisor about it at the time, although in our next meeting I did admit to him that I found the client attractive. With his help I began to give myself permission not just to allow, but also to search around for an extended range of feelings towards my clients. This was a liberating experience. I slowly discovered that I didn't just feel compassion, empathy, boredom or dislike when with clients. On occasions I began to let myself feel the bigger feelings of disgust, abandonment, revulsion, fury, anguish, terror, sexual excitement and love. I gradually learned to notice and incubate these responses in myself and value their importance in bringing me closer to my clients' experience.

When considering the realm of strong feelings in counselling relationships, the subject of sexual responses to clients is perhaps the most taboo and the one which most frequently has its dwelling in the shadows. It is the one that I think needs greatest airing, not least because its suppression makes it more likely that therapists who feel sexual with their clients will keep this a secret from themselves and their supervisors, and thereby disavow feelings that can be a source of benefit to their clients.

SEXUAL RESPONSES AND THE USE OF SELF

Little has been written about sexual feelings towards clients and Virginia Hilton (1997b) suggests why this may be. 'If sexual feelings for clients are difficult enough to acknowledge, then surely it would be considered risky to expose oneself in writing about such responses in the therapeutic process' (p. 201). As Page (1999: 69) has astutely commented: 'if we do not allow ourselves the feelings of sexual desire towards clients we do not have to deal with the discomfort this creates'. Herlihy and Corey (1992) have observed that although sexual feelings in counselling, including sexual attraction, are likely to occur frequently, there has been a lack of systematic research into the topic. They suggest that 'this silence gives a misleading impression that counselors are somehow immune from this experience or that those who do encounter it are unusual, aberrant, or guilty of therapeutic error' (p. 32). The danger then arises that 'counselors who believe that their feelings are "abnormal" or "wrong" may resist getting help in dealing with them and may be left feeling overwhelmed by an attraction and increasingly tempted to act it out with the client' (ibid.).

Pope and colleagues (1986) have conducted one of a small number of research studies that have examined the extent of therapists' sexual attraction to clients. Their survey data from 575 registered psychologists working in private practice in the United States revealed that 95% of men and 76% of women therapists (87% overall) had felt sexually attracted to clients on at least one occasion. Although only a small number (9.4% of men and 2.5% of women) had acted on these feelings, 63% of those surveyed disclosed that they felt anxiety, confusion and guilt about having such feelings. Pope and colleagues suggest that approaches to training must start to lift the taboo on the subject by acknowledging that sexual feelings are a normal and natural aspect of therapist responses towards clients and do not in themselves constitute unethical behaviour. '[T]he phenomenon of therapist–client sexual intimacy must be clearly differentiated from the experience of sexual attraction to clients. The latter seems to suffer from guilt by association, and the general failure to discuss the experience openly does little to clarify the situation' (p. 157).

In order to give ourselves permission to bring our sexual selves into our counselling relationships I think it helps to acknowledge that, while both may be legitimate responses, there is a crucial difference between feeling sexual attraction *towards* a client and feeling sexually aroused when *with* a client. If I feel sexual attraction towards my client, and particularly if this persists, it is likely that I need to attend to something about myself or my relationship with my client. It may be that I genuinely feel attracted to the client, in which case it would probably be helpful for me to talk this through with my supervisor and check out if I am managing myself appropriately within the relationship – in particular whether I am able to contain my feelings towards the client sufficiently to continue to work effectively with them. Or it could be that the client is acting in a provocative or seductive manner towards me, in which case it is important for me to consider, again preferably with the help of my supervisor, what this might mean and what is the best way to respond – whether by confrontation or a gentler exploration of the dynamic. If, on the other hand, I have not previously felt sexually attracted to the client and, unusually, find myself experiencing sexual arousal when I am with him or her, it is probably important for me to pay closer attention to what the client is dealing with. Rather than trying to suppress my responses, I would do well to ask myself whether they might throw any light on the client's experience and issues. Here is an example to illustrate my point.

My client had been horrifically and extensively abused as a child. Gradually she began to be able to reveal the extent of the abuse to me and to recount it in some detail. For some weeks and months I was able to listen calmly and fully to her disclosures. One day I found myself beginning to feel sexually aroused as she recounted yet another occasion where she had been sexually molested. Initially I felt disconcerted and alarmed at my response. Fortunately I had learned to begin to trust that whenever I encountered unexpected emotional and physical responses with my clients the source of these was often to be found in the client's experience. I asked my client in clear and explicit language about her own physical and sexual responses to the abuse and she was able to tell me that she had sometimes experienced sexual arousal and had even, on occasion, invited the abuse because of the pleasurable bodily sensations it brought with it. She had wanted to tell me about this, but felt too ashamed and 'dirty' to do so. She was relieved when I was then able to assure her that it is not uncommon for someone who is abused to feel sexually stimulated by the experience and that this is a natural response that the body has and does not imply that the abuse was welcomed or freely chosen. Once my client had acknowledged the response as her own I did not need to carry it for her any longer and whilst her disclosures of abuse continued for many more months, I did not again feel sexually aroused when with her.

An experience like this can bring us very much closer to understanding the feelings of our clients. My response is a direct mirror of the client's and an example of what is sometimes called projective identification. I didn't want to feel aroused by what was happening and neither did my client. I felt ashamed and wanted it to stop and so did she. Having these feelings gives me a glimpse of what my client experienced although I know that what she endured was a thousand times worse. My understanding is broadened and my acceptance of myself and my client is deepened so that I am less likely to condemn or judge either of us for having these feelings. I also learn to accept that I am having these responses because I am willing to feel them. I know that I am able to suppress uncomfortable or unacceptable feelings through retreating into distractions and thereby staying on safe and familiar ground. Yet by resonating with my client in this way I choose to go with her into her nightmare world of restimulation and chaos. And having gone into this world with her I will not be the same again. As I emerge I know that I am changed. I have become a sadder and more pessimistic person and I now carry the weight of a knowledge of what one human being can do to another that I would rather not have. Jourard (1971: 150) has wisely asserted that as the price of therapist authenticity is to be changed 'those who wish to leave their being and their growth unchanged should not become therapists'.

I showed the draft of this section to the client who is referred to in the vignette above in order for her to decide if she was willing for me to include it. This felt risky and exposing as I was thereby disclosing to her a powerful and intimate response that I had experienced in a session and had not at the time shared with her. Her comments on reading it were: 'I'm pleased that you trust me enough to let me know that went on for you – I could see how nervous you were while I was reading it. I'm glad I know that you had that response because some of the stuff I've told you about, under different circumstances, would be quite natural. Something I really hope for is that one day I'll be able to have a normal sexual relationship with someone, and to know that was how you felt makes my own responses feel more normal and natural. It makes me more hopeful and I don't feel so abnormal for having had those responses to the abuse'.

It is sometimes hard to convey to trainees – even advanced ones – the value for the counsellor of allowing strong authentic feelings to be part of their way of being with clients. I remember conducting a tutorial with a student who was writing a dissertation on the impact on counsellors of working with clients who have been sexually abused. The student had drafted a questionnaire asking counsellors about a range of feelings they might experience whilst doing, or as a result of doing, such work. It was a well designed questionnaire but omitted the issue of sexual arousal for counsellors. When I suggested to the student that she might ask counsellors about their sexual feelings in working with this client group she was horrified. Even when I explained my reasons for this she resisted and said that she did not think anyone would fill in the questionnaire if she asked them such questions. Yet, as Virginia Hilton (1997b: 183) has observed, 'sexuality is central to human existence, and therefore it is central to the therapeutic process. Whether we are comfortable with it or not, our task as therapists is to be present with our *feelings* as well as our awareness, when the client's sexual issues emerge in the relationship' (original emphasis).

I don't think we can prepare trainees in advance for all the strong feelings that client work will arouse in them or convince them by argument or example that it is acceptable to have such feelings. What we can do is be around for them, as trainers and supervisors, to give them permission to accept these feelings when they do occur and, very importantly, help them to make sense of and contain them. If they are educated in a climate where such feelings are stifled and suppressed their clients will suffer. Strong feelings that are not allowed expression will fester and leak as personal fallout, either on to our clients, our colleagues, or our families. Concealed and repressed feelings contain the seeds of burnout and the roots of client abuse and exploitation. One expression of emotion that, curiously, seldom seems to find a place in the literature on counselling and psychotherapy is that of humour, which is considered in the next section.

THE JOY OF HUMOUR

It seems to me that humour is excluded from accounts of therapy to the extent that one might almost assume that it never happens – or if it does, that it has crept in uninvited, as a breach of therapeutic etiquette. Counselling is a serious business – or is it? As therapists we are put on this earth to alleviate distress and to unburden others of what gives them sorrow and pain. As we go about our business does this mean that our clients become people who are robbed of the capacity for joy and laughter, by dint of their suffering, while we are endeavouring to help them? Should I somehow learn to park my mischievous and humorous self outside the counselling room in order to prepare myself properly to meet my client? If the answer to these questions is 'yes', I've clearly been getting something badly wrong and should possibly seek a change of profession.

If you have never come across a humourless therapist I hope that you will continue to be spared, as it is a depressing experience. Counsellors lacking in a sense of humour usually materialise as over-earnest and very careful. Each phrase is carefully weighed and delivered in measured tones, often in immaculate jargonese. Any hint of a smile in response to something jolly the client has foolishly ventured is quickly suppressed and replaced with a stony, if earnest, gaze which is justified as not colluding in 'gallows laughter' (whatever that means). I once had a client who came for counselling feeling distraught after a close and unexpected bereavement. We worked together for several months and when we reviewed the work before ending she said that one of the unexpected bonuses she had gained had been the fun that we had experienced with one another. She particularly commented on the times when we had laughed aloud together as having been healing and as helping her to feel that she would eventually get through the acute pain of her bereavement.

There is a place for the life-giving breath of humour in even the most harrowing of therapeutic encounters, as I hope the following account makes clear.

I have been with my client for four hours whilst she has been re-living and thereby clearing events from her childhood of great horror. During this time she has experienced a terrifying panic attack where she has felt as if she is suffocating. She has twice had to leave the room to vomit in the nearby toilet. She has felt so close to passing out that I have helped her to lie in a recovery position on the floor until she can bear to come back to full consciousness and continue the work. She has been struck dumb in a trance-like state for half an hour and then been possessed by an immense fury where paper and tissues are shredded until they carpet the floor of the counselling room like white feathers escaped from a quilt.

Now, in the last twenty minutes of the session, we have reached a place of calm together. I am sitting next to her on the floor, amongst the debris, and she reaches for my hand and holds it. We chat about soap operas on TV and laugh about how awful the actors' accents in some of them are. Then we joke about how hard we are working when nearly everyone else has gone home and together we imagine what the evening cleaner would think if he came into the room and saw the mess. We have an ordinary conversation and it feels wonderfully releasing for us both. I venture to say: 'I'm beginning to think we will get through this together'. She replies: 'In moments like this, I dare to think it too'. We agree it will be important for us to remember such moments when the going gets tough again, as we both know that it will. Our shared laughter allows us to keep a sense of perspective in a landscape that would otherwise be dominated with events of almost unspeakable horror. We have hauled ourselves out of the noisome pit of her abusive childhood through the laughter we create together and the joy we take in one another's presence. In such moments we dance a dance of defiance in the face of her abusers and it reinvigorates and renews us both.

When I showed the above extract to the client who features in it, to ask how she felt about my using it in the book, she gave her permission with the following comments: 'It reminds me of just how much we got through in those sessions and how far you were prepared to go with me and to stay with me. Like the bit about having to put me in a recovery position. I don't think a lot of counsellors would do what you did and it might be dangerous if they weren't as competent. Perhaps you need to say that too'. I think, in saying this, that she was wise to remind me to emphasise again that the use of self is about observing limits as well as about seeking expansion. The BAC Code of Ethics and Practice for Counsellors (BAC 1998) is careful to alert counsellors that they are required to work within their known limits of competence (in this instance I had some first-aid training, as well as my counselling training, to guide me) and to monitor these. The need for careful monitoring of shadow side influences is nowhere more apparent than in the area where therapy begins to meet the needs of the counsellor as well as those of the client.

THE USE OF SELF AND THE THERAPIST'S UNMET NEEDS

A number of writers and researchers have taken the view that the therapist's personal history and search for identity are largely influential in the decision to become, and continue working, as a counsellor or psychotherapist (Dryden and Spurling 1989; Ford 1963; Guy 1987; Hillman 1979; Hilton R. 1997a, 1997b; Kottler 1986; McCarley 1975; Pines 1982; Raskin 1978; Skovholt and Rønnestad 1992). This perspective is perhaps exemplified most clearly by Raskin's (1978: 362) stark assertion that 'I became a therapist before I became a person'.

Others have taken the specific view that the legacy of a troubled or repressed childhood will significantly determine therapeutic attitudes and characteristics (Burton and Associates 1972; Farber 1985; Goldberg 1986; Goldklank 1986; Henry 1966; Lowen 1985; Miller 1997; Pilgrim 1987; Racusin *et al.* 1981). Here again we are looking at coins that have two sides. Alice Miller has suggested that many psychotherapists can be said to 'suffer from an emotional disturbance' arising from the experience of unmet needs in childhood, yet it is precisely this experience that nourishes innate therapeutic competencies. 'The therapist's sensibility, empathy, responsiveness, and powerful "antennae" indicate that as a child he probably used to fulfill other people's needs and to repress his own' (Miller 1997: 22).

It may be true, as Herron and Rouslin (1984: 120) suggest, that 'all patients help their therapist's emotional growth'. One way in which this manifests is, I believe, that many counsellors are able to offer compassion to their clients and help them to do difficult 'original pain work' (Bradshaw 1991: 66) almost as a displacement activity (much as in Britain, in the late summer of 1997, many members of the general public were able to express their own unresolved losses in the extra-ordinary demonstrations of grief that were displayed over the death of Princess Diana). Therapists learn to take care of the wounded inner children of their clients in the same way as their own wounded inner children may need to be attended to. Hillman (1979: 17) is one therapist who has acknowledged this drive in confessing: 'I may bring to my work a need to redeem the wounded child, so that every person who comes to me for help is my own hurt childhood needing its wounds bound up by good parental care'.

There is a myth that abused children grow up to be abusers. No doubt some do. I have also commonly experienced the profound empathy, protectiveness and sensitivity that an adult survivor of abuse conveys to children who, in turn, often appear drawn to this person. The adult survivor will come to have a profound sense of what was denied to them as a child and, as an adult, will therefore frequently champion the rights and needs of children around them. Similarly, the counsellor may be particularly sensitive to their own needs that were not met as a child (and all of us to some extent have dependency needs that were not attended to), and utilise this awareness of what they needed and did not get in attempting to provide nurturance and a corrective emotional experience for their clients. I think this can also amount to a corrective emotional experience for the counsellor who may be compensating for their own developmental lacunae and inadequate parenting through the care they bestow on their clients. This can be a helpful *modus operandi* as long as the counsellor doesn't over-function for the client, give priority to their own healing, or get caught up in some grandiose fantasy of curing or reparenting that is more about pathologising or infantalising clients than helping them to make a healthy transition into autonomous adulthood.

Herron and Rouslin (1984) maintain that the narcissism (the need to be loved and admired) which is innate in the personality of all therapists governs the use of self and determines whether it is misused or used to good effect. Therapists who develop an inflated sense of grandiosity as a defence against feelings of helplessness and inadequacy and who are unable to tolerate and integrate injury to this narcissistic (constructed) self, are likely to side-step with practised dexterity any intimate engage-ment with clients that could unveil their true and vulnerable self, even when the client might well benefit from such an unveiling.

On the other hand, therapists who are open to being challenged by their clients may be able to achieve a level of authentic reciprocity that is as healing for the therapist as it is for the client. Robert Hilton

(1997a) has suggested that 'the therapist needs her role challenged in order to recover her true self' (p. 83) which will have become submerged in her role as a helper – a role that she may well have had thrust upon her from childhood. In what amounts to a role reversal, the therapist who is open to dropping her professional mask has the hope of being released from the prison of her professional persona and having her authentic self validated by her client. 'We cannot release ourselves, but perhaps a client will see the phoniness in this role, the inauthenticity. Or perhaps the client will take us seriously enough to demand more than we can give' (p. 83).

I have mentioned already that I have had the dual role within my work setting of counsellor and resident tutor. Whilst in this position I had a client who had suffered terrible damage as a child and for many months was almost inconsolably distressed as she began to confront the source of her difficulties. During these months her despair often found expression in the demands she made on me whilst I was on call in the role of resident tutor and whenever I was on duty she would, directly or indirectly, ask for my assistance. She had a series of accidents and illnesses that required hospitalisation and took several overdoses that resulted in the two of us spending the night in the local casualty ward together on more than one occasion. Often she would call me in a desperate state of mind in the middle of the night and ask me to come to her. One evening she phoned when I had just fallen asleep after a long and demanding day at work. I felt exhausted and was very reluctant to go to her. I wanted to refuse and yet I pulled some clothes on over my nightdress and went to her room. She was in a highly anxious and distressed state when I arrived and I felt utterly hopeless in her presence and unable to assume even the pretence of professional poise. I said to her: 'I am not here as your counsellor. I do not know how to help you or what I can do to make you feel better. I am willing to sit with you for a while and that is all I can do'. We had a cup of tea together and after about twenty minutes she said: 'I feel calmer now. I think I will be able to sleep and I will not harm myself. Thank you for coming'. I left and went back to bed.

We moved on from this chaotic period of our work, which my client later referred to as the time when 'my unconscious was working overtime'. She talked about how greatly it had mattered to her that I had been prepared to come out of my role as a counsellor and come to her, when I could have chosen not to do so. It had not mattered at all that I couldn't think of what to do when I came. The important thing for her was that I had come to meet her in an authentic and human way. She told me that it was an unexpected relief for her to experience me as consistent and 'the same' in whatever situation we found ourselves – whether it was in the counselling room, in the back of an ambulance, in casualty as she lay on a trolley waiting for a doctor to see her, or in a psychiatric ward, to which she was briefly admitted. She had expected me to be angry whenever she called me out and the fact that I was not enabled her to begin to trust that I would still be around if she dared to speak about what really troubled her – which she eventually and bravely did.

And for me such moments of meeting were in themselves releasing. My client had indeed liberated me from the confines of my role as her therapist and although we then continued to meet only as counsellor and client, I always thereafter felt that I never had to assume a role with her. We had, in the words of Hilton (1997a: 84), 'come together to discover each other without the adaptive selves interfering'. We had met and survived a moment where I had nothing to offer her and I had found that to be myself was enough. Neither my client nor I would have chosen this dual relationship. When I stopped being a resident tutor she said that she was glad we didn't have to manage the complication of two relationships any longer. Yet together we somehow found a way of creating a productive mutuality out of the confusion of two muddled selves.

PERSONAL FALLOUT AND THE USE OF SELF

As well as looking to their clients to redeem aspects of the self that were repressed in childhood, therapists may unwittingly look to their clients to compensate for unfulfilled aspects of self in the present. At worst, as Guggenbühl-Craig (1979: 56) has intimated, clients may come to be 'expected to fill the gap left by the [therapist's] own loss of contact with warm dynamic life' and the conduct of therapy may then become a form of vicarious living for the therapist (Miller 1997) characterised by a kind of one-way intimacy (Bugental 1964). It can be tempting for therapists to fall into this seductive trap for not only do clients' stories provide a rich and stimulating source of surrogate experience, they promise to supply this at little personal risk to the therapist him or herself. Counsellors who find themselves immersed in their clients' worlds to the exclusion of extratherapeutic interests and relationships would do well, in colloquial parlance, to 'get a life', for as Guggenbühl-Craig (1979: 57) asserts, it is only the therapist 'who is passionately engaged in his own life [who] can help his patients to find theirs'.

Few eminent therapists seem to have taken the risk of writing about their own personal fallout. Kottler, who coined this term, proves to be an exception in that he is extraordinarily frank in writing about aspects of his shadow-side that intrude into his work with clients. As my own experience of researching this topic (see Chapters 5, 6 and 7) has confirmed, we can choose to open ourselves up or close ourselves down to examining this area of self and there are plenty of attractive side-tracks we can take to avoid this murky and swampy territory in order to stay on firmer and more familiar ground. In particular I admire the way that Kottler allows himself (and by inference, therefore, me too) to have less than squeaky clean motives for the clinical work that we do. It comes as a relief to read words like the following from a distinguished figure in the field of psychotherapy:

> I frequently catch myself saying and doing things in sessions for my own entertainment. I ask questions only to satisfy my curiosity. I let clients dig themselves in holes just to see how they will get out. I inflate my sense of importance so clients will admire me more. I probably see clients longer than is absolutely necessary because I need the money. Oh, I justify all of these actions, convincing myself they are all for the client's good. I do not worry as much about this personal fallout because I am aware of it. I do genuinely worry about those instances when I do not catch myself meeting my own needs.
>
> (Kottler 1986: 41)

I imagine that we could all draw up our own list of shadowy manoeuvres and it might prove to be a cleansing and releasing exercise for each of us to set them down for sober contemplation – if only to serve as a healthy reminder of our imperfections when we are tempted to gaze adoringly at our own 'perfect' therapist self-image.

LOSS ISSUES FOR THE THERAPIST

Without our clients and patients we do not exist as therapists. We need them in order to define and confirm ourselves. 'Others tell one who one is' (Laing 1977: 94). Working as a therapist, as we have seen, brings many rewards and is frequently experienced by the counsellor as emotionally satisfying, identity enhancing, growthful and healing. I like the way Herron and Rouslin (1984: 81) put it – that 'doing psychotherapy can be zestful, fascinating, and packed with jumbo shrimp for the spirit'.

Counselling is a profession that also brings deprivation and loss. Perhaps we are willing to deal with so much loss, grief and anguish in what our clients bring to us as a way of rehearsing our own losses. Kottler (1986) has confronted this issue in writing about his own motivation as a therapist:

> I am afraid of dying, and worse, of being forgotten. I feel as though I am in the process of immortalizing myself with every disciple who goes out in the world with a part of me inside them. It is as if I can cheat the terror of death if only I can keep a part of me alive.
>
> (pp. 53–4)

If we go through enough loss that belongs to another we may come to bear our own losses, even the great and final one of our own mortality, more tolerably. If I can bear the pain of this person's anguish and stay with it, enormous as it is, I will be better equipped to bear my own losses when they come (and surely mine won't be as bad as this). In this way the wounded healer may be attempting to immunise themselves against further injury. The more I see that others are able to survive and grow through their losses, the more it becomes possible that this may be true for me too. I have witnessed this and there is hope.

Foremost among their own losses that an experienced counsellor will undergo is the forfeiture of innocence and naïvety. Our principal role is to listen to our clients unburden themselves of distressing and disturbing feelings and experiences. Our clients can only divest themselves of their burdens if we are open and receptive to receiving them. This demands full engagement and unfiltered listening which can leave us feeling unprotected. The challenge for the counsellor is the hugely demanding one of witnessing trauma without being overwhelmed or traumatised oneself. This is particularly true for counsellors who work to any extent with clients who have been abused, where they will need to 'contain material that will be of a deeply disturbing nature' and 'make contact at a deep level whilst remaining intact themselves' (Walker 1992: 197). The essence of this difficult task it to provide containment that is also experienced by the client as empathic companionship. The counsellor needs to be strong, resilient, and yet open to being moved and affected by the client's experience. If I can only hold the material and provide containment by switching off or dissociating from it, I may well be modelling and reinforcing the client's original response to their experience of abuse through discounting the impact of it, not only on myself but for my client.

A client gave me to read an account she had written of being sexually abused as a child. She had not felt able to speak aloud about this and writing it down became a way of separating herself sufficiently from the experience to begin to articulate it. I was very moved by what she had written and could not at first find any useful words to describe my response. I struggled with tears and knew that when I spoke she would hear a tremor in my voice. It felt very risky to let her see how affected I was. I said: 'My insides are lurching around as I read what you have written and I cannot begin to imagine what it was actually like for you to have experienced that' and I looked at her with tears in my eyes. She had been looking into her lap and fidgeting nervously as I read from the paper. Now she returned my gaze and her eyes were shining. She said: 'It means so much to me to see you are affected by what happened to me. It helps me to begin to feel that I am not wrong to feel so bad about it, and maybe that it *does* matter that this has been done to me'.

In another session with this client we talked about what it is like for her when she sees I am moved to tears by her predicament. These are her words: 'It's like you are giving me a present. It feels like a gift to me when you cry. When I see you are upset I can't pretend it isn't important any longer – it seems so real and it means you must respect me. When I see you crying I want to comfort you and when I think about it afterwards I think you must feel like that about me and it helps me to think "maybe *I'm* worth comforting"'. I asked her whether it became a burden for her when I became tearful and she replied: 'No, it is never that – I know you can look after yourself. It helps me – I know you must really care'. When this happens am I, I wonder, crying for my client as a counsellor in the grip of a strong countertransference, or as another human being who finds loss hard to bear? I'm not sure the theoretical distinction matters as much as the reality of the giving of the very human response.

In the course of our work we are likely to hear about many acts of human wickedness and depravity and to witness the open wounds and scars that these inflict. We cannot help but feel contaminated by such experiences and will, at some level, feel angry with our clients for soiling us with their pernicious material. It is important that we are able to acknowledge these feelings openly and discuss them with a trusted colleague or supervisor otherwise they are likely to fester as resentment and infiltrate the counselling relationship in insidious and destructive ways.

I find that my dreams often provide clues to my unacknowledged responses to clients or to the unexpressed dynamic between us. For example, when working with a client who had been neglected as a child I had several vivid dreams of mothering and protecting small children. This helped me to acknowledge my maternal feelings towards him and become freer to choose how to use or not use this impulse within our relationship. Clients can also populate our dreams with stories and images that are disturbing and which arise from their material. I will dream of things that I would never have dreamed of if they had not been pictured for me by my client. These are scenes from which I would rather have averted my eyes and in a sense they become the stigmata of my role. In this way I bear the scars of my clients' wounds.

I notice that I tend to dream about a client when I am carrying material from the client that I need to debrief. It can also happen in what seems to be a more direct response to the client's immediate needs. I worked with a client who for several weeks experienced relentless and horrific flashbacks of abuse that seriously disturbed his sleep to the point of utter exhaustion. One night I had a nightmare that was populated with spectres from my client's story and which gave me a restless and anxious night. I saw the client the following day and he told me that for the first time in weeks he had enjoyed a dreamless and relatively undisturbed sleep.

A further price we pay for involving ourselves fully with our clients and allowing them to matter to us is the pain of loss and separation that we experience when they leave us or let us down. I have had some of the most rewarding relationships of my life with my clients and often it is hard for me to say good-bye, even as I willingly let them go. I think these words of Rice's sum up for me the client's experience and my own at the end of a profitable period of counselling: 'I see that we don't just leave bad homes, but we leave good homes too. It's not an empty, lonely feeling, but a full sadness of losing them' (Rice 1994). Counsellors are aware of the built-in mortality of their therapeutic alliances and know that they will need to survive the death of cherished relationships many times over in the course of their professional careers. The challenge that arises from this awareness is how much I come to protect myself from the pain of separation by holding myself aloof and at a distance from my clients and how much I am willing to experience a depth of mutuality with my clients that may leave *me* feeling bereft as they move on to other relationships (or indeed leave me in precipitous ways including, even, suicide).

I notice that as we move towards the negotiated end of a counselling relationship I often begin to feel shyer, more self-conscious and rather vulnerable with my client. This is sometimes in marked contrast to how I have generally felt with the client when we have been in mid-process. Even when the client may have been feeling chaotic, defensive, distressed or disturbed, I have overall maintained a sense of calmness wherein I have felt still and settled. It is as if I feel more sure of my role and my place in the process when my client is clearly and deeply engaged in their own process of 'working through'. As the client reaches stiller waters and the harbour of our journey's end comes into view something shifts for me personally. This is something about meeting the client differently, in a more equal relationship, and it can feel exposing. My client comes to see me more as a real and fallible person as their need to construct me as a figure they have needed to work something through with dissolves and gradually melts away. Perhaps it is that whereas we first met as counsellor and client, now we part as two equally vulnerable human beings.

Chapter 9

On the use of self in supervision

A therapist who is not in supervision should be regarded either with suspicion or awe.

(LeShan 1996)

Supervision that is to encourage the therapeutic use of self by the counsellor will emphasise attention given to the person of the counsellor as he or she lives in relationship with the client. Such supervision will focus primarily on the counsellor's own dynamics and reactions to clients rather than on case discussion, analysis of client problems, case work management, or counselling skills and techniques. Whilst acknowledgement and consideration of these aspects of the therapeutic work will need to take precedence on occasion, as a rule the counsellor will be principally encouraged to examine their own needs, drives, motivations and personal responses to clients as a way of developing their internal supervisor (Casement 1985) and enhancing their use of self.

It seems noteworthy to mention that although respondents in the therapist survey that is included in Chapters 5, 6 and 7 of this book were not asked about supervision, over half of them (thirty-four) mentioned the significance of supervision in the experiences of unorthodox practice that they wrote about. Thirty-one therapists wrote about the importance of good supervision in helping them to manage issues relating to unorthodox practice and the therapeutic use of self and three mentioned difficulties experienced where supervision had been inadequate or inappropriate (e.g. where supervision was provided by a line manager who represented the interests of an organisation rather than acted as an impartial consultant).

One researcher and writer who has considered supervision as a vehicle for the development of individual styles of counselling is Alvin

Mahrer (1996a, 1997). Mahrer has, over a period of forty years, developed and refined an approach to supervision designed to enhance the therapist's use of self which he terms 'experiential supervision'. Mahrer's approach[1] is concerned with helping the supervisee/trainee to consider deeply and explicitly the question 'how do I think about psychotherapy?' as a means of helping her or him develop an individual, authentic and personal framework for counselling. Mahrer asserts that people become different kinds of therapists depending on what is inside them and that the most effective therapists are those who have developed an individual style that most comfortably fits with their deeper, internal, personal framework. The essential question that guides Mahrer's interventions as a supervisor is 'can we probe inside you and find a deeper, inner framework for your thinking?'

This question is explored through the use of audio tapes of counselling sessions which therapists bring to group supervision. The supervisee is asked to select a portion of the tape that they find compelling in some way – it might be the part of a session they feel really good about, or embarrassed or bad about, or maybe it is a part they feel unsure, confused or bewildered about. Alternatively the supervisee might be encouraged to select a portion of tape that illustrates the part of the session where the therapist began knowing what change consists of for their client – perhaps that part where they first notice the beginning of possibilities for change and glimpse the direction that change might take in the client.

The supervisee is then asked probing (often 'why?') questions to lead them deeper and deeper into an exploration of their rationale of helping until the bedrock of principles governing their own methodology and philosophy of counselling is uncovered and made explicit. So, for example, a member of the supervision group might ask the presenting supervisee: 'Why do you consider that to have been a bad intervention?', followed by supplementary probes that help the person expand on the aims and assumptions governing their own personal theory of therapy. If the supervisee selects a section of tape they feel good about it can be useful for all the members of the supervision group to write down or say why they think it is good. In this way more than one person can begin to articulate their own principles of change from the material presented. Supervisees are encouraged to keep an ongoing log or journal of their emerging personal framework and principles and to experiment with applying these more explicitly in their therapeutic work as a way of helping them to develop and integrate a consistent and clearly articulated personal theory and style of counselling.

Mahrer's approach has been outlined here because it seems to me to convey two essential features relating to the use of self in supervision – the first being the immediate and challenging quality of the dialogue which takes place between supervisor and supervisee, and the second being the way that supervisees are encouraged to look inside and trust that they will find their own way forward. Supervisees undergoing Mahrer's method of supervision are likely to uncover more about themselves as they turn their attention inward and examine their personal reactions to clients. The following section of this chapter focuses on the supervisee in attempting to articulate the quality of learning that may arise for counsellors when they are open to exploring and utilising their emotional responses to clients as a means of extending and deepening the range of their therapeutic interventions.

MANAGING EMOTIONAL RESPONSES TO CLIENTS

In Chapter 8 I discussed the importance of trainee counsellors receiving permission to have strong feelings in response to their clients. Here I will consider how supervisors can help their supervisees formulate their own immediate responses into interventions that can benefit their clients.

Having a powerful emotional or physical feeling with a client is perhaps the clearest and most immediate way that we can make use of ourselves in our counselling work. Our clients will usually know when we are experiencing a feeling with them, even when our words cannot do justice to the experience. When someone tells me of deeply anguished, despairing or humiliating experiences they have undergone – and may be reliving in my presence – there comes a point where I know I cannot share their unique agony and when I sense that to attempt an empathic response in words would be futile and shallow. This person is taking me beyond what I have experienced. How can I presume to walk in their moccasins? To attempt it would be a pretence at understanding. To say at such times: 'I know how you're feeling' may be experienced by the client as incongruent, patronising and manifestly untrue.

On such occasions I would contend that remaining congruent is paramount over all other attitudes and responses and pre-determines my ability to be authentically empathic. Maintaining congruence is likely to give rise to what Bozarth (1984: 69) has termed emergent and idiosyncratic forms of empathy – those which are anchored in the client's experience, rather than the counsellor's skills of reflection. Such responses, he asserts, emphasise: '(1) the transparency of the therapist in relationship to the other person; (2) the person-to-person encounter in the relationship; and (3) the intuition of the therapist'. Whilst we cannot always be sure of truly empathising in the sense of understanding our clients' experience and conveying that understanding in words, we *can* constantly strive to achieve congruence – that is extending a genuine response to our clients through remaining open to our own responses. As Lietaer (1993: 23) has remarked 'there can be no openness to the client's experience if there is no openness to one's own experience. And without openness there can be no empathy either. In this sense, congruence is the "upper limit" of the capacity for empathy'. Congruence, if it can be experienced at relational depth rather than merely portrayed (Mearns 1997a, 1997b), is likely to be more genuinely compassionate and therapeutic than a glib or assumed empathy. Here is an example of what I mean.

My client is recalling in anguished words the relived agony of very early childhood abuse. He says: 'I can just see this tiny child with a blank face lying on the bed. It's overwhelming. I have this hollow inside me but it feels so heavy at the same time'. If I had attempted an empathic response to this, probably the best I could have mustered would have been something like: 'You feel unbearable sadness and pain at seeing this image of yourself being hurt as a tiny child'. However this would be an incongruent response to the extent that I do not in any way know what it feels like, as a two-year-old, to be abused as my client has been abused and, further, it is not an intervention that genuinely conveys my own feelings which are, predominantly, outrage and horror. I cannot understand or know what one person's unique and individual trauma is like and to make a pretence of so doing can be patronising and insulting. What I actually say to my client is: 'I cannot imagine what you feel when you look at that image of yourself as a two-year-old. When I think about a tiny child being hurt in that way I just wish I had been there to save you from it'. My client responds: 'No one came and saved me. I desperately wanted someone to come and stop it happening'. Until then my client has been dry eyed and numb. Now his face crumples and he begins to weep and thereby takes a first small step towards the gargantuan task that lies ahead of mourning the murder of his childhood.

At this point I think it is useful to state that I see a difference between sympathy, empathy and compassion in relation to the use of self. When

I am merely sympathetic to my client's predicament I may feel their anguish but am in a more or less static position in relation to them. Sympathy disempowers both me and the client because in expressing sympathy I am just feeling awful with them and have largely lost my ability to think and act on their behalf. I might say something like: 'My God, how terrible that this happened to you' and this brings us up against the experience but does not provide a way of loosening or exploring it. When I am able to experience empathy with my client, in contrast, I am able to be separate and objective and simultaneously think and feel my way into what they might be experiencing. Whilst I can never know exactly what this is like, I have sufficient understanding to make an 'as if' response that may offer them a symbol or metaphor that can serve to illuminate their experience more clearly to them, for example when I say something like: 'It is as if this despair is so huge that it might swallow you up if you dare to talk about it'.

Yet if we remain capable only of empathic resonance our capacity for helping will be limited. Casement has captured the essence of this limitation.

> Empathic identification is not enough, as it can limit a therapist to seeing what is familiar, or is similar to his own experience. Therapists therefore have to develop an openness to, and respect for, feelings and experiences that are quite unlike their own.
>
> (Casement 1985: 95)

Compassion, on the other hand, has a quality of engagement and investment in the relationship that takes the therapist's responses beyond the limits of empathy. Lewin (1996: 28) has asserted that 'compassion is the core value that animates psychotherapy and gives it soul and staying power'. Brazier (1995: 191) states that 'compassion means to wish others free of suffering' and in this sense it seems to me that compassion is a higher order form of empathy that involves greater mutuality. In compassion the experiencing of emotion often precedes, but does not preclude, the ability to think and act, as sympathy often does. When I experience compassion I am hit first by my feelings as a response to whatever is going on for the client, and may need to allow these to form more fully before I can make sense of them sufficiently to make a verbal response. I may experience a shudder, a lump in my throat, a lurch in my stomach, the sense of tears welling up, a sensation of coldness or hotness, a feeling of heaviness or of lightness, a sense of nausea or panic. Frequently there will be a feeling of being struck dumb in that instance as if the strength and impact of the feeling have moment-arily robbed me of my ability to say anything meaningful. After that the thinking comes and may produce words that are clumsy and tentative as I struggle to give form to my feeling and offer it to my client.

At such moments I am so aware of my own sensations that I am likely to respond in 'I' rather than 'you' terms: 'I felt like a weight fell on my chest as you described your busy weekend. And then I thought "it sounds so bleak and empty in all that activity"'. Often in these moments it feels as if I register the impact of something that is the client's almost as if they need first to locate it in me before they can take it back and experience it as their own. To the words spoken above my client responded: 'It doesn't mean anything, all that activity. I just keep going because I'm terrified that if I stop I will just feel like killing myself again – although I know that thought is always there, anyway, in the background'. I suppose I am saying here that compassion is a form of countertransference, although I think it devalues a very human and authentic response to think of it only in these terms, as something which the client projects into the therapist.

Compassion has been said to be 'about succouring without smother-ing' (Lewin 1996: 85) and while countertransference may be experi-enced from a position of detached objectivity, compassion only comes to life in moments of true intimacy where therapist and client are fully accessible to, and involved with, one another within the relationship. Where compassion feeds the relationship therapist and client are im-pelled to search for meaning together rather than feeling that one has to look to the other for answers. 'Compassion always insists that we stay in the difficult area of doubt. Compassion requires of us a healing measure of felt uncertainty that allows us to keep on trying' (Lewin 1996: 329). Compassion comes to life in the way that the therapist uses themselves and in so far as they are able to become a resonating chamber for the client's emotions. Congruence and compassion open the way to using what Kopp (1974: 3) considers to be the therapist's primary in-strument of healing: 'the personal vulnerability of his own trembling self'.

I have said that compassion often takes away my speech. If I can't, in the moment, muster adequate words, I try instead to stay with the fullness of my emotional response to what the client is revealing to me, without diluting or distancing myself from it in order to protect myself. This may, as Lietaer has suggested, involve 'a regressive contact with one's own deeper feeling levels' (Lietaer 1993: 27). Contrary to what is often said about the need for counsellors to disengage from their own personal issues when they are with clients, here I may need instead to allow the intrusion of my own painful experiences and feelings in order to provide a full and congruent response to my client. For example, I may not be able to experience fully my feelings about my client being abused unless there is resonance with my own feelings of being used, exploited or betrayed. In these moments I will sit quietly with my client and trust that what I am feeling will come through in my gaze towards them. Maintaining gaze is important even if the client is unable to look back as he or she is usually able to sense being held or dropped in the counsellor's attention. I think these words which clients have spoken to me are illustrative of such moments:

> 'Even though you couldn't know how unbearable it was for me then, I felt you came there with me, rescued me, and brought me back'.

> 'I know you can't really understand what it was like for me but I sense that you have had losses too and so you know what it feels like'.

> 'Your eyes are very expressive. I can see you're upset and that helps me to feel cared for. If you care for me I might be worth caring about'.

> 'I cannot bear to look at you today. If I do I will have to see how much you care about me when all I want is to be left alone to curl up in a corner and die'.

> 'You held me in your arms when I was really upset – even though you sat on the other side of the room and never ever touched me'.

Even experienced counsellors are sometimes scared of feeling strong emotions with their clients. The supervisor has a vital role to play in helping supervisees to live in and with their feelings, to make sense of them and to use them as a guide to how they might intervene with their clients. The supervisor's task, as Charney puts it, is to help supervisees read their feelings 'as signposts for what the patient evoked' which can then be used 'to advance the therapy' (Charney 1986: 20). The supervision space, as Williams (1995: 19) has asserted, 'must be able to contain storms, distress, despair at humanity and oneself, hard-headed planning, and tough mutual evaluation'. Thus the task of the supervisor is frequently concerned with enabling the counsellor to remain buoyant and clear thinking in the midst of much turbulence. Supervision is often about how the supervisor helps the therapist to stay 'poised' (Bramley 1996) and to hold their nerve when faced with distressed, demanding and difficult clients. For instance, it may be that my supervisee is frightened of 'losing it' and falling apart if they feel upset with a client. Or they may be scared of their own negative feelings as if these might damage the client or the counselling relationship if they are acknowledged. It is hard at first to know that damage is more likely to occur through covert responses stemming from suppressed feelings than through the authentic living of strong emotions in the fullness of the moment in which they arise.

If I am really furious with my client for, yet again, arriving twenty minutes late and then trying to keep me over time and I do not allow myself to know this I am likely to lapse into any number of indirect or diluted responses. I may be generally a bit huffy; I may smile as sweetly as ever but hold myself in a tense and ungiving posture; I may get into explaining the importance of clear time boundaries and reasoning with the client to keep to them in future; I may give the appearance of attending to the client whilst secretly fantasising about how to get even – I am thinking of calling her bluff next time and demanding to know what's going on, or of joining the game by not hurrying back from lunch myself; perhaps I'll make sure I have my nose buried in a book next time she arrives late so that she sees my time is precious. All of these responses are ways that I diminish myself and my client by being inauthentic and not responding from my genuine feelings.

I am not suggesting that counsellors should be encouraged by their supervisors to blurt out any strong emotional response that the client triggers in them. There is a common misperception amongst people who have not read the work of Carl Rogers carefully that he advocates telling the client 'straight' what you are feeling, whether it is boredom or any other feeling. In discussing genuineness Rogers in fact advised caution against unbridled self-disclosure:

> Since this concept [i.e. genuineness] is liable to misunderstanding, let me state that it does not mean that the therapist burdens his client with overt expression of all his feelings. Nor does it mean that the therapist discloses his total self to his client. It does mean, however, that the therapist denies to himself none of the feelings he is experiencing and that he is willing to experience transparently any *persistent* feelings that exist in the relationship and to let these be known to the client.
>
> (Rogers, cited in Lietaer 1993: 17)

This is what Rogers said on this subject in an interview towards the end of his life and I think it sets the record straight.

> When I am with a client, I like to be aware of my feelings, and if there are feelings which run contrary to the conditions of therapy and occur persistently, then I am sure I want to express them. But there are also other feelings. For instance, sometimes, with a woman client I feel: 'this woman is sexually attractive, I feel attracted to her.' I would not express that unless it comes up as an issue in therapy. But, if I felt annoyed by the fact that she was always complaining, let us say, and I kept feeling annoyed, then, I would express it.
>
> The important thing is to be aware of one's feeling and then you can decide whether it needs to be expressed or is appropriate to express.
>
> (Rogers, in Baldwin 1987: 46)

The important sequence, to which Rogers alludes here, is first, the awareness of feelings (which is crucially determined by the counsellor's willingness to feel them); second, a period of incubation of those feelings (which may just be a few seconds, or several weeks that perhaps incorporate a visit to one's supervisor to discuss them); and third, the decision about what response to make arising from the feelings.

Normally, in the face of persistent feelings, I do not make a one-off response, but rather embark on a gradient of responding that gradually moves up 'through the gears'. It is important to give the client every opportunity to come forth of their own accord rather than being dragged out into the light of exposure by the counsellor. The best counselling is that which occurs through invitation rather than demand. In order to be able to do this I have learned that I need first to spend some time with my feeling, in this case my fury, and get through it sufficiently to emerge the other side into clearer air that will give me some thinking space. Supervision is a place where this can happen. My supervisor can help me to express my feelings without censure and absorb what I need to debrief or get rid of. She might then ask a facilitative question that we can both consider together, such as: 'I wonder what it means for the client to provoke such fury in you?' This helps me to switch from my own dynamic to that of the client and releases me from the pressure to do something to relieve myself of my fury. We can then explore some possibilities together. Is my client so sure that I cannot like spending time with her that she lets me off the hook by arriving late? Is she provoking my fury in the hope that I will vent it on her and 'prove' how unlikeable she is? Does she inveigle me to go over time because she knows I probably have someone else to see and she wants to keep me to herself? (All of these things have proved to be the case with different clients I have worked with.)

With my imaginary client I would probably begin by simply letting her know that I had noticed we were starting late, as we had done in previous sessions, and allow her to respond if she wished. One of the most wise and fruitful interventions a counsellor can make is that of letting the client know that you have 'noticed' something. It is an indirect intervention that both invites the client to respond and also allows them the choice of not responding, or of making a partial or indirect response. As Hycner (1991) has observed 'the human condition is to be both revealed and "hidden"' and therefore 'indirectness may sometimes be a compassionate stance' (p. 40). Allowing a space for the client to comment, but not pressuring them to do so, may bring forth a direct response from the client that clears the air and immediately lets me know what the difficulty is so that I can begin to help. This happened with a client to whom I said: 'I notice that we are starting fifteen minutes after your appointment time, as we did last week'. She replied: 'That's because I was hiding in the bushes outside, like I did last week, because I was too frightened to come in. I was hoping you'd hear me and come out to find me'. Clearly with such a response we are back in business and can begin to explore why bushes seem to provide more of a sanctuary than does the counselling room. With another person who was habitually ten minutes late for his session I made an observation about this and he told me that he always hid in the toilets downstairs until there was nobody around before he came up as he could not bear anyone to look at him. We were then able to move to talking about how difficult he found it to stay in the room and be looked at by me.

If an observation seems insufficient to engage a response I will, the next time I broach the subject, move to providing a more direct, if still gentle, invitation. So I might say: 'It strikes me that we do not use twenty minutes at the start of your session and yet we seem to run out of time at the end. I'd be interested to know how you feel about this'. Again I am leaving the client room to manoeuvre. It is not the counsellor's task to unmask the client before she is ready to divest herself of her protective armour. She is more likely to reveal the real difficulty if she is not backed into a corner where, quite understandably, she would become more pre-occupied with fighting me off and making her escape than in coming out for a direct meeting with me.

To link all of this back to supervision – is to say that we may at times need a hand from our supervisor to help with acknowledging our feelings, clearing a space for our thinking, considering the client's perspective, and formulating possible responses. Carroll (1998) in speaking about supervision and spirituality has described supervision as a 'form of retreat'. He suggests that in supervision 'we retreat in order to return differently and of course when we are different so are others'. Supervision provides a forum for therapist reflexivity that parallels client reflexivity. If reflexivity is a turning back on self (Rennie 1992) then supervision can create an environment in which the therapist actively turns their attention inward and, with the supervisor's help, searches out that which was missed, overlooked, or only partially formed in the therapy session. In this way the therapist learns to work actively on their own and the client's material both in and out of counselling sessions, in the same way that the client is encouraged to continue exploring their internal world between sessions in order to make the most of the therapeutic process and relationship. I have written elsewhere about a model of supervision that can be used to guide the supervisee through such a process (Page and Wosket 1994).

As a supervisor, there is one intervention that I use again and again which I have found to be key in helping supervisees to respond to clients from their own feelings. It is this:

'What would it be like if you found a way of communicating that [feeling] to your client?'

Although this is a simple question it is potentially a very powerful one. The fact that the counsellor has needed their supervisor to help them discover their feeling towards the client means that something has been missed or suppressed. I would not need to ask this question if the counsellor was able to be fully congruent with themselves and their client. What the question does is to help the counsellor gain or regain their therapeutic connection to the client where this has been blocked or disrupted. It invites the supervisee to consider what impact the client is having on them as well as how they might respond to the client. The question creates a bridge between the authentic self of the counsellor and the authentic self of the client when it may be that the dialogue between them has degenerated to the point of two false and constructed selves interacting from fixed positions (for example, where the counsellor had become the bestower of wisdom and the client the supplicant).

At such times it is as if I need my supervisor to help me find and articulate what my real self wants to say to the real self of my client. In order to do this the supervisor needs to be able, with sensitivity, to attune themselves to picking up what the counsellor might be missing, or what the counsellor's underlying feeling may be, or what it is that the client may need, or be trying to say. The question then becomes the means by which the relationship or the process can become more intact. There are many variations of this question. Here are a couple of examples of dialogue from supervision sessions that illustrate how the question might be asked and the impact it can have.

In this first example the supervisor is Val and the supervisee is Ben.

BEN: My dilemma is that I feel very stuck with this client. We seem to be getting nowhere. I keep trying to find ways of challenging her strengths but she won't listen. She doesn't think she has any strengths.

VAL: What does that feel like when you are with your client and you experience that sense of getting nowhere?

BEN: I feel like I am running out of things to say. I get anxious that I am not helping her and I wonder if I should call it a day and stop seeing her.

VAL: If you could find a way of communicating some of that to your client so that it became a gift that she could receive from you, rather than giving her a burden, what might you do?

BEN: My first thought was that I would stop trying to think of things to say.

VAL: And what might happen then?

BEN: I would sit quietly with her and look at her.

VAL: And if you sit quietly here and imagine yourself doing that now, with your client, what is it like?

BEN: I feel quite emotional and I notice I'm starting to well up. I think I would look at her tenderly and she would see that I care about her. [Stays with his feelings in silence for a few moments.] Now I feel like I want to say: 'I don't think I've heard how hard it is for you to keep going and you have been trying to tell me'.

In the next example the supervisor is Val and the supervisee is Ali.

ALI: I think my difficulty is about how to manage the ending with this client, now that we have contracted to finish after four more sessions.

VAL: What's going on for you in that dilemma?

ALI: I feel quite anxious and I think it's about how much of myself to bring into the ending.

VAL: How would it be if you found a way of saying that to your client, in a way that she could hear it?

ALI: We've had a good working relationship and I'm not sure she knows how much I like her and will miss her. I think I'd like her to know that before she leaves but it would be moving to a different level.

VAL: It would be more personal and you are wondering what that would be like for both of you?

ALI: I think it would be OK. My hunch is that it would mean a lot to her to know that I like her and will miss her. I think I need to say it in the next session so that we've got time to deal with anything that comes up for her and that she'd like to say to me.

VAL: It could be quite significant for her and you want to be careful.

ALI: She came with such low self esteem and didn't think anyone would like her. I'd really like her to know that I like her a lot as a person. It wasn't right to say it earlier because she needed to work out for herself that she is likeable, rather than me tell her.

VAL: So would you just come out and say it, or do you need to prepare the ground in some way?

ALI: I think I probably need to negotiate with her first that it would be OK for us to say something about our relationship as part of the ending. Then she would know I might want to say something more personal and she would have a chance to think about anything she wanted to say to me. I don't want to catch her off her guard or just dump my feelings on her.

These examples illustrate what I consider to be the essence of supervision, which is to encourage counsellors to bring more of themselves into their interactions with clients. This usually amounts to helping them find the courage to be more immediate and congruent with their clients. Inexperienced counsellors, in particular, can be fearful of burdening their clients with their own uncertainty or vulnerability and do not see that by allowing clients to see their humanity they may be bestowing a gift on the client that he or she may be glad to receive and well able to make use of. When the client is someone who inhabits an internal world where loving feelings towards the self are experienced as alien or quickly suppressed it can be a revelation for them to know that they have made an emotional impact on their counsellor.

THE SUPERVISOR'S FEELINGS

If supervisees need to be helped and encouraged to respond from their feelings, I think the same is also true of supervisors. I have learned that my internal responses when with a supervisee usually provide the best clue to what is going on for the counsellor, the client, or both. It is as if I am in some way 'standing in for the client' and listening out for what the counsellor might have missed or what the client is trying to get the counsellor to hear, but is unable to say directly. I am sure that this ability has its roots in my own experience of being a client, more than in what I have learned about the skills and processes of being a counsellor or supervisor. It is akin to the process that Casement (1985, 1990) calls 'trial identification', wherein the supervisee is encouraged to consider the client's perspective whilst contemplating possible interventions. Here, as the supervisor, I strive to gain a sense of what may be going on for the client in the relationship with their counsellor. This is a step further removed from the client in one sense yet it can bring the client back into focus in an immediate and powerful way. It is as though the supervisor, through attending to their own 'internal client', acts as a conduit for the needs of the supervisee's client and gives a voice to those needs. It normally occurs when I find myself saying something that arises from a certain quickening of my internal responses – a sensation more familiar to me from being in the client role than from being a counsellor or supervisor – rather than from any external frame of knowing about theory or process. At these moments I am likely to say 'if I was your client I might need [or want, or feel, or dread, or avoid . . .]'. Here is an example of what I mean.

My supervisee, Mati, was discussing her work with a very distressed young woman who had many anxiety symptoms, including a phobia about death. She had made a number of para-suicide attempts and frequently self-harmed. The client's mother had just been diagnosed with a serious illness and the client was avoiding talking about this with her mother. With the client's agreement Mati had spoken to her doctor about the possibility of a psychiatric referral.

MATI: I feel as if we've had a bit of a breakthrough. She took some tablets again a few weeks ago and ended up at casualty and I've been quite challenging with her about this.

VAL: You confronted her about it.

MATI: Yes, and it helped that in the last supervision session we had spent some time looking at my feelings about whether I felt I could help her or not and how committed I was to the relationship. I felt more confident about what I could offer her and I think that helped me to put my cards on the table. I let her know that I cared about her and told her that she didn't need to keep having crises in order to come and see me. I told her that I would be happy to see her, at least until the end of the academic year, if she would like to come.

VAL: You made a clear offer of help and challenged the acting out in a very supportive way.

MATI: I think she heard it like that. She really seemed to listen, especially when I said that I know she feels very isolated and lonely and that I would really like to listen and try to understand how she is feeling. She even became tearful, very briefly, and I think that's the first time she's shown her feelings. Normally she tries to be strong in the session.

VAL: I can see how you feel you've made a breakthrough.

MATI: And the next time she came she seemed more optimistic. She said she would like to continue with the counselling. When we looked at what she might like to get from seeing me she said she'd like to try to tell me more about how she felt when her dad left, which was a very difficult time in her life. She even looked ahead and said that she'd like to get to the point where perhaps she'd be able to go and see the psychiatrist to talk about her fear of death.

VAL: And what did you say when she said that?

MATI: I said that it was really good that she is beginning to think about what she wants and that I would support her in going to see the psychiatrist if that happened.

VAL: I asked you that because I was thinking: 'Why can't she talk to *you* about her fear of death?' If I was your client I think I might like to know that it would be alright for me to talk to you about that, even though I might not dare to think that I could.

MATI: Oh my God! Of course – I totally missed that! She's scared about her mother dying and can't talk to her about it and I'm giving her the same message – 'this is too awful and scary for us to talk about, you'll have to take it to the psychiatrist'. How could I have missed that? It's so important.

VAL: I think it would be easy to miss it. It's such a scary subject for her that it would be hard for her to let you come close to it. How do you feel about the possibility of her talking to you about it?

MATI: It would be OK. I'm sure I could manage it and I know I could get help in supervision when I needed it.

VAL: Well perhaps it's not too late to say something.

MATI: Yes, I definitely want to do that. Next time I see her I'll say that
if the time comes when she wants to talk about her feelings about
death and her mum being ill, I hope she will consider talking to me
as I'd really like to hear about what that's like for her.

This process of trial identification by the supervisor can also be applied
to a consideration of what might be going on for the supervisee, that he
or she is finding difficult to acknowledge or express.

My supervisee, Aisha, a part-time student counsellor, was bringing me
up to date on her case load of clients. She talked briefly about Bren who
hadn't turned up for the last two sessions and who, she had now heard
from a tutor, would be deferring for a semester and soon leaving college. She appeared ready to move on to tell me about another client. As
she spoke I was aware of saying to myself : 'I'd feel pretty pissed off if
a client of mine who I'd been working with for twenty sessions just
stopped coming. I'd probably want to follow them up to try to find out
what was happening'. Rather than dismissing this thought as irrelevant
or simply my own issue about non-attending clients, I was prompted to
ask my supervisee: 'How do you feel about him just leaving without
letting you know?'
    In response, Aisha said that she felt OK about the client going as
they seemed to have reached an impasse. She was, in any case, feeling
overworked and losing Bren would leave her with more energy to
give to her remaining two clients who were making better progress. I
responded by saying: 'You sound almost relieved that he has gone.
Like it's easier to let him go than stay connected'.
    Aisha looked uncomfortable and said 'I know I'm squirming at what
you just said. I feel very resistant in my belly to the thought of following him up in any way'. I encouraged her to stay with her resistance
and talk from it. Aisha talked about her feelings for the client in the last
few sessions. While she thought she had been empathic, in talking about
him now she realised that what she had actually felt was irritation. She
traced this feeling to the fact that the client darts from one issue to
another in different sessions and this makes it hard for her to stay with
him and develop the relationship. The dialogue developed as follows:

VAL: What are the issues that he brings?
AISHA: He talks a lot, but not in any depth, about past relationships and
how they never work out. He says they are either too intense or too
undemanding.

VAL: And which of these was your relationship with him most like?

AISHA: [After some thought] I think it was becoming too intense. We were starting to get a bit too close to feelings that it is difficult for him to talk about. I can see now that I'm in danger of allowing him to repeat the pattern and just drop out of our relationship.

As we talked more about the client Aisha began to notice that her feelings of irritation towards him dissipated and she felt both more empathic and more in tune with what the client needed – which she now realised was someone to stick with him through the impasse. At the following supervision session she related that she had sent the client a brief letter wishing him well and inviting him, if he wished, to come back to see her on his return to college.

PARALLEL PROCESSES AND THE USE OF SELF

Readers of this book are likely to be familiar with the concept of the parallel process in supervision (Calligor 1984; Doehrman 1976; Mattinson 1977; Searles 1955). It occurs where something in the relationship and the encounter between the supervisor and the supervisee appears to mirror or parallel something of what is occurring between the counsellor and client. It can work in a number of directions and is, as Williams (1995: 7) has observed, 'more of a multi-lane highway than a one-way valve'. For instance, a dynamic that originates between a supervisor and her supervisee may come to be played out in the counselling session, as in the following example. The supervisor is feeling anxious because of organisational pressures in her place of work. She conducts supervision in her office at work where some of her anxiety spills over into the supervision session and is conveyed towards the supervisee as he discusses his client work. As a consequence, the supervisee then acts in an apprehensive or agitated manner towards his client in the next counselling session.

The parallel process in supervision is frequently activated by the supervisor's internal responses – thoughts, feelings, sensations, fantasies, images – to what the supervisee is presenting. Even though, as Williams (1995) observes, 'supervisors may fear imposing what might only be their own whimsical narcissism when they introduce "off the wall" statements of personal feelings' (p. 157), they do well to be alert to this manifestation of the use of self which can provide a potent source of learning for both supervisor and supervisee. When supervisors avoid the risks involved in disclosing personal responses 'not only are their own sessions flat, but their trainees follow their example and never bring forward in sessions with clients "what is going on" for them; a sterile orthodoxy rules up and down the line, a dissociative parallel process starting from the top' (Williams 1995: 157). The following example from a supervision session illustrates the use of an 'off the wall' statement, the effect of which the reader may judge. Commentary to the dialogue is given in brackets. The supervisor is Val, the supervisee is Shaun.

SHAUN: I feel as if I'm not being as helpful to my client as I would like to be. I feel we're stuck although he says he is getting a lot out of the counselling.

VAL: What does your client say he is getting out of the counselling?

SHAUN: We had a review session recently and he said: 'I feel that when I come to counselling it is as if I confess to you and am forgiven and then I can manage to keep going until the next time I see you'. I feel really uncomfortable with this. He is investing so much in me and I feel scared that I will not be able to do enough to prevent him from sinking into a decline or even killing himself.

[Shaun then proceeds to give me an enormous amount of detail about the client, his family background and present circumstances. His words come thick and fast and move us away from the previous focus. I open my mouth several times and attempt to speak. Whenever I do so Shaun speaks more rapidly and loudly as if he is afraid I will interrupt him before he has finished. I feel overloaded with information and cannot take any more in and I give up trying to intervene and start listening to myself instead of trying to listen to Shaun. A voice inside me is saying 'I wish you'd shut up'. I start to smile at the thought of saying this as it seems so rude and yet I am nearly bursting with it. Shaun notices my smile and stops in mid flow.]

SHAUN: You're smiling at me. Why?

VAL: Because I want to say: 'I wish you'd shut up. I need some space to think about what you said at the start'. [We both laugh.]

SHAUN: And I'm not letting you by giving you all this stuff that you don't want.

VAL: I'm just getting confused. I can't make sense of it all – but I *am* wondering if this is what your client does – gives you lots of stuff

to keep you from thinking about what you need to think about
when you are with him.

SHAUN: He does it all the time! Every week he brings something different and I don't know what it will be. He just pours it out, like a
confessional.

VAL: And what do you do with it?

SHAUN: I guess I just receive it. It's quite flattering to feel that I am the
only person that he tells any of this to.

[We are then able to talk about how the client has seduced Shaun
into colluding that he has the power to give his client 'absolution'.
We consider together how Shaun has allowed the client to give
him a great deal of power which then leaves his client feeling very
dependent on him. In turn Shaun feels responsible for the client's
safety and welfare. We explore how Shaun might start to invite the
client to take some of his own power back, so that next time the
client asks for absolution Shaun might say to him something that
promotes more reflexivity, like: 'It is difficult for you to forgive
yourself and to feel that you can find your own way ahead'.]

This vignette gives a sense of the powerful and immediate learning that
can arise in supervision when interpersonal cues are picked up and used
by the supervisor. This kind of learning is unique to supervision in that
it arises from the opportunity for supervisor and supervisee to experience and thereby recapture the underlying dynamic being played out
between therapist and client which the counsellor may previously have
missed. Williams (1995: 266) has rightly observed that this kind of
learning 'cannot take place in the ivory tower of one's study, nor can it
be achieved exclusively in the vortex of client's difficulties. Supervision seems a useful "middle ground" between the two for challenge
and reflection on practice'.

Counsellors need the safeguards provided by regular, ongoing supervision if they are to give themselves, safely, permission to work in
uniquely creative and sometimes unorthodox ways. It is important for a
counsellor who is intent on liberating aspects of their unique helping
potential to have a supervisor who will be supportive of the development
of their use of self, rather than someone who has a fixed and intractable
or model-bound approach. Such work demands flexibility, humility,
forbearance and the toleration of difference on the part of the supervisor. These qualities are needed in good measure so that the supervisor
can enter the supervisee's frame of reference and allow them to venture
into territory which they themselves may be unfamiliar with without

feeling unduly anxious, punitive or envious. In short, as Villas-Boas Bowen (1986) has asserted 'supervisors need to create an atmosphere where supervisees [can] experience their own expertise and power' (p. 292) and discover their own personally authentic style. Paradoxically, in order to create such an atmosphere, a supervisor also needs a well developed sense of authority together with the ability to closely monitor their supervisees' practice. Clients will thrive safely on the unique helping capabilities of their counsellors when therapists have supervisors who can ensure that the work that is taking place is disciplined and ethical as well as being liberating and creative.

EPILOGUE

As I reach the point of concluding this book I am conscious of the difficulty of bringing to a close a subject that I feel I have only just begun to explore – both in these pages and also within myself and my counselling practice. So it feels not so much that I am finished, more that this is where I have to stop.

I am aware of having turned the spotlight only briefly on to small and selected aspects of what is a huge area needing illumination. Much more remains to be said about the therapeutic use of self. As I look back over what I have written, the thought comes to mind that I hope readers who have ventured this far will have the sense of having taken part in a stimulating conversation. Parts of good conversations tend to be repeated, embellished and used to prompt further reflection and discussion. I like to think that what I have said here about the use of self in counselling will be carried forward and may become part of other conversations, and particularly those that occur between therapists and their clients.

NOTE

1 Material in this section is derived from information given by Professor Alvin Mahrer at his workshop on Experiential Supervision held in June 1997 at Sheffield Hallam University.

Bibliography

Aebi, J. (1993) 'Nonspecific and specific factors in therapeutic change among different approaches to counselling', *Counselling Psychology Review*, 8, 3: 19–32.

AGC and PLB (1995) Advice, Guidance, Counselling and Psychotherapy Lead Body, *First Release of Standards*, Welwyn.

Anderson and Grimm (1985) *The Classic Fairy Tales of Anderson and Grimm*, London: Bracken Books (first published 1935).

Andrews, J. (1991) *The Active Self in Psychotherapy: an Integration of Therapeutic Styles*, Boston: Allyn and Bacon.

Angus, L. E. and Rennie, D. L. (1988) 'Therapist participation in metaphor generation: collaborative and noncollaborative styles', *Psychotherapy*, 25, 4: 552–60.

Aponte, H. J. (1982) 'The person of the therapist: the cornerstone of therapy', *Family Therapy Networker*, 6, 2: 19–21 and 46.

Aponte, H. J. and Winter, J. E. (1987) 'The person and practice of the therapist: treatment and training', in M. Baldwin and V. Satir (eds) *The Use of Self in Therapy*, Binghamton, NY: Haworth Press.

Ashworth, P. D. (1997) 'The variety of qualititative research. Part one: introduction to the problem', *Nurse Education Today*, 17: 215–8.

Atkinson, D. and Schein, S. (1986) 'Similarity in counseling', *The Counseling Psychologist*, 14, 2: 319–54.

Atkinson, D., Brady, S. and Casas, J. (1981) 'Sexual preference similarity, attitude similarity, and perceived counselor credibility and attractiveness', *Journal of Counseling Psychology*, 28, 6: 504–509.

BAC (1996a) *Criteria for Counsellor Accreditation*, Rugby: British Association for Counselling.

—— (1996b) *Ethical Guidelines for Monitoring, Evaluation and Research in Counselling*, Rugby: British Association for Counselling.

—— (1998) *Code of Ethics and Practice for Counsellors*, Rugby: British Association for Counselling.

Baldwin, D. C., Jr (1987) 'Some philosophical and psychological contributions to the use of self in therapy', in M. Baldwin and V. Satir (eds) *The Use of Self in Therapy*, Binghamton, NY: Haworth Press.

Baldwin, M. (1987) 'Interview with Carl Rogers on the use of self in therapy', in M. Baldwin and V. Satir (eds) *The Use of Self in Therapy*, Binghamton, NY: Haworth Press.

Baldwin, M. and Satir, V. (eds) (1987) *The Use of Self in Therapy*, Binghamton, NY: Haworth Press.

Barker, C. (1985) 'Interpersonal Process Recall in clinical training and research', in F. Watts (ed.) *New Developments in Clinical Psychology*, Leicester: British Psychological Society.

Barlow, D. H., Hayes, S. C. and Nelson, R. O. (1984) *The Scientist Practitioner: Research and Accountability in Clinical and Educational Settings*, New York: Pergamon.

Bergin, A. E. and Garfield, S. L. (1994) 'Overview, trends and future issues', in A. E. Bergin and S. L. Garfield (eds) *Handbook of Psychotherapy and Behavior Change* (4th edn), New York: John Wiley.

Bergin, A. E. and Strupp, H. H. (1972) *Changing Frontiers in the Science of Psychotherapy*, Chicago: Aldine.

Berman, J. S. and Norton, N. C. (1985) 'Does professional training make a therapist more effective?', *Psychological Bulletin* 98: 401–6.

Beutler, L. E. and Consoli, A. J. (1993) 'Matching the therapist's interpersonal stance to clients' characteristics: contributions from systemic eclectic psychotherapy', *Psychotherapy* 30, 3: 417–22.

Beutler, L. E., Machado, P. P. and Neufeldt, S. A. (1994) 'Therapist variables', in A. E. Bergin and S. L. Garfield (eds) *Handbook of Psychotherapy and Behavior Change* (4th edn), New York: John Wiley.

BIIP (1997) British Institute of Integrative Psychotherapy, *The Assessment of Practitioner Competence*, (Draft Consultative Document), London.

Blatt, S. J., Sanislow, C. A., Zuroff, D. C. and Pilkonis, P. A. (1996) 'Characteristics of effective therapists: further analysis of data from the National Institute of Mental Health Treatment of Depression Collaborative Research Program', *Journal of Consulting and Clinical Psychology*, 64, 6: 1276–84.

Bloom, J. W. (1998) 'The ethical practice of WebCounseling', *British Journal of Guidance and Counselling*, 26, 1: 53–9.

Bond, T. and Shea, C. (1997) 'Professional issues in counselling', in S. Palmer and G. McMahon (eds) *Handbook of Counselling* (2nd edn), London: Routledge.

Bowlby, J. (1969) *Attachment and Loss*, vol. 1: *Attachment*, London: Hogarth Press.

Bozarth, J. D. (1984) 'Beyond reflection: emergent modes of empathy', in R. F. Levant and J. M. Shlien (eds) *Client-Centred Therapy and the Person-Centred Approach: New Directions in Theory, Research and Practice*, New York: Praeger.

Bradshaw J. (1991) *Homecoming: Reclaiming and Championing Your Inner Child*, London: Piatkus.

Brady, J. P., Davison, G. C., Dewald, P. A., Egan, G., Fadiman, J., Frank, J. D., Gill, M. M., Hoffman, I., Kempler, A. A., Lazarus, A. A., Raimy, V., Rotter, J. B. and Strupp, H. H. (1982) 'Some views on effective principles of psychotherapy', in M. R. Goldfried (ed.) *Converging Themes in Psychotherapy: Trends in Psychodynamic, Humanistic and Behavioral Practice*, New York: Springer.

Bragan, K. (1996) *Self and Spirit in the Therapeutic Relationship*, London: Routledge.

Bramley, W. (1996) *The Supervisory Couple in Broad-Spectrum Psychotherapy*, London: Free Association Books.

Brazier, D. (1993) 'The necessary condition is love: going beyond self in the person-centred approach', in D. Brazier (ed.) *Beyond Carl Rogers: Towards a Psychotherapy of the 21st Century*, London: Constable.

—— (1995) *Zen Therapy*, London: Constable.

Breakwell, G. M. (1989) *Facing Physical Violence*, London: BPS Books and Routledge.

Brightman, B. (1984) 'Narcissistic issues in the training experience of the psychotherapist', *International Journal of Psychoanalytic Psychotherapy*, 10: 293–317.

Buber, M. (1937) *I and Thou*, trans. R. G. Smith, Edinburgh: T. & T. Clark.

Bugental, J. F. (1964) 'The person who is the psychotherapist', *Journal of Consulting Psychology*, 28: 272–7.

—— (1987) *The Art of the Psychotherapist*, New York: Norton.

Burton, A. and Associates (1972) *Twelve Therapists: How They Live and Actualise Themselves*, San Francisco: Jossey-Bass.

Butler, S. F. and Strupp, H. H. (1986) 'Specific and nonspecific factors in psychotherapy: a problematic paradigm for psychotherapy research', *Psychotherapy*, 23, 1: 30–40.

Butler, S. and Zelin, S. L. (1977) 'Sexual intimacies between therapists and patients', *Psychotherapy: Theory, Research and Practice*, 14: 139–45.

Callaghan, G. M., Naugle, A. E. and Follette, W. C. (1996) 'Useful constructions of the client–therapist relationship', *Psychotherapy*, 33, 3: 381–90.

Calligor, L. (1984) 'Parallel and reciprocal processes in psychoanalytic supervision', in L. Calligor *et al.*, *Clinical Perspectives in the Supervision of Psychoanalysis*, New York: Plenum Press.

Carkhuff, R. R. (1969a) *Helping and Human Relations: Vol. 1. Selection and Training*, New York: Holt, Rinehart and Winston.

—— (1969b) *Helping and Human Relations: Vol. 2. Practice and Research*, New York: Holt, Rinehart and Winston.

Carkhuff, R. R. and Anthony, W. A. (1979) *The Skills of Helping: An Introduction to Counseling*, Amherst, MA: Human Resource Development Press.

Carroll, M. (1998) 'Spirituality, values and supervision', Keynote Address, British Association for Supervision Practice and Research, Third International Conference on Supervision, 25 July 1998, St Mary's College, Strawberry Hill, London.

Casement, P. (1985) *On Learning From the Patient*, London: Routledge.

—— (1990) *Further Learning From the Patient: The Analytic Space and Process*, London: Routledge.

Cash, D. and Kehr, J. (1978) 'Influence of non-professional counselors' physical attractiveness and sex on perceptions of counselor behavior', *Journal of Counseling Psychology*, 25, 4: 336–42.

Cashdan, S. (1988) *Object Relations Therapy: Using the Relationship*, New York: Norton.

Charney, I. W. (1986) 'What do therapists worry about: a tool for experiential supervision', in F. W. Kaslow (ed.) *Supervision and Training: Models, Dilemmas and Challenges*, Binghampton, NY: Haworth Press.

Christensen, A. and Jacobson, N. S. (1994) 'Who (or what) can do psychotherapy: the status and challenge of nonprofessional therapies', *Psychological Science*, 5, 1: 8–14.

Clarkson, P. (1989) *Gestalt Counselling in Action*, London: Sage.

—— (1990) 'A multiplicity of psychotherapeutic relationships', *British Journal of Psychotherapy*, 7, 2: 148–63.

—— (1992) Chapter 1 in W. Dryden (ed.) *Hard-Earned Lessons from Counselling in Action*, London: Sage.

—— (1994a) 'The nature and range of psychotherapy', in P. Clarkson and M. Pokorny (eds) *The Handbook of Psychotherapy*, London: Routledge.

—— (1994b) 'The psychotherapeutic relationship', in P. Clarkson and M. Pokorny (eds) *The Handbook of Psychotherapy*, London: Routledge.

—— (1995) *The Therapeutic Relationship*, London: Whurr.

—— (1996) *The Bystander: An End to Innocence in Human Relationships?*, London: Whurr.

—— (1998) 'Researching the "therapeutic relationship" in psychoanalysis, counselling psychology and psychotherapy', in P. Clarkson (ed.) *Counselling Psychology: Integrating Theory, Research and Supervised Practice*, London: Routledge.

Clarkson, P. and Aviram, O. (1998) 'Phenomenological research on supervision: supervisors reflect on "Being a supervisor"', in P. Clarkson (ed.) *Counselling Psychology: Integrating Theory, Research and Supervised Practice*, London: Routledge.

Cohen, L. H., Sargent, M. M. and Sechrest, L. B. (1986) 'Use of psychotherapy research by professional psychologists', *American Psychologist*, 41: 198–206.

Collier, H. V. (1987) 'The differing self: women as psychotherapists', in M. Baldwin and V. Satir (eds) *The Use of Self in Therapy*, Binghamton, NY: Haworth Press.

Connor, M. (1994) *Training the Counsellor: an Integrative Model*, London: Routledge.

Connor-Greene, P. A. (1993) 'The therapeutic context: preconditions for change in psychotherapy', *Psychotherapy*, 30, 3: 375–82.

Cooper, T. (1997) 'The self as therapist', in UKCP (United Kingdom Council for Psychotherapy) *Development through Diversity: The Therapist's Use of Self* (3rd Professional Conference Proceedings), London: UKCP.

Corey, G. (1996) *Theory and Practice of Counseling Psychology* (5th edn), Pacific Grove, CA: Brooks/Cole.

Corey, G., Corey, M. S. and Callanan, P. (1993) *Issues and Ethics in the Helping Professions* (4th edn), Pacific Grove, CA: Brooks/Cole.

Coyle, A. (1998) 'Qualitative research in counselling psychology: using the counselling interview as a research instrument', in P. Clarkson (ed.) *Counselling Psychology: Integrating Theory, Research and Supervised Practice*, Routledge: London.

Crits-Christoph, P., Baranackie, K., Kurcias, J. S., Beck, A. T., Carroll, K., Perry, K., Luborsky, L., McLellan, A. T., Woody, G. E., Thompson, L., Gallagher, D. and Zitrin, C. (1991) 'Meta-analysis of therapist effects in psychotherapy outcome studies', *Psychotherapy Research*, 1, 2: 81–91.

Crouch, A. (1997) *Inside Counselling: Becoming and Being a Professional Counsellor*, London: Sage.

Davis, J. (1997) 'Commitment: the price of keeping faith. An interview with John Davis', in W. Dryden (ed.) *Therapists' Dilemmas* (revised edn), London: Sage.

Dawes, R. M. (1994) *House of Cards: Psychology and Psychotherapy Built on Myth*, New York: Free Press.

Delroy, S. (1996) *Just Beneath the Surface: The Process of Counseling and Psychotherapy*, London: Dobro.

Deurzen-Smith, E. van (1988) *Existential Counselling in Practice*, London: Sage.

Doehrman, M. G. (1976) 'Parallel processes in supervision and psychotherapy', *Bulletin of the Menninger Clinic*, 40, 1: 9–104.

Dolan, R. T., Arnkoff, D. B. and Glass, C. R. (1993) 'Client attachment style and the psychotherapist's interpersonal stance', *Psychotherapy*, 30, 3: 408–12.

Douglass, B. G. and Moustakas, C. (1985) 'Heuristic inquiry: the internal search to know', *Journal of Humanistic Psychology*, 25, 3: 39–55.

Draucker, C. B. (1992) *Counselling Survivors of Childhood Sexual Abuse*, London: Sage.

Driscoll, M., Newman, D. and Seals, J. (1988) 'The effect of touch on perception of counselors', *Counselor Education and Supervision*, 27, 4: 344–54.

Dryden, W. (1980) 'The relevance of research in counselling and psychotherapy for the counselling practitioner', *British Journal of Guidance and Counselling*, 8, 2: 225–32.

—— (1991) *Dryden on Counselling Volume 3: Training and Supervision*, London: Whurr.

—— (ed.) (1996) *Research in Counselling and Psychotherapy: Practical Applications*, London: Sage.

Dryden. W. and Feltham, C. (eds) (1992) *Psychotherapy and its Discontents*, Buckingham: Open University Press.

Dryden, W. and Feltham, C. (1994) *Developing Counsellor Training*, London: Sage.

Dryden, W. and Spurling L. (eds) (1989) *On Becoming a Psychotherapist*, London: Routledge.

Dryden, W., Horton, I. and Mearns, D. (1995) *Issues in Professional Counsellor Training*, London: Cassell.

Duncan, B. L., Solovey, A. D. and Rusk, G. S. (1992) *Changing the Rules: A Client-Directed Approach to Therapy*, New York: Guilford.

Durlak, J. A. (1979) 'Comparative effectiveness of paraprofessionals and professional helpers', *Psychological Bulletin*, 86, 1: 80–92.

Eckler-Hart, A. (1987) 'True self and false self in the development of the psychotherapist', *Psychotherapy*, 24, 4: 683–92.

Egan, G. (1997) *The Skilled Helper: A Problem-Management Approach to Helping* (6th edn), Monterey, CA: Brooks/Cole.

Ellingham, I. (1996) 'Person-centred counselling/psychotherapy versus psychodynamic counselling and psychotherapy', in S. Palmer, S. Dainow and P. Milner (eds) *Counselling: The BAC Counselling Reader*, London: Sage.

Elliot, R. (1986) 'Interpersonal Process Recall (IPR) as a psychotherapy process research method', in L. Greenberg and W. Pinsof (eds) *The Psychotherapeutic Process: A Research Handbook*, New York: Guilford Press.

Elliott, R. and Shapiro, D. A. (1992) 'Client and therapist as analysts of significant events', in S. G. Toukmanian and D. L. Rennie (eds) *Psychotherapy Process Research: Paradigmatic and Narrative Approaches*, Newbury Park: Sage.

Erwin, E. (1997) *Philosophy and Pyschotherapy*, London: Sage.

Etherington, K. (1996) 'The counsellor as researcher: boundary issues and critical dilemmas', *British Journal of Guidance and Counselling*, 24, 3: 339–46.

Eysenck, H. J. (1952) 'The effects of psychotherapy: an evaluation', *Journal of Consulting Psychology*, 16: 319–21.

—— (1966) *The Effects of Psychotherapy*, New York: International Sciences.

Farber, B. (1985) 'The genesis, development, and implications of psychological-mindedness in psychotherapists', *Psychiatry*, 22: 170–7.

Fear, R. and Woolfe, R. (1996) 'Searching for integration in counselling practice', *British Journal of Guidance and Counselling*, 24, 3: 399–411.

Feltham, C. (1995) *What is Counselling?*, London: Sage.

—— (1996a) 'Psychotherapy's staunchest critic: an interview with Hans Eysenck', *British Journal of Guidance and Counselling*, 24, 3: 423–35.

—— (1996b) 'Beyond denial, myth and superstition in the counselling professions', in R. Bayne, I. Horton and J. Bimrose (eds) *New Directions in Counselling*, London: Routledge.

—— (1997a) 'Counselling and psychotherapy: differentiation or unification', in I. Horton and V. Varma (eds) *The Needs of Counsellors and Psychotherapists*, London: Sage.

—— (ed.) (1997b) *Which Psychotherapy?*, London: Sage.

—— (1998a) 'In search of meaning and sanity', in C. Feltham (ed.) *Witness and Vision of the Therapists*, London: Sage.

—— (1998b) 'Introduction', in C. Feltham (ed.) *Witness and Vision of the Therapists*, London: Sage.

Festinger, S. (1957) *A Theory of Cognitive Dissonance*, New York: Harper and Row.

Fiedler, F. E. (1950) 'A comparison of therapeutic relationships in psychoanalytic, nondirective and Adlerian therapy', *Journal of Consulting Psychology*, 14: 436–45.

Ford, E. (1963) 'Being and becoming a psychotherapist: the search for identity', *American Journal of Psychotherapy*, 17: 472–82.

Frank, J. D. (1961) *Persuasion and Healing*, Baltimore, MD: Johns Hopkins Press.

—— (1971) 'Therapeutic factors in psychotherapy', *American Journal of Psychotherapy*, 25: 350–61.

—— (1982) 'The present status of outcome research', in M. R. Goldfried (ed.) *Converging Themes in Psychotherapy: Trends in Psychodynamic, Humanistic and Behavioral Practice*, New York: Springer.

—— (1989a) 'Non-specific aspects of treatment: the view of a psychotherapist', in M. Shepherd and N. Sartorius (eds) *Non-Specific Aspects of Treatment*, Toronto: Hans Huber.

—— (1989b) 'Discussion', in M. Shepherd and N. Sartorius (eds) *Non-Specific Aspects of Treatment*, Toronto: Hans Huber.

Friedman, M. (1992) *Religion and Psychology: A Dialogical Approach*, New York: Paragon House.

Gabbard, G. and Pope, K. (1988) 'Sexual intimacies after termination: clinical, ethical, and legal aspects', *Independent Practitioner*, 8, 2: 21–6.

Garrett, T. (1994) 'Sexual contact between psychotherapists and their patients', in P. Clarkson and M. Pokorny (eds) *The Handbook of Psychotherapy*, London: Routledge.

Geller, J. D., Cooley, R. S. and Hartley, D. (1981–2) 'Images of the psychotherapist: a theoretical and methodological perspective', *Imagination, Cognition and Personality*, 1, 2: 123–46.

Gendlin, E. T. (1981) *Focusing* (2nd edn), New York: Bantam.

—— (1984a) 'The client's client: the edge of awareness', in R. F. Levant and J. M. Shlien (eds) *Client-Centred Therapy and the Person-Centred Approach*, New York: Praeger.

—— (1984b) 'The politics of giving therapy away: listening and focusing', in D. Larson (ed.) *Teaching Psychological Skills: Models for Giving Psychology Away*, Monterey, CA: Brooks/Cole.

—— (1990) 'The small steps of the therapy process: how they come and how to help them come', in G. Lietaer, J. Rombauts and R. Van Balen (eds) *Client-Centred and Experiential Psychotherapy in the Nineties*, Leuven, Belgium: Leuven University Press.

—— (1996) *Focusing-Oriented Psychotherapy: A Manual of the Experiential Method*, New York: Guilford.

Gergen, K. (1996) 'The healthy, happy human being wears many masks', in W. T. Anderson (ed.) *The Fontana Postmodernism Reader*, London: Fontana Press.

Goldberg, C. (1986) *On Being a Psychotherapist: The Journey of the Healer*, New York: Gardner Press.

Goldfried, M. R. (ed.) (1982a) *Converging Themes in Psychotherapy: Trends in Psychodynamic, Humanistic and Behavioral Practice*, New York: Springer.

—— (1982b) 'Towards the delineation of therapeutic change principles', in M. R. Goldfried (ed.) *Converging Themes in Psychotherapy: Trends in Psychodynamic, Humanistic and Behavioral Practice*, New York: Springer.

Goldfried, M. R. and Pradawar, W. (1982) 'Current status and future directions in psychotherapy', in M. R. Goldfried (ed.) *Converging Themes in Psychotherapy: Trends in Psychodynamic, Humanistic and Behavioral Practice*, New York: Springer.

Goldklank, S. (1986) 'My family made me do it: the influence of family therapists' families of origin on their occupational choice', *Family Process*, 25: 309–19.

Goldman, L. (1977) 'Toward more meaningful research', *Personnel and Guidance Journal*, 55: 363–8.

—— (ed.) (1978) *Research Methods for Counsellors: Practical Approaches in Field Settings*, New York: Wiley.

Goldstein, A. P. (1982) 'Psychotherapy research and psychotherapy practice: independence or equivalence?', in M. R. Goldfried (ed.) *Converging Themes in Psychotherapy: Trends in Psychodynamic, Humanistic and Behavioral Practice*, New York: Springer.

Gomez, L. (1995) 'Satanist abuse', *Counselling*, 6, 2: 116–20.

Goodwin, J. M. (1994) 'Sadistic abuse: definition, recognition and treatment', in V. Sinanson (ed.) *Treating Survivors of Satanist Abuse*, London: Routledge.

Gottlieb, M. C. (1993) 'Avoiding exploitive dual relationships: a decision-making model', *Psychotherapy*, 30, 1: 41–8.

Grafanaki, S. (1996) 'How research can change the researcher: the need for sensitivity, flexibility and ethical boundaries in conducting qualitative research in counselling/psychotherapy', *British Journal of Guidance and Counselling*, 24, 3: 329–38.

Guggenbühl-Craig, A. (1979) *Power in the Helping Professions*, Irving, TX: Spring (first published 1971).

Gutheil, T. G. and Gabbard, G. O. (1993) 'The concept of boundaries in clinical practice: theoretical and risk-management dimensions', *American Journal of Psychiatry*, 150, 2: 188–96.

Guy, J. (1987) *The Personal Life of the Psychotherapist*, New York: Wiley.

Hall, L. and Lloyd, S. (1993) *Surviving Childhood Sexual Abuse* (2nd edn), London: Falmer Press.

Hartmann, E. (1997) 'The concept of boundaries in counselling and psycho-therapy', *British Journal of Guidance and Counselling*, 25, 2: 147–62.

Hattie, J. A., Sharpley, C. F. and Rogers H. J. (1984) 'Comparative effective-ness of professional and paraprofessional helpers', *Psychological Bulletin*, 95, 3: 534–41.

Hedges, L. E. (1997) 'In praise of dual relationships', in L. E. Hedges, R. Hilton, V. W. Hilton and O. B. Caudill *Therapists at Risk: Perils of the Intimacy of the Therapeutic Relationship*, Northvale, NJ: Jason Aronson.

Hedges, L. E., Hilton, R., Hilton, V. W. and Caudill, O. B. (1997) *Therapists at Risk: Perils of the Intimacy of the Therapeutic Relationship*, Northvale, NJ: Jason Aronson.

Henry, W. (1966) 'Some observations of the lives of healers', *Human Develop-ment*, 9: 47–56.

Heppner, P. and Dixon, D. (1981) 'A review of the interpersonal influence process in counseling', *Personnel and Guidance Journal*, 59: 542–50.

Heppner, P. and Heesacker, M. (1982) 'Interpersonal influence process in real-life counseling: investigating client perceptions, counselor experience level, and counselor power over time', *Journal of Counseling Psychology*, 29, 3: 215–23.

Herlihy, B. and Corey, G. (1992) *Dual Relationships in Counseling*, Alexan-dria, VA: American Counseling Association.

Hermansson, G. (1997) 'Boundaries and boundary management in counselling: the never-ending story', *British Journal of Guidance and Counselling*, 25, 2: 133–46.

Heron, J. (1996) *Co-operative Inquiry: Research into the Human Condition*, London: Sage.

Herron, W. G. and Rouslin, S. (1984) *Issues in Psychotherapy* (Volume 1), Washington, DC: Oryn Publications.

Hewson, J. (1996) 'Obituary: Ruth Hunt', *Counselling*, 7, 3: 183.

Hillman, J. (1979) *Insearch: Psychology and Religion*, Dallas, TX: Spring.

Hilton, R. (1997a) 'The perils of the intimacy of the therapeutic relationship', in L. E. Hedges, R. Hilton, V. W. Hilton and O. B. Caudill *Therapists at Risk: Perils of the Intimacy of the Therapeutic Relationship*, Northvale, NJ: Jason Aronson.

—— (1997b) 'The healing process for therapists', in L. E. Hedges, R. Hilton, V. W. Hilton and O. B. Caudill *Therapists at Risk: Perils of the Intimacy of the Therapeutic Relationship*, Northvale, NJ: Jason Aronson.

—— (1997c) 'Touching in psychotherapy', in L. E. Hedges, R. Hilton, V. W. Hilton and O. B. Caudill *Therapists at Risk: Perils of the Intimacy of the Therapeutic Relationship*, Northvale, NJ: Jason Aronson.

Hilton, V. W. (1997a) 'The devil, the shadow, and the therapist's dilemma', in L. E. Hedges, R. Hilton, V. W. Hilton and O. B. Caudill *Therapists at Risk: Perils of the Intimacy of the Therapeutic Relationship*, Northvale, NJ: Jason Aronson.

—— (1997b) 'Sexuality in the therapeutic process', in L. E. Hedges, R. Hilton, V. W. Hilton and O. B. Caudill *Therapists at Risk: Perils of the Intimacy of the Therapeutic Relationship*, Northvale, NJ: Jason Aronson.

Hobson, R. F. (1985) *Forms of Feeling: The Heart of Psychotherapy*, London: Routledge.

Holdstock, L. (1993) 'Can we afford not to revision the person-centred concept of self?', in D. Brazier (ed.) *Beyond Carl Rogers*, London: Constable.

Holmes, P., Paul, S. and Pelham, G. (1996) 'A Relational Model of counselling', *Counselling*, 7, 3: 229–31.

Holroyd, J. C. and Brodsky, A. (1980) 'Does touching patients lead to sexual intercourse?', *Professional Psychology*, 11, 5: 807–11.

Horton, I. (1997) 'The needs of counsellors and psychotherapists', in I. Horton and V. Varma (eds) *The Needs of Counsellors and Psychotherapists*, London: Sage.

Horton, I. and Varma, V. (eds) (1997) *The Needs of Counsellors and Psychotherapists*, London: Sage.

House, R. (1996) 'The professionalization of counselling: a coherent "case against"?', *Counselling Psychology Quarterly*, 9, 4: 343–58.

—— (1997) 'The dynamics of professionalism: a personal view of counselling research', *Counselling*, 8, 3: 200–4.

Howard, A. (1996) *Challenges to Counselling and Psychotherapy*, Basingstoke: Macmillan.

Howard, G. S. (1986) 'The scientist-practitioner in counseling psychology: toward a deeper integration of theory, research and practice', *The Counseling Psychologist*, 14, 1: 61–105.

Howarth, I. (1989) 'Psychotherapy: who benefits?', *The Psychologist*, 2, 4: 150–2.

Howe, D. (1993) *On Being a Client: Understanding the Process of Counselling and Psychotherapy*, London: Sage.

Hunter, M. and Struve, J. (1998) *The Ethical Use of Touch in Psychotherapy*, Thousand Oaks, CA: Sage.

Hutterer, R. (1993) 'Eclecticism: an identity crisis for person-centred therapists', in D. Brazier (ed.) *Beyond Carl Rogers*, London: Constable.

Hycner, R. H. (1991) *Between Person and Person: Towards a Dialogical Psychotherapy*, Highland, NY: The Gestalt Journal.

Imber, S. D., Glanz, L. M., Elkin, I., Sotsky, S. M., Boyer, J. L. and Leber, W. R. (1986) 'Ethical issues in psychotherapy research', *American Psychologist*, 41, 2: 137–46.

Johns, H. (1996) *Personal Development in Counsellor Training*, London: Cassell.

—— (1997) 'Self-development: lifelong learning?', in I. Horton and V. Varma (eds) *The Needs of Counsellors and Psychotherapists*, London: Sage.

Johnston, S. H. and Farber, B. A. (1996) 'The maintenance of boundaries in psychotherapeutic practice', *Psychotherapy*, 33, 3: 391–402.

Jourard, S. M. (1971) *The Transparent Self* (revised edn), New York: Van Nostrand Reinhold.

Jung, C. G. (1983) *Jung: Selected Writings* (selected and introduced by Anthony Storr), London: Fontana.

Kagan, N. (1967) *Studies on Human Interaction: Interpersonal Process Recall Stimulated by Videotape*, Michigan: Education Publications.

—— (1984) 'Interpersonal process recall: basic methods and recent research', in D. Larsen (ed.) *Teaching Psychological Skills: Models for Giving Psychology Away*, Monterey, CA: Brooks/Cole.

Kagan, N. I. and Kagan, H. (1990) 'IPR – a validated model for the 1990s and beyond', *The Counseling Psychologist*, 18, 3: 436–40.

Kahn, M. (1997) *Between Therapist and Client: The New Relationship* (revised edn), New York: Freeman.

Karasu, T. B. (1996) *Deconstruction of Psychotherapy*, Northvale, NJ: Jason Aronson.

Kazdin, A. E. (1986) 'Comparative outcome studies of psychotherapy: methodological issues and strategies', *Journal of Consulting and Clinical Psychology*, 54, 1: 95–105.

Keith, D. V. (1987) 'The self in family therapy: a field guide', in M. Baldwin and V. Satir (eds) *The Use of Self in Therapy*, Binghamton, NY: Haworth Press.

Kiesler, D. J. (1966) 'Some myths of psychotherapy research and the search for a paradigm', *Psychological Bulletin*, 65, 2: 110–36.

King, E. (1996) 'The use of self in qualitative research', in J. T. Richardson (ed.) *Handbook of Qualitative Research Methods for Psychology and Social Sciences*, Leicester: BPS Books.

King, S. A., Engi, S. and Poulos, S. T. (1998) 'Using the Internet to assist family therapy', *British Journal of Guidance and Counselling*, 26, 1: 43–52.

Kitchener, K. S. (1988) 'Dual role relationships: what makes them so problematic?', *Journal of Counseling and Development*, 67: 217–21.

Kline, P. (1992) 'Problems of methodology in studies of psychotherapy', in W. Dryden and C. Feltham (eds) *Psychotherapy and its Discontents*, Buckingham: Open University Press.

Kopp, S. (1974) *If you Meet the Buddah on the Road, Kill Him!*, London: Sheldon Press.

Kottler, J. A. (1986) *On Being a Therapist*, San Francisco: Jossey-Bass.

Kottler, J. A. and Blau, D. S. (1989) *The Imperfect Therapist: Learning from Failure in Therapeutic Practice*, San Francisco: Jossey-Bass.

Kreinheder, A. (1980) 'The healing power of illness', *Psychological Perspectives*, 11, 1: 9–18.

Kwiatkowski, R. (1998) 'Counselling and psychotherapy are they different and should we care?', *Counselling Psychology Quarterly*, 11, 1: 5–14.

Lago, C. (1996) 'Computer therapeutics', *Counselling*, 7, 4: 287–9.

Laing, R. D. (1977) *Self and Others* (2nd edn), Harmondsworth: Penguin (first published 1961).

—— (1990) *The Divided Self: An Existential Study in Sanity and Madness*, London: Penguin (first published 1959).

Lambert, M. J. (1989) 'The individual therapist's contribution to psychotherapy process and outcome', *Clinical Psychology Review*, 9: 469–85.

Lambert, M. J. and Bergin, A. E. (1994) 'The effectiveness of psychotherapy', in A. E. Bergin and S. L. Garfield (eds) *Handbook of Psychotherapy and Behavior Change* (4th edn), New York: John Wiley.

Lambert, M. J., Shapiro, D. A. and Bergin, A. E. (1986) 'The effectiveness of psychotherapy', in S. L. Garfield and A. E. Bergin (eds) *Handbook of Psychotherapy and Behavior Change* (3rd edn), New York: John Wiley.

Lawson, H. (1985) *Reflexivity: A Post-modern Predicament*, La Salle, IL: Open Court.

Lazarus, A. A. (1993) 'Tailoring the therapeutic relationship or being an authentic chameleon', *Psychotherapy*, 30, 3: 404–7.

Leijssen, M. (1993) 'Creating a workable distance to overwhelming images: comments on a session transcript', in D. Brazier (ed.) *Beyond Carl Rogers*, London: Constable.

Lemma, A. (1996) *Introduction to Psychopathology*, London: Sage.

LeShan, L. (1996) *Beyond Technique: Psychotherapy for the 21st Century*, Northvale, NJ: Jason Aronson.

Lewin, R. A. (1996) *Compassion: The Core Value that Animates Psychotherapy*, Northvale, NJ: Jason Aronson.

Lidmila, A. (1997) 'Professional training: politics and needs', in I. Horton and V. Varma (eds) *The Needs of Counsellors and Psychotherapists*, London: Sage.

Lietaer, G. (1993) 'Authenticity, congruence and transparency', in D. Brazier (ed.) *Beyond Carl Rogers*, London: Constable.

Lomas, P. (1981) *The Case for a Personal Psychotherapy*, Oxford: Oxford University Press.

Lowen, A. (1985) *Narcissism*, New York: Collier Macmillan.

Luborsky, L., Singer, B. and Luborsky, L. (1975) 'Comparative studies of psychotherapies: is it true that "everyone has won and all must have prizes"?', *Archives of General Psychiatry*, 32: 995–1008.

Luborsky, L., McClellan, A. T., Woody, G. E., O'Brien, C. P. and Auerbach, A. (1985) 'Therapist success and its determinants', *Archives of General Psychiatry*, 42: 602–11.

Lynch, G. (1997) 'Words and silence: counselling and psychotherapy after Wittgenstein', *Counselling*, 8, 2: 126–8.

McCarley, T. (1975) 'The psychotherapist's search for self-renewal', *American Journal of Psychiatry*, 123: 221–4.

McConnaughy, E. A. (1987) 'The person of the therapist in psychotherapeutic practice', *Psychotherapy*, 24, 3: 303–14.

McKinstry, L. (1997) 'Today Britain employs more counsellors than soldiers. Is self-obsession now our greatest enemy?', *Daily Mail*, 20 January 1997.

McLennan, J. (1996) 'Improving our understanding of therapeutic failure: a review', *Counselling Psychology Quarterly*, 9, 4: 391–7.

McLeod, J. (1993) *An Introduction to Counselling*, Buckingham: Open University Press.

—— (1994) *Doing Counselling Research*, London: Sage.

—— (1996a) 'Qualitative approaches to research in counselling and psychotherapy: issues and challenges', *British Journal of Guidance and Counselling*, 24, 3: 309–16.

—— (1996b) 'The research agenda for counselling', in S. Palmer, S. Dainow and P. Milner (eds) *Counselling: The BAC Counselling Reader*, London: Sage.

—— (1997a) *Narrative and Psychotherapy*, London: Sage.

—— (1997b) 'Research and evaluation in counselling', in S. Palmer and G. McMahon (eds) *Handbook of Counselling* (2nd edn), London: Routledge.

Mahoney, M. J. and Norcross, J. C. (1993) 'Relationship styles and therapeutic choices: a commentary on the preceding four articles', *Psychotherapy*, 30, 3: 423–6.

Mahrer, A. R. (1988) 'Discovery-oriented psychotherapy research: rationale, aims, and methods', *American Psychologist*, 43: 694–702.

—— (1989) *The Integration of Psychotherapies: A Guide for Practicing Therapists*, New York: Human Sciences Press.

—— (1993) 'The experiential relationship: is it all-purpose or is it tailored to the individual client?', *Psychotherapy*, 30 (3): 413–6.

—— (1996a) *The Complete Guide to Experiential Psychotherapy*, New York: John Wiley.

—— (1996b) 'Discovery-oriented research on how to do psychotherapy', in W. Dryden (ed.) *Research in Counselling and Psychotherapy: Practical Applications*, London: Sage.

—— (1997) 'Experiential supervision', in C. E. Watkins (ed.) *Handbook of Psychotherapy Supervision*, New York: John Wiley.

Mahrer, A. R. and Nadler, W. P. (1986) 'Good moments in psychotherapy: a preliminary review, a list, and some promising research avenues', *Journal of Consulting and Clinical Psychology*, 54, 1: 10–15.

Mair, K. (1992) 'The myth of therapist expertise', in W. Dryden and C. Feltham (eds) *Psychotherapy and its Discontents*, Buckingham: Open University Press.

Mann, D. W. (1994) *A Simple Theory of the Self*, New York: Norton.

Marmor, J. (1953) 'The feeling of superiority: an occupational hazard in the practice of psychotherapy', *American Journal of Psychiatry*, 110: 370–6.

Martin, J. (1992) 'Cognitive-mediational research on counseling and psychotherapy', in S. G. Toukmanian and D. L. Rennie (eds) *Psychotherapy Process Research: Paradigmatic and Narrative Approaches*, Newbury Park: Sage.

Maslow, A. H. (1982) 'Abstracting and Theorizing', in M. R. Goldfried (ed.) *Converging Themes in Psychotherapy: Trends in Psychodynamic, Humanistic and Behavioral Practice*, New York: Springer.

Masson, J. (1992) 'The tyranny of psychotherapy', in W. Dryden and C. Feltham (eds) *Psychotherapy and its Discontents*, Buckingham: Open University Press.

Mattinson, J. (1977) *The Reflection Process in Casework Supervision*, London: Institute of Marital Studies, Tavistock Institute of Human Relations.

Mays, D. T. and Franks, C. M. (eds) (1985) *Negative Outcome in Psychotherapy and What to Do About It*, New York: Springer.

Meara, N. M. and Schmidt, L. D. (1991) 'The ethics of researching counseling/therapy processes', in C. E. Watkins, Jr and L. J. Schneider (eds) *Research in Counseling*, Hillsdale, NJ: Lawrence Erlbaum Associates.

Mearns, D. (1992) Chapter 6 in W. Dryden (ed.) *Hard-Earned Lessons from Counselling in Action*, London: Sage.

—— (1997a) 'Achieving the personal development dimension in professional counsellor training', *Counselling*, 8, 2: 113–20.

—— (1997b) *Person-Centred Counselling Training*, London: Sage.

Mearns, D. and McLeod, J. (1984) 'A Person-Centred approach to research', in R. F. Levant and J. M. Schien (eds) *Client Centred Therapy and the Person-Centred Approach: New Directions in Theory, Research and Practice*, New York: Praeger.

Miller, A. (1997) *The Drama of Being a Child: The Search for the True Self* (revised edn), London: Virago (first published 1979).

Miller, G. D. and Baldwin, D. C., Jr (1987) 'Implications of the wounded-healer paradigm for the use of self in therapy', in M. Baldwin and V. Satir (eds) *The Use of Self in Therapy*, Binghamton, NY: Haworth Press.

Miller, S. D., Duncan, B. L. and Hubble, M. A. (1997) *Escape from Babel: Toward a Unifying Language for Psychotherapy Practice*, New York: Norton.

Morrow-Bradley, C. and Elliott, R. (1986) 'Utilization of psychotherapy research by practicing psychotherapists', *American Psychologist*, 41, 2: 188–97.

Mowbray, R. (1995) *The Case Against Psychotherapy Registration: A Conservation Issue for the Human Potential Movement*, London: Trans Marginal Press.

Murphy, L. J. and Mitchell, D. L. (1998) 'When writing helps to heal: e-mail as therapy', *British Journal of Guidance and Counselling*, 26, 1: 21–32.

Norcross, J. C. (ed.) (1986) *Handbook of Eclectic Psychotherapy*, New York: Bruner/Mazel.

—— (1991) 'Prescriptive matching in psychotherapy: an introduction', *Psychotherapy*, 28, 3: 439–43.

—— (1993) 'Tailoring relationship stances to client needs: an introduction', *Psychotherapy*, 30, 3: 402–3.

Norcross, J. C. and Grencavage, L. M. (1989) 'Eclecticism and integration in counselling and psychotherapy: major themes and obstacles', *British Journal of Guidance and Counselling*, 17 (3): 227–47.

Norcross, J. C. and Prochaska. J. O. (1986) 'Clinicians' theoretical orientations: selection, utilization, and efficacy', *Professional Psychology*, 14: 197–208.

Ogles, B. M., Lambert, M. J. and Masters, K. S. (1996) *Assessing Outcome in Clinical Practice*, Boston: Allyn and Bacon.

O'Hara, M. and Anderson, W. T. (1996) 'Psychotherapy's own identity crisis', in W. T. Anderson (ed.) *The Fontana Postmodernism Reader*, London: Fontana Press.

Olio, K. A. and Cornell, W. F. (1993) 'Therapeutic relationship as the foundation for treatment with adult survivors of sexual abuse', *Psychotherapy*, 30, 3: 375–82.

Orlinsky, D. E. and Howard, I. (1986) 'The psychological interior of psychotherapy: explorations with the therapy session reports', in L. Greenberg and W. Pinsof (eds) *The Therapeutic Process*, New York: Guilford Press.

Orlinsky, D. E., Grawe, K. and Parks, B. K. (1994) 'Process and outcome in psychotherapy – noch einmal', in A. E. Bergin and S. L. Garfield (eds), *Handbook of Psychotherapy and Behavior Change* (4th edn), New York: John Wiley.

Owen, I. R. (1997) 'Boundaries in the practice of humanistic counselling', *British Journal of Guidance and Counselling*, 25, 2: 163–74.

Page, S. (1999) *The Shadow and the Counsellor*, London: Routledge.

Page, S. and Wosket, V. (1994) *Supervising the Counsellor: A Cyclical Model*, London: Routledge.

Palmer, S. and McMahon, G. (eds) (1997) *Client Assessment*, London: Sage.

Palmer, S. and Szymanska, K. (1994) 'How to avoid being exploited in counselling and psychotherapy', *Counselling*, 5, 1: 24.

Palmer, S. and Varma, V. (eds) (1997) *The Future of Counselling and Psychotherapy*, London: Sage.

Patterson, C. H. (1974) *Relationship Counseling and Psychotherapy*, New York: Harper and Row.

Patterson, C. H. and Hidore, S. C. (1997) *Successful Psychotherapy: A Caring, Loving Relationship*, Northvale, NJ: Jason Aronson.

Patterson, C. H. and Watkins, C. E. (1996) *Theories of Psychotherapy* (5th edn), New York: HarperCollins.

Peavy, R. V. (1996) 'Counselling as a culture of healing', *British Journal of Guidance and Counselling*, 24, 1: 141–50.

Peck, M. S. (1989) *The Road Less Travelled*, London: Century Hutchinson (first published 1978).

Persaud, R. D. (1993) 'The "career" of counselling: careering out of control?', *Journal of Mental Health*, 2: 283–85.

Pilgrim, D. (1987) 'Some psychodynamic aspects of helping: a critical overview', in E. Karas (ed.) *Current Issues in Clinical Psychology, Vol. 3*, New York: Plenum Press.

—— (1996) 'British psychotherapy in context', in W. Dryden (ed.) *Handbook of Individual Therapy*, London: Sage.

Polkinghorne, D. E. (1991) 'Qualitative procedures for counselling research', in C. E. Watkins, Jr and L. J. Schneider (eds) *Research in Counseling*, Hillsdale, NJ: Lawrence Erlbaum Associates.

Pope, K. S. and Bouhoutsos, J. C. (1986) *Sexual Intimacy between Therapists and Patients*, New York: Praeger.

Pope, K. S. and Vetter, V. (1992) 'Ethical dilemmas encountered by members of the American Psychological Association', *American Psychologist*, 47, 3: 397–411.

Pope, K. S., Keith-Spiegel, P. and Tabachnick, B. G. (1986) 'Sexual attraction to clients: the human therapist and the (sometimes) inhuman training system', *American Psychologist*, 41, 2: 147–58.

Rachman, S. and Wilson, G. (1980) *The Effects of Psychological Therapy*, New York: Wiley.

Racusin, G., Abramowitz, S. and Winter, W. (1981) 'Becoming a therapist: family dynamics and career choice', *Professional Psychology*, 12: 271–9.

Ram Dass and Gorman, P. (1985) *How Can I Help? Stories and Reflections on Service*, New York: Knopf.

Rappaport, R. L. (1991) 'When eclecticism is the integration of therapist postures, not theories', *Journal of Integrative and Eclectic Psychotherapy*, 10, 2: 164–72.

Raskin, N. (1978) 'Becoming – a therapist, a person, a partner, a parent, a . . .', *Psychotherapy: Theory, Research and Practice*, 15: 362–70.

Real, T. (1990) 'The therapeutic use of self in constructionist systemic therapy', *Family Process*, 29: 255–72.

Reason, P. and Rowan, J. (eds) (1981) *Human Inquiry: A Sourcebook of New Paradigm Research*, Chichester: Wiley.

Rennie, D. L. (1992) 'Qualitative analysis of the client's experience of psychotherapy', in S. G. Toukmanian and D. L. Rennie (eds) *Psychotherapy Process Research: Paradigmatic and Narrative Approaches*, Newbury Park: Sage.

—— (1994a) 'Clients' accounts of resistance in counselling: a qualitative analysis', *Canadian Journal of Counselling*, 28, 1: 43–57.

—— (1994b) 'Storytelling in psychotherapy: the client's subjective experience', *Psychotherapy*, 31, 2: 234–43.

—— (1998) *Person-Centred Counselling: An Experiential Approach*, Newbury Park: Sage.

Rennie, D. L. and Toukmanian, S. G. (1992) 'Explanation in psychotherapy process research', in S. G. Toukmanian and D. L. Rennie (eds) *Psychotherapy Process Research: Paradigmatic and Narrative Approaches*, Newbury Park: Sage.

Rice, L. N. (1992) 'From naturalistic observation of psychotherapy process to micro theories of change', in S. G. Toukmanian and D. L. Rennie (eds) *Psychotherapy Process Research: Paradigmatic and Narrative Approaches*, Newbury Park: Sage.

Rice, L. N. and Greenberg, L. S. (1990) 'Fundamental dimensions in experiential therapy: new directions in research', in G. Lietaer, J. Rombauts and R. Van Balen (eds) *Client-Centred and Experiential Psychotherapy in the Nineties*, Leuven, Belgium: Leuven University Press.

Rice, R. (1994) 'Surprise', Chapter 11 in E. Messner, J. E. Groves and J. H. Schwartz, (eds) *What Therapists Learn about Themselves and How they Learn it: Autognosis*, Northvale, NJ: Jason Aronson.

Robson, D. and Robson, M. (1998) 'Intimacy and computer communication', *British Journal of Guidance and Counselling*, 26, 1: 33–41.

Bibliography 245

Rogers, C. R. (1967) *On Becoming a Person: A Therapist's View of Psycho-* *therapy*, London: Constable (first published 1961).
—— (1980) *A Way of Being*, Boston, MA: Houghton Mifflin.
—— (1989) *Client-Centred Therapy: Its Current Practice, Implications, and* *Theory*, London: Constable (first published 1951).
—— (1994) 'The interpersonal relationship: the core of guidance', in C. R. Rogers and B. Stevens *Person to Person: The Problem of Being Human*, London: Souvenir Press (first published 1967).
Ross, P. (1996) 'The impact of research upon practice', in S. Palmer, S. Dainow and P. Milner (eds) *Counselling: The BAC Counselling Reader*, London: Sage.
Russell, J. (1993) *Out of Bounds: Sexual Exploitation in Counselling and* *Therapy*, London: Sage.
—— (1996) 'Sexual exploitation in counselling', in R. Bayne, I. Horton and J. Bimrose (eds) *New Directions in Counselling*, London: Routledge.
Russell, R. (1981) *Report on Effective Psychotherapy: Legislative Testimony*, New York: R. R. Latin Associates.
Rutter, P. (1989) *Sex in the Forbidden Zone*, London: Mandala.
Samuels, A. (1992) 'Foreword', in W. Dryden and C. Feltham (eds) *Psycho-* *therapy and its Discontents*, Buckingham: Open University Press.
Sanders, P. and Liptrot, D. (1994) *An Incomplete Guide to Qualitative* *Research Methods for Counsellors*, Manchester: PCCS.
Sanders, P. and Rosenfield, M. (1998) 'Counselling at a distance: challenges and new initiatives', *British Journal of Guidance and Counselling*, 26, 1: 5 – 10.
Schafer, R. (1968) *Aspects of Internalization*, New York: International Univer- sities Press.
Schön, D. A. (1983) *The Reflective Practitioner: How Professionals Think in* *Practice*, New York: Basic Books.
—— (1987) *Educating the Reflective Practitioner: Towards a New Design for* *Teaching and Learning in the Professions*, San Francisco: Jossey-Bass.
Searles, H. F. (1955) 'The informational value of the supervisor's emotional experience', *Collected Papers on Schizophrenia and Related Subjects*, Lon- don: Hogarth Press.
—— (1958) 'The schizophrenic's vulnerability to the therapist's unconscious processes', *Collected Papers on Schizophrenia and Related Subjects*, London: Hogarth Press.
Sedgwick, D. (1994) *The Wounded Healer: Countertransference from a Jung-* *ian Perspective*, London: Routledge.
Shapiro, D. A. and Firth, J. (1987) 'Prescriptive vs. exploratory psychotherapy: outcomes of the Sheffield Psychotherapy Project', *British Journal of Psy-* *chiatry*, 151: 790–9.
Shapiro, D. A. and Shapiro, D. (1982) 'Meta-analysis of comparative psycho- therapy outcome studies: a replication and refinement', *Psychological Bulletin*, 92: 581–604.

Shapiro, D. A., Firth-Cozens, J. and Stiles, W. B. (1989) 'Therapists' differential effectiveness: a Sheffield Psychotherapy Project addendum', *British Journal of Psychotherapy*, 154: 383–5.

Sharaf, M. and Levinson, D. (1964) 'The quest for omnipotence in professional training', *Psychiatry*, 27: 135–49.

Shepherd, M. and Sartorius, N. (eds) (1989) *Non-Specific Aspects of Treatment*, Toronto: Hans Huber.

Shillito-Clarke, C. (1996) 'Ethical issues in counselling psychology', R. Woolfe and W. Dryden (eds) *Handbook of Counselling Psychology*, London: Sage.

Shipton, G. (1996) 'Working with resistance to research', in S. Palmer, S. Dainow and P. Milner (eds) *Counselling: The BAC Counselling Reader*, London: Sage.

Skovholt, T. M. and Rønnestad, M. H. (1992) *The Evolving Professional Self: Stages and Themes in Therapist and Counselor Development*, Chichester: Wiley.

Sloane, R. B., Staples, F. R., Cristol, A. H., Yorkston, N. J. and Whipple, K. (1975) *Psychotherapy versus Behavior Therapy*, Cambridge, MA: Harvard University Press.

Smail, D. (1978) *Psychotherapy: A Personal Approach*, London: Dent.

Smith, D. and Fitzpatrick, M. (1995) 'Patient–therapist boundary issues: an integrative review of theory and research', *Professional Psychology: Research and Practice*, 26, 5: 499–506.

Smith, M. L. and Glass, G. V. (1977) 'Meta-analysis of psychotherapy outcome studies', *American Psychologist*, 32: 752–60.

Smith, M. L., Glass, G. V. and Miller, T. I. (1980) *The Benefits of Therapy*, Baltimore, MD: Johns Hopkins University Press.

Spinelli, E. (1994) *Demystifying Therapy*, London: Constable.

Stein, D. M. and Lambert, M. J. (1984) 'On the relationship between therapist experience and psychotherapy outcome', *Clinical Psychology Review*, 4: 127–42.

Stevens, R. (1996a) 'The reflexive self: an experiential perspective', in R. Stevens (ed.) *Understanding the Self*, London: Sage in Association with the Open University.

—— (ed.) (1996b) *Understanding the Self*, London: Sage in Association with the Open University.

Stiles, W. B. (1993) 'Quality control in qualitative research', *Clinical Psychology Review*, 13: 593–618.

Stiles, W. B., Shapiro, D. A. and Elliott, R. (1986) 'Are all psychotherapies equivalent?', *American Psychologist*, 41: 165–80.

Strong, S. (1968) 'Counseling: an interpersonal influence process', *Journal of Counseling Psychology*, 15: 215–24.

Strupp, H. H. (1982) 'Psychotherapists and (or versus?) researchers', in M. R. Goldfried (ed.) *Converging Themes in Psychotherapy: Trends in Psychodynamic, Humanistic and Behavioral Practice*, New York: Springer.

—— (1986) 'Psychotherapy: research, practice and public policy (how to avoid dead ends)', *American Psychologist*, 41, 2: 120–30.

—— (1989) 'Psychotherapy: can the practitioner learn from the researcher?', *American Psychologist*, 44, 4: 717–24.

Strupp, H. H. and Hadley, S. W. (1979) 'Specific vs nonspecific factors in psychotherapy: a controlled study of outcome', *Archives of General Psychiatry*, 36: 1125–36.

Szymanska, K. and Palmer, S. (1997) 'Counsellor–client exploitation', in S. Palmer and G. McMahon (eds) *Handbook of Counselling* (2nd edn), London: Routledge.

Tait, M. (1997) 'Dependence; a means or an impediment to growth?', *British Journal of Guidance and Counselling*, 25, 1: 17–26.

Talley, P. F., Strupp, H. H. and Morey, L. C. (1990) 'Matchmaking in psychotherapy: patient–therapist dimensions and their impact on outcome', *Journal of Consulting and Clinical Psychology*, 58: 182–8.

Thorne, B. (1987) 'Beyond the core conditions', in W. Dryden (ed.) *Key Cases in Psychotherapy*, Beckenham: Croom Helm.

—— (1995) 'New directions in counselling: a roundtable', in I. Horton, R. Bayne and J. Bimrose (eds) *Counselling*, 6, 1: 34–40.

—— (1997) 'Where are the boundaries? An interview with Brian Thorne', in W. Dryden (ed.) *Therapists' Dilemmas* (revised edn), London: Sage.

Toukmanian, S. G. (1996) 'Clients' perceptual processing: an integration of research and practice', in W. Dryden (ed.) *Research in Counselling and Psychotherapy: Practical Applications*, London: Sage.

Toukmanian, S. G. and Rennie, D. L. (eds) (1992) *Psychotherapy Process Research: Paradigmatic and Narrative Approaches*, Newbury Park: Sage.

Treacher, A. (1983) 'On the utility or otherwise of psychotherapy research', in D. Pilgrim (ed.) *Psychology and Psychotherapy: Current Trends and Issues*, London: Routledge and Kegan Paul.

Trepper, T. S. (1990) 'In celebration of the case study', *Journal of Family Psychotherapy*, 1, 1: 5–13.

UKCP (United Kingdom Council for Psychotherapy) (1997) *Development through Diversity: The Therapist's Use of Self* (3rd Professional Conference Proceedings), London: UKCP.

Vanaerschot, G. (1993) 'Empathy as releasing several micro-processes in the client', in D. Brazier (ed.) *Beyond Carl Rogers*, London: Constable.

Villas-Boas Bowen, M. C. (1986) 'Personality differences and person-centred supervision', *Person-Centred Review*, 1, 3: 291–309.

Viorst, J. (1987) *Necessary Losses*, New York: Fawcett/Ballantine.

Walker, M. (1992) *Surviving Secrets: The Experience of Abuse for the Child, the Adult and the Helper*, Buckingham: Open University Press.

Watkins, C. E., Jr and Schneider, L. J. (eds) (1991) *Research in Counseling*, Hillsdale, NJ: Lawrence Erlbaum Associates.

Webb, S. B. (1997) 'Training for maintaining appropriate boundaries in counselling', *British Journal of Guidance and Counselling*, 25, 2: 175–88.

Weldon, F. (1997) 'Mind at the end of its tether', *Guardian*, 11 January 1997.

Welwood, J. (ed.) (1985) *Awakening the Heart: East/West Approaches to Psychotherapy and the Healing Relationship*, Boston: Shambhala.

Wessler, R. L. and Wessler, S. H. (1997) 'Counselling and society', in Palmer, S. and Varma, V. (eds) *The Future of Counselling and Psychotherapy*, London: Sage.

West, W. (1998) 'Critical subjectivity: use of self in counselling research', *Counselling*, 9, 3: 228–30.

Wetherell, M. and Maybin, J. (1996) 'The distributed self: a social constructionist perspective', in R. Stevens (ed.) *Understanding the Self*, London: Sage in Association with the Open University.

Wheeler, S. (1991) 'Personal therapy: an essential aspect of counsellor training, or a distraction from focussing on the client?' *International Journal for the Advancement of Counseling*, 14: 193–202.

—— (1996) *Training Counsellors: The Assessment of Competence*, London: Cassell.

Wilkins, P. (1997) *Personal and Professional Development for Counsellors*, London: Sage.

Williams, A. (1995) *Visual and Active Supervision: Roles, Focus, Technique*, New York: Norton.

Wills, T. A. (1982) 'Nonspecific factors in helping relationships', in T. Wills (ed.) *Basic Processes in Helping Relationships*, New York: Academic Press.

Wilson, J. E. and Barkham, M. (1994) 'A practitioner-scientist approach to psychotherapy process and outcome research', in P. Clarkson and M. Pokorny (eds) *The Handbook of Psychotherapy*, London: Routledge.

Winnicott, D. W. (1965) *The Family and Individual Development*, London: Tavistock.

—— (1986) *Home is Where We Start From: Essays by a Psychoanalyst*, Harmondsworth: Penguin.

Woolfe, R. (1996) 'The nature of counselling psychology', in R. Woolfe and W. Dryden (eds) *Handbook of Counselling Psychology*, London: Sage.

Woolsey, L. (1986) 'Research and practice in counseling: a conflict of values', *Counselor Education and Supervision*, 26, 2: 84–94.

Wosket, V. (1989) 'An exercise in Person-Centred research focusing on four case studies and examining client antecedents, role expectations, perceived counsellor characteristics and satisfaction with counselling', unpublished Advanced Diploma in Counselling Research Project, University College of Ripon and York St John.

—— (1990) 'Therapist motivation: A neglected factor in helping relationships', unpublished MA dissertation, University of Keele.

Yalom, I. D. (1980) *Existential Psychotherapy*, New York: Basic Books.

Zweig, C. (1996) 'The death of self in a postmodern world', in W. T. Anderson (ed.) *The Fontana Postmodernism Reader*, London: Fontana Press.

Index